# Corpus

WITHIN LIVING MEMORY

*Life in a Cambridge College*

# Corpus

## WITHIN LIVING MEMORY

*Life in a Cambridge College*

M.E. Bury and E.J. Winter

THIRD MILLENNIUM PUBLISHING

Copyright © 2003 Corpus Christi College and
Third Millennium Publishing Limited

First published in 2003 by Third Millennium Publishing Limited,
an imprint of Third Millennium Information Limited

Farringdon House
105–107 Farringdon Road
London EC1R 3BU
United Kingdom
www.tmiltd.com

ISBN 1 903942 17 9

Edited by M.E. Bury and E.J. Winter
Copy-edited by Honeychurch Associates, Cambridge, UK
Designed by Third Millennium Information Limited
Produced by Third Millennium Publishing, an imprint of
Third Millennium Information Limited

Reprographics by News S.p.a., Italy

# Contents

# FOREWORD

## John Hatcher, Vice-Master

*Old Court in 1952.*

Much of life passes unrecorded, and so is all but lost to future generations. In the flood of histories of institutions, major events and long-term processes, life as it was lived for most of the time frequently gets left out of the picture. As the previously published histories of Corpus show, it is possible to reconstruct many aspects of the College's past from surviving official administrative and financial documents, but what would we give for a student's diary or a Fellow's journal of life here in centuries gone by? It is to be hoped that this book of personal memories and reminiscences of everyday life in Corpus will fill part of the gap left unfilled by more conventional histories. The picture that emerges from the contributions is, of course, a far from comprehensive or even consistent record, since it is composed of a multitude of personal views and experiences, most of which have been recalled from a distance of many decades. Readers perusing the pages that follow, will note differences of view and perspective and occasional conflicts of evidence. This is as it should be. For this is not a strictly-edited, highly-structured official record but a miscellany of views from the inside, written by the individuals who lived and worked in Corpus in the decades from the 1920s to the 1950s and later, and their personal statements of what the College meant to them at the time and since.

The first step in the production of this book was taken by Liz Winter, our current Director of Development, while she was organizing a reunion of Old Members who had matriculated before 1950. It seemed to Liz that this was the ideal age group to provide the foundations for a modest book of memories of their time at Corpus, and their eager responses to her request for contributions indicated that such a project would be both worthwhile and feasible. The next step was to gain the willing and expert assistance of Betty Bury to edit the submissions and structure them for publication. This was a splendid choice, for Betty is of the same generation as many of the contributors and knows a good number of them personally, and her intimate knowledge of the history of the College during much of this era is readily apparent in the informative introductions which she has written to the flood of memories from the 1920s to the 1950s. In fact, with the enthusiastic support of Karen Aarestad, the former Development Director, so encouraging had the progress of this venture become that it was decided to produce a much more ambitious, commercially published volume, with copious illustrations and additional sections highlighting some of the subsequent changes which have occurred in College life. It was at this stage that Third Millennium was chosen as publisher, and the project began to benefit from the expertise and enthusiasm lent by Julian Platt and Matt Wilson to the production process, and by Lindsey Shaw-Miller and Catherine Walston of Honeychurch Associates to editorial tasks. In the production of the final draft Betty Bury and Liz Winter received assistance from two recent Old Members of the College, John Lee and Flora McCabe. I hope that you will agree that the quality of this volume has justified the delays encountered in its production, and join with me in thanking all those – contributors, editors and publishers – who have brought the project to a fitting conclusion.

# WHY CORPUS CHRISTI?

Oliver Rackham

*Old Court in 1934.*

**The Shadow of Catastrophe**

Corpus Christi College was a response to catastrophe: the Black Death of 1349. It is almost impossible to overestimate the fear and grief which were to hang over many succeeding generations: for example, plague returned twelve years later and carried off Henry, Duke of Lancaster, one of our original benefactors. This went on for 315 years. Three seventeenth-century Old Members were heroes of the plague. Henry Butts (Master of the College), Sir Henry Morse, and Thomas Tenison (later Archbishop of Canterbury) distinguished themselves by caring for their fellow-citizens in the plagues of 1625, 1637, and 1665. The last was the final epidemic: the plague mysteriously disappeared as suddenly as it had begun.

Bubonic plague appeared in southern Europe in 1347. It spread inexorably northwards, and reached these parts in March 1349. It finished its ravages by December 1349 (though people would not have known that for some time) and moved on into Scotland.

One-third of the population of England were dead, perhaps more in Cambridge, when, in January 1350, William Horwode, future Mayor of Cambridge, got up at a meeting of the new Gild of Corpus Christi and said, 'Now that we have finished with the latest batch of funerals, let us move on to the chief item on the agenda, the founding of a new college'. Our College was founded in far worse circumstances than any other: it was born of an act of heroic fortitude and defiant faith on the part of ordinary people.

The fourteenth century was not a nice time in other ways. But cold and hunger and overpopulation notwithstanding, this was the Age of Chivalry, one of the great ages of achievement, especially in Cambridge and Ely.

At Ely half a dozen great building projects were going on at the same time, including the Octagon, Lady Chapel, and Prior Crauden's Chapel. In Cambridge, six new colleges had been founded in the 25 years before the Black Death. Churches built at that time include St Botolph, Little St Mary, St Michael, and Grantchester chancel.

The Black Death was the worst catastrophe ever to hit England. There must have been some relation between it and the founding of the College three years later, but this has been curiously overlooked by earlier historians. Only in recent years, through the researches of Catherine Hall and Patrick Zutshi, drawing on the earlier work of Mary Bateson, have the details come to light. For what follows I am especially indebted to Mrs Hall.

Philip Ziegler, historian of the Black Death, flatly stated in *The Black Death* (Harmondsworth, 1969) that this College and the slightly earlier Gonville Hall and Trinity Hall were all founded in consequence. Trinity Hall was founded expressly in order to make good losses among the clergy. Corpus Christi was founded by the two town gilds in order to reduce the cost of saying masses for departed members by using what he calls 'cheap labour among the students'. However, Trinity Hall was founded to provide lawyers rather than priests and, although Corpus Christi did specialize in training priests, students were not qualified to say mass and would not have been of direct help to the gilds.

**Corpus Christi**

The Body of Christ, Corpus Christi, has two mystical meanings. It means the corporate society of Christian believers, an idea developed by St Paul. This has been written into the twentieth-century liturgy: Anglicans tell themselves, Sunday by Sunday, 'We are the Body of Christ' (I Corinthians 12). Although this would have been familiar in the Middle Ages, the College is concerned with that other sense, based on our Lord's words at the Last Supper, 'Take, eat, this is my Body which is given for you' (Matthew 26 26). Corpus Christi is a symbol of the redeeming sacrifice of Jesus on the Cross, especially as expressed through the bread which is offered at the Communion service.

This sense of the Body of Christ is present in all Christian liturgies except the most extremely Protestant. It was specially developed by the visions seen by Juliana de Cornillon in the 1230s. This eccentric Belgian nun was responsible for Corpus Christi as the subject of a cult and of special devotions. The cult of Corpus Christi was slow to get going. It was made official in 1264 by Pope Urban IV, who had worked in Belgium and may have known Juliana. By popular demand it gradually spread through western Christendom, reaching England in the early fourteenth century: masses were sung, followed by processions and feasting, on the Thursday after Trinity Sunday (varying between 21 May and 24 June).

## Gilds

Corpus Christi College, uniquely, was founded, not by an individual benefactor, but by the Gild of Corpus Christi and the Gild of the Blessed Virgin Mary. Gilds were of two kinds: trade gilds and civic gilds. A trade gild was a sort of combination of employers' association and trade union: the University was, in effect, a trade gild of scholars. Civic gilds, which began more than a thousand years ago, were voluntary bodies, associations of townspeople. Their functions were social, devotional, festive, funerary, and sometimes civic. Among their functions were the jobs now done by the Rotary Club, the Women's Institutes, mutual insurance companies, the Amateur Dramatic Society, sickness insurers, the Parish Council, the Freemasons, the Internal Drainage Board, and (most important of all) a burial club. They usually had a gildhall: a public hall with a kitchen and shops attached, as survives in use to this day at Hadleigh, Suffolk. Typically they were not only for the rich: their members included relatively poor people.

Much is known of our two gilds because they not only founded the College, they turned into the College and gave it their property, including their archives, which the College still has. The Alderman, Brethren,

**Plate A.**
*End of the bede-roll of the Gild of St Mary. From top to bottom:*

1 *Names of the last few members to die ordinary deaths, in three different hands.*

2 Kyrie eleison *and the collects for the living and the dead, in a formal hand.*

3 *'Item, [pray] for the souls of those who died in the mortality and after, anno domini mcccxlix', followed by about ninety-two names.*

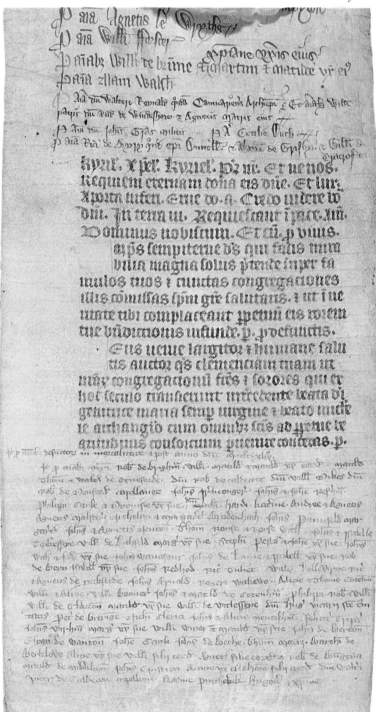

and Sisters of the Gild of Merchants of the Blessed Virgin Mary had been in existence for about a hundred years. Despite their name they were not really a trade gild, although they had some connections with brewing. They met in Great St Mary's, and held an annual feast after Christmas at which they commemorated departed members.

Gilds of Corpus Christi were not uncommon: there were at least 50 gilds with that dedication. Ours, however, was founded by a group of Cambridge businessmen during the Black Death itself and its main business was the founding of a college. The earliest record of this gild is a bequest to it in May 1349, two months after the plague reached Cambridge. In 1348 or early in 1349 John Hardy, the University stationer, William Horwode, later to be Mayor, and Henry de Tangmere, the goldsmith and banker, would have seen the plague rolling towards Cambridge. Their reaction was to found a Gild of Corpus Christi and to raise funds for some as yet undefined purpose.

### Founding the College

The year 1349, however, was not a good time to hold public meetings. With the coming of the first glimmers of hope that the plague would stop before everyone was dead, the first meeting of the Corpus Christi Gild was held: it was officially launched on 31 January 1350.

The idea of founding a college was probably present by then. Hardy, Horwode, and Tangmere were all still alive. Many of the funds they had raised would have been given in order to commemorate the departed, whether by plague or otherwise. There were already plenty of chantry colleges, endowments of priests whose duty was to sing masses for the souls of those who had endowed them. If they had given all their funds for this, the result would have been a few little houses attached to St Bene't's Church, for three or four priests. Henry VIII would have stolen the assets at the Reformation, and the College would not be here today.

Hardy, Horwode, and Tangmere devised something new and much more ambitious: another *academic* college, that should have students as well as chantry priests. There were already seven colleges in Cambridge, six in Oxford, and one in Salisbury, so they would have known what to do. The new Gild had among its members at least two, Thomas Campes and John Raysoun, who were to be among the first Fellows of the College.

Corpus Christi Gild first consolidated its position in the town by taking over St Mary's Gild. How could they do this? The answer may be in a sinister little roll of parchment which still lies in the College archives: the bede-roll of St Mary's Gild. It is a beautifully written list of deceased members of the Gild for whose souls the Gild had to pray: Robert de Madingley, Godfrey the Haymonger, Margaret Fyndesylver, Thomas and Beatrix Outlaw, and so on. It was added to over the years until it was nearly full with some 850 names (Plate A). But at the bottom the calligraphy stops and there is a hair-raising addition: 'Item, [pray] for the souls of the dead in the mortality and after, anno domini mcccxlix'. There are about ninety-two names squeezed into the last blank 3½ inches. The three and a half of the Virgin Mary had plenty of property and probably not many members left alive.

Finding a site was a problem for all new urban institutions, especially houses of friars. An academic college needed at least half an acre of land in one ownership. To get this in inner-city Cambridge needed a lot of wheeling and dealing, involving not only the Gilds but the two other infant colleges, Gonville Hall and Trinity Hall.

The united Gild needed an important patron. Their connections with the nobility got them a very exalted knight, Henry Duke of Lancaster. One of his jobs was to go to King Edward III and get a licence for founding a college – the equivalent of planning permission.

### Property and Functions of the College

The united Gild last admitted new members in 1358 and is last heard of in the 1360s. The Gild functions were taken over by other gilds in Cambridge, of which there were at least seven including four gilds of St Mary. St Bene't's and St Botolph's Churches each had gilds. The College inherited the property of the united Gild, its feasts, and its public functions.

The Corpus Christi procession was a grand civic event. Members carried around the Body of Christ in a silver-gilt tabernacle worth £20, accompanied by a mysterious treasure called a Beryl. The Master and twelve Fellows (not that there were twelve Fellows) and seven lesser clergy each carried something called a shield or a stocking, made of silver and azure, decorated with the weapons of the Passion of Christ. These were presumably some sort of badge or ornament for the staves of the canopy held over the officiating priest. They were given by Henry, Duke of Lancaster, who was far more than a nominal benefactor, even though he was one of the busiest men of the Age of Chivalry.

From the Gilds and from benefactors the College inherited some splendid objects. In an inventory of *c.*1385 the precious church vestments, minutely described, are curiously mixed up with secular textiles. The Rector of Over's dosser was embroidered with leopard's heads and 'papiliones of divers colours, called in English boterflyes'. There was a bedspread depicting a woodwose (a rude and hairy personage who does not shave or dress) and a woodwosess; a vestment called a quilt depicted a foxhunt – foxes out hunting with arrows – and an ape looking in an urinal; a cushion with a devil piping and a woman trumpeting.

The plate was fabulous: two 'vultures' eggs', the Cup of the Three Bears, seven chalices and patens, all lovingly described; six spoons of silver with maidens' heads in hairnets; twelve precious mazers (maple-wood cups); and many others. Much of this was the plate of the Gild of St Mary, of which the College still has two items.

The Great Horn, from which most members of the College have drunk on graduating, is the horn of an aurochs, an extinct animal, a kind of super-bull. The Pharaohs and kings of Assyria liked to be depicted hunting him when they were not spearing lions. In Julius Cæsar's time aurochsen still roamed the dread Hercynian Wood, where Bayreuth and Pilsen now stand. 'They are in size a little below elephants… Great is their strength and great their speed.' For a young man to kill one was a mark of great valour. The horns were surrounded with silver on the mouths and used as cups in the grandest feasts. (Cæsar, *De Bello Gallico*, vi.28)

By the thirteenth century aurochsen were confined to Eastern Europe. The horns were rare and mysterious objects of legend: only about fifteen are known in Britain. They had long been a symbol of royalty. Two were found in the ship-burial of an Anglo-Saxon king at Sutton Hoo; on the Bayeux Tapestry King Harold and his lords quaff out of two horns very like ours at his feast at Bosham. How did a modest town gild come to possess such a fabulous and mystical object?

The other item surviving from this period is the Coconut Cup, a silver-mounted coconut shell. Coconuts came from India at nearest, and thus had the air of rarity and romance that moon-rock had during the Space Age.

**Later History of the Corpus Christi Feast**
Corpus Christi was celebrated for the rest of the Middle Ages. Yet at the Reformation the Body of Christ became very contentious, especially the relation between the physical body of Our Lord and the wafers over which the priest spoke the words of consecration at Mass. If you got the details wrong, you got burnt. Not surprisingly, Protestants disapproved of the cult of Corpus Christi as savouring of popery. The feast of Corpus Christi was dropped from the Anglican Prayer Book.

In Cambridge, at the procession in 1535, there was a bad omen: the canopy over the officiating priests caught fire. Was God venting his wrath at an idolatrous festival? Or did a dissident woman cast fire from an upper window? The procession was abandoned; the Duke of Lancaster's stockings, the Beryl, and the Tabernacle were melted down and never heard of again.

Matthew Parker, Queen Elizabeth's Archbishop of Canterbury, was a Reformer: his vestments had been splashed with Anne Boleyn's blood, he had sniffed the fires which burnt several of his colleagues, and he had to pay the bill for the combustion of Archbishop Cranmer, his predecessor. But he was not a fundamentalist, and still had much affection for the old ways. He continued to inscribe 'Collegium Corporis Christi' on all the plate that he gave the College. He introduced the heraldic Pelican, an ancient symbol of Corpus Christi and of Corpus Christi College Oxford, though not of the Cambridge Gild. The College had no coat-of-arms, so he got Clarencieux King-of-Arms to provide one and put pelicans on it.

The College still held the feast of Corpus Christi, without the procession, until Parker died in 1575, when it was transferred to Parker's birthday. It nearly lost the name Corpus Christi and

*Right: Statue of Matthew Parker 1504–1575, Archbishop of Canterbury and Master of the College.*

turned into Bene't (i.e. St Benedict's) College; Corpus Christi was relegated to official occasions, and did not return to ordinary use until the College built the New Court in the 1820s.

## Future Questions

Much is now known about how the College acquired a formal existence; much less about how it began functioning. Should it celebrate the centenary of 1352, when the Gild got a licence? Or 1355, when the statutes were ratified? Or 1353, when it acquired 'all the vessels and utensils needed for brewing'? Or again in 1353 when it began its career as a patron of drama by putting on a play called *The Children of Israel*?

How did the College do its work? We have little to go on. Susanna Gregory's novels portray early Corpus as a very nasty place, containing nearly as many murderers as Michaelhouse, the predecessor of Trinity. This I cannot confirm but there are three lines of research.

## Archives

The early College archives still have some secrets. The early inventory owes its survival to falling into the hands of a frugal Bursar, who used blank pages and bits of

pages for drafting the College accounts. Scholars have studied the inventory, but not what is written on the back of the pages. They are a dog's dinner. They have got wet and the ink has run; the handwriting is awful; and the accounts themselves seem utterly chaotic, even by the standards of the University's latest financial system. Roof and gutter repairs on the College itself, College hostels, commercial properties in the town, agricultural properties at Landbeach and Grantchester, are mixed up together and interspersed with kitchen expenses, oddments of income, rabbits and mutton for feasts, hire of minstrels, loads of firewood, purchase of 9s. 4d. worth of 'Clobber', purchases, sales, and repairs of plate, and the College barber paid by contract at so much a term. They would be well worth sorting out for what they can tell of how the early College functioned.

## Buildings

The College is proud of still having the original Old Court, but has not treated it well, especially in the twentieth century. This wonderful building has become dingy and dilapidated and institutional. At least it has not been much restored, apart from a regrettable episode in the 1950s. Most of the historic features are

**Plate B.**
*Reconstruction of the Old Court before it was finished, looking south. The Hall is in the middle of the far side. To the left (where the parlour would be in an ordinary house) is the present B staircase, then consisting of an upstairs great hall. To the right (as in an ordinary house) are the buttery and pantry; the kitchen is further to the right. The other buildings are Fellows' and students' rooms.*

**Plate C.**
*Original Old Court windows
of earlier phase (a) and later
phase (b).*

still there, even if covered up or decayed. To see them, one looks in cupboards or crawls in the roof space or waits until someone pulls down a ceiling, pulls up the floorboards or takes out a built-in recess.

The Old Court tells us that the early College was conceived as a domestic, not a monastic building: an extension of a private house of the time (Plate B). It was a single household, not what would now be called a House in Multiple Occupation. The standard house of eastern England at the time – at all social levels from the nobleman's hall to the humble terrace house – has a central hall open to the roof, which is soot-blackened on the underside from the fire on a hearth in the middle. At one end are the buttery and pantry and access to what was often a detached kitchen, with rooms above. At the other end are the private rooms: the parlour and a bedroom above. By adding further private rooms this generated a college court, of which the Old Court is apparently the prototype.

The College must have had students. The well-known theory that medieval colleges had no undergraduates has been disproved by recent research. (*See* A.B. Cobban, 'Commoners in medieval Cambridge colleges', 1983.) Undergraduates apart from Scholars play little part in the College archives until the late sixteenth cen-

tury; but that is because they were not technically members of the College, not because they did not exist. The original establishment was probably intended for a Master and twelve Fellows, although in practice there were seldom more than eight Fellows. The Old Court as originally built contained 22 sets of rooms; for much of the time each Fellow could have had a whole staircase. Although some rooms may have been occupied by College servants, much of the space would have been difficult to fill except with students. More than this, early College accounts are full of references to hostels belonging to the College, such as the Angel and the Lilypot, attached to the College or in surrounding streets. Medieval Corpus would have had at least several dozen students.

When was the Old Court built? The only known written evidence is from Josselyn, Parker's secretary, who says it was finished in the Mastership of John Kynne. It would thus have been built over 26 years, *c.*1352 to *c.*1378, which is not unreasonable. However, Josselyn was writing nearly 200 years later. Most of what he says is based on his reading or misreading of fourteenth-century documents, most of which still exist. This about the Old Court is a statement for which Mrs Hall has found no documentary corroboration.

The Old Court looks as if it was conceived as a whole. The staircases were designed to be more or less identical, and were not constrained by having to incorporate buildings already there. However, there are obvious discrepancies between the details of original windows, most easily explained by supposing that the Old Court was built over many years and that a succession of architects and builders did the windows in slightly different ways (Plate C). Over the years I have investigated the timber construction, on the strength of which I worked out the various phases in which the Old Court could have been built staircase by staircase, beginning at the south-east corner. The earliest part was the south range, which was built before the plan emerged of building a complete court. In consequence there is an awkward join, visible both externally (Plate D) and in the roof timbers, where the east range was added on to a south range that had not been planned to receive it. A more recent chance exposure shows that whereas P staircase was conceived much as it is now, M staircase was originally different from P and was later altered to resemble P.

On the outside of the Old Court are several curious blocked windows (Plate E). They are not original: they are Victorian or even twentieth-century, in modern carved stone artfully blackened to match the dirt of the rest of the wall. Why should someone go to the trouble of inserting a fancy dummy window into a fourteenth-century wall? The answer must be that there was a blocked window there already; it was badly decayed by acid rain and the Victorians took offence at it; they hacked it out and replaced it with a crude copy; and they kept no record of what they had destroyed. The original window probably came to be blocked to protect the College from rioters.

During the Peasants' Revolt of 1381, the College was sacked not by peasants but by workers, presumably members of some of the rival town gilds. They stole a lot of plate, or so the Fellows said, though the inventory does not confirm this. Less well known is an incident in 1460, a nasty moment in the Wars of the Roses, when the College accounts record the expenditure of 12d on 'the safeguard of the College plate and treasury, with title-deeds'. They laid in saltpetre and sulphur, protective clothing, artillery, and twelve arrows, and 'defended' some of the windows. The deterrent theory worked. These warlike preparations kept out what was called the 'tempestuous riot'. This incident may well have left a permanent record in the blocking of most of the external windows. Security precautions, then as now, tend to be kept up long after the reason for them has disappeared.

### Dendrochronology

The Old Court contains several hundred medieval timbers, each one made out of a whole oak tree. The growth of oak trees depends on the weather. For example, 1975 and 1976 were bad years, in which most oaks grew a narrow annual ring followed by a very narrow one; similar narrow rings are characteristic of the

**Plate D.**
*The join at the south-east corner of the Old Court. A recess has been made in the wall of N staircase (left) in order to avoid obstructing the window of B staircase. B is therefore earlier, and was built without taking thought for adding N.*

**Plate E.**
*Blocked window on Free School Lane side of Old Court. Note the slight change in the surrounding rubble masonry (e.g. to the right of the down-pipe) resulting from the replacement of the original window.*

**Plate F.**

*Section of a rafter
from the Old Court,
given to the author
by the late Professor
Bruce Dickens. The
tree grew fast for its
first dozen years, fol-
lowed by three bad
years (marked), then
a number of less bad
years, then a very
bad year (marked),
and so on. In princi-
ple it would be possi-
ble to identify these
specific years.*

drought years 1989, 1990, and 1995. This particular pattern of bad years will be recognized by future scholars as distinctive of the late twentieth century. The process is extended backwards in time by comparing the good and bad years from the early decades of trees still living with the later decades of timbers in eighteenth- and nineteenth-century buildings, and so on, back to the Middle Ages and beyond. In good conditions this might reveal, for example, that a tree was felled in May 1352 (Plate F).

If no cross-section is available to measure the annual rings, a core is extracted with a special hollow drill and with difficulty, for medieval oak is nearly as hard as iron.

The Old Court, like other medieval structures, is made from a multitude of small and fast-grown oak-trees. (Timber from big slow-grown oaks was normally imported from Poland and Lithuania.) I hope to find out from the age of the timbers how many years there are between the apparent phases of the Old Court. For this limited and unconventional purpose 40 rings may well be enough, although professional dendochronologists usually need at least 100 rings to overcome random variations and give an absolute date. Tree-ring dating is helped by the medieval practices of felling the trees and using them at once without seasoning, and of not discarding the sapwood, so that with luck the last ring of the tree's life may be present.

The south-east corner of the Old Court (B staircase) is an anomaly. It was originally a big upstairs hall, adjacent to the original College Hall and nearly as big, long since subdivided. A strange window projecting through the garret floor is a relic of this. Why did the infant College need two Great Halls? Was this hall built as a gildhall? Or, as Catherine Hall has suggested, did the infant Gonville Hall start building on the site and hand over its hall in the exchange of sites?

Dendrochronology may reveal, independently of the documents, the date of the Old Court; how long it took to build; its relation to other fourteenth-century structures such as St Botolph's Church; and whether B staircase is older than the College.

### In Piam Memoriam

We still pray for the repose of the souls of our Founders (as far as the Anglican Church allows us to) at the Commemoration of Benefactors and on Corpus Christi Day. We recite a list of their names, but it is a strangely haphazard list. Of the three heroic principal Founders, Henry de Tangmere, the banker, has always been on the list, and we have recently restored William Horwode the Mayor. But John Hardy, the stationer, is still not there, nor is Margaret Andrew, who probably died of the plague and counts as our earliest identifiable benefactor.

*Requiem eternam dona eis, Domine, et lux.… A porta inferi erue Domine animas.… Deus venie largitor et humanae salutis auctor, quesumus clemenciam tuam ut nostrarum congregationum fratres et sorores qui ex hoc seculo transierunt, intercedente beata Dei genetrice Maria semper virgine et beato Michaele archangelo cum omnibus sanctis ad perpetue beatitudinis consorcium pervenire concedes.*

*Rest eternal grant unto them, O Lord, and [let] light [perpetual shine upon them]. Deliver their souls from the gate of the pit… O God, who art the bestower of pardon and author of human salvation, we beseech thee of thy clemency to grant that by the intercession of Mary ever-Virgin the blessed Mother of God, and blessed Michael the Archangel with all the Saints, the brethren and sisters of our confraternities who have passed over from this world may come unto the fellowship of everlasting blessedness.*

[From the bede-roll of the Gild of St Mary]

CORPUS

# MEMORIES:

## Introduction by Betty Bury

## 1920–27 *Years of quite exceptional distinction and prosperity*

It is a splendid tribute to the staying-power of Corpus men that we should have received no fewer than four contributions from Old Members who were admitted to the College in the twenties. Dr Pearce, the then Master, had been elected in September 1914, but it was not until 1919 that the very necessary recovery in the College's reputation could be resumed. Between 1914 and 1918 the Master and Mr Pollock had been in sole charge of a College filled almost exclusively with the HQ staff of the two Divisions and then with military cadets. Mr Spens and Mr Butler had served in the Foreign Office; Mr Thomson fought in France and then researched for the RFC and the RAF; Mr Pickthorn fought in France and Macedonia and was severely wounded; Sir Edwyn Hoskyns became Chaplain to the Forces in Egypt, India and on the Western Front; Mr Morris, debarred from military service by poor eyesight, taught at Sherborne School; Mr Goodhart served in the United States Army from 1917 to 1919; Mr Campbell Smith fought in France and was promoted Lieutenant-Colonel, Mr Thouless served with the British Salonica Forces; and Dr Clark-Kennedy was a member of the RAMC in Mesopotamia and on the Western Front. Furthermore, of these post-war Fellows, Mr Butler, Mr Thomson, Mr Morris; and Mr Goodhart had all been undergraduates at Trinity, Mr Spens at King's and Sir Edwyn Hoskyns at Jesus. In fact, the breach of continuity had, as the *Association Letter* of 1922 described it, 'been more than ordinarily large'.

Patrick Bury, in his *History* of the College between 1822 and 1952, describes the Society as having 'to rebuild its corporate existence almost *de novo*', but nevertheless is able to describe 1919 to 1927 'as years of quite exceptional distinction and prosperity' in the history of the College as a whole. Under Dr Pearce's post-war Mastership, priority continued to be given to the educational needs of the College and to the establishment of new and wider connections outside its walls. In 1922 the government had for the first time agreed to granting funds on a regular basis for university education, and a gradual influx of grant-aided students began. In Corpus, a remarkable number of benefactions enabled the College to fund scholarships and prizes and so induce able young men to compete for entry and in due course become candidates for Fellowships on their home ground. In 1920 demand for places rose to 133, against an average of 80 or 90 in pre-war years; nevertheless, our first contributor would still have found himself housed in College, as were the whole of the first two years – and Scholars of the third. The fourteen sets of attic rooms on the west and north sides of the New Court had providentially been completed in 1920.

---

In writing the short introductions to the four groups of years between 1922 and 1952, I have especially relied on the following books:

*A History of Corpus Christi College Cambridge from 1822 to 1952* by Patrick Bury

*A History of the County of Cambridge and The Isle of Ely.* The Victoria History of the Counties of England, Volume 3, edited by J.P.C. Roach

*Cambridge Between Two Wars* by T.E.B. Howarth

*Letters from Cambridge* by A.S.F. Gow

*Old Court in 1900.*

In some colleges, Corpus amongst them, the conservative ethos hardly altered until the Second World War. At the same time the 1920s witnessed an unprecedented increase in the number of teachers, in facilities for research in the arts and sciences, the extraordinary achievements of the Cavendish Laboratory, the introduction of a multiplicity of new courses and, of necessity, a vast building programme. In 1926 the introduction of new University statutes also brought major changes; they created the faculty system which reorganized teaching, until then mainly in the care of the colleges; they stated that teaching staff were to be paid by the University, were to retire at specific ages and be entitled to proper pensions; stipendiary college Fellowships were to be conditional on holders being occupied in teaching, research or college administration. Women also became eligible for University teaching posts and a certain number were at once appointed to lectureships.

Many of our contributors, not surprisingly, deplore the almost complete absence of girls during term-time. Oxford had approved the admission of women to full membership of the University in 1920; Cambridge in the same year appointed a syndicate to discuss the matter, six of its members being conservative and six liberal. Mr Spens argued that Tripos results showed that the Cambridge examination system was not suited to women, and in the view of the Master of Corpus, women could not be admitted on equal terms simply because they were not content with equality. They meant to rule, he thought, and usually did so in the end. Sir Geoffrey Butler observed that women were handicapped in the Natural Science Tripos because it lasted for three weeks and, although J.T. Sheppard secured a majority of 99 in the Union for full equality and separate colleges for women (Corpus voted 48–8 against), the report in the Senate in 1920 was defeated by 904 votes to 712. A year later, after a further adverse vote, H.P. (Pussy) Hart, MA of Corpus and vicar of Ixworth, yelling 'Now go and tell Girton and Newnham', led a mob of some 300 undergraduates against the bronze memorial gates at Newnham. He was severely reprimanded for doing so and a number of freshmen were sent down but, as we know, women were not admitted to full membership of the University until a quarter of a century later. There were, of course, a small number of girls at Girton and Newnham but access to them seems to have required courage and their existence was largely ignored by their male contemporaries.

A.J. Beamish in his *Association Letter* of 1955 looked back on life in Cambridge during the early post-war 'Renaissance' and recalled 'the passionate enthusiasm to revive every form of civilised activity'. Boris Ord and his student and professional friends set a musical standard hitherto undreamt of in undergraduate clubs, while the 'intensity of artistic effort… was nowhere more striking than in the theatre'. In the course of 1926–7 no fewer than fifty-four different productions were put on at the ADC and the New and Festival Theatres. There were the 'flicks' too which Christopher Isherwood described as anything but silent since the audience supplied the popping of champagne corks, the puffing of trains, the sound of horses' hooves and the kisses. If, as Isherwood also recalled, 'we young writers of the middle twenties' were all suffering, more or less subconsciously, from a feeling of shame that we hadn't been old enough to take part in the European war, the shame was subconscious. 'In my case, at any rate, it was suppressed by the strictest possible censorship.'

John Roach in his Victoria History volume writes that the true religion of the inter-war years in the University was devotion to international causes and the principles connected with them. The greatest of these was unsurprisingly the League of Nations; a Corpus freshman in his diary for 12 October 1927 records going 'to the Guildhall to hear Professor Gilbert Murray give a League of Nations address…. The meeting was at 8.30: there was no charge for admission and the large Guildhall was almost packed. The Vice-Chancellor was in the chair'. And on 19 February 1928 he was disappointed to find that there was 'no getting in to hear the PM on "Our Country's Opportunity" because of the vast queue'.

Christianity was also a very live issue. A mission led by Charles Gore in 1920 attracted between two and three thousand undergraduates to prayer meetings, again in the Guildhall, and when Dean Inge of St Paul's Cathedral came to preach in Cambridge long queues formed along King's Parade. The evangelical Cambridge Inter-Collegiate Christian Union (CICCU) and the more liberal Student Christian Movement both revived after the First World War, and it was at this time that Corpus also began to be influenced by the Anglo-Catholic revival. The allegiance of the declared agnostics was to the Heretics' Society that was in its hey-day in the 1920s and well known for the absolute freedom of its discussions.

There was also at this time much emphasis on the ennobling influence of team sports when, says T.E.B. Howarth, the quality of Cambridge athletics 'was a great deal more impressive than the inept moralizing to which it often gave rise'. Corpus boasted Blues of many kinds and in 1922 an international rugby player; in 1920 and 1921 Corpus men captained the University Soccer and Hockey Clubs and in 1927 the Water-polo team. Men also represented the University against Oxford in golf, lawn tennis, winter sports, shooting and archery although the fortunes of the Boat Club did not begin to revive until the 1930s.

Dr Pearce, who presided over these remarkable years of post-war recovery, resigned his Mastership in 1927 upon his appointment as first Bishop of the new See of Derby. Born in 1870, elected a Fellow of Corpus in 1895, appointed to a classical lectureship and to the living of St Bene't's in 1900, he served as Dean of Chapel until his election as Master in 1914. As a junior Fellow he helped to lower the barriers between dons and undergraduates and as Dean played an important part in modifying Chapel services in accordance with the Anglo-Catholic revival. An *Association Letter* commented on his 'gift of sympathy, his remarkable pastoral gifts and his clear, telling public speaking' which were said to have 'made his Deanship memorable in the history of the College and not without its effect in the University'. It is not surprising that he was a brisk man, a briskness tempered by a saving grace of humour: he was exemplary in answering all his letters at once and with his own hands! Dr Pearce benefited the College

*College rooms in 1900.*

by skilfully encouraging hospitality and, in 1926, the College revived the practice of having its own Audit Ale specially brewed. However, in 1921 the Corpus Christi feast was cancelled because of the coal strike and during the General Strike in 1926, when over half the University's undergraduates enthusiastically volunteered for service, there can have been no entertaining. One hopes that it was not a Corpus man who, having been given a tip by a grateful old lady at Liverpool Street to which he had driven her train, revealed that it was only at Bethnal Green that he had discovered how the brakes worked.

Dr Pearce was unique among the Heads of Oxford and Cambridge colleges. Strongly Conservative in both local and national politics, no other clerical Master had ever held all the offices of Mayor, Vice-Chancellor of his University and Chairman of his County Council, and no-one since the early eighteenth century had been elected for a third term as Vice-Chancellor. This election was partly due to a shortage of eligible candidates but was nevertheless a recognition of his outstanding administrative ability. His interests were wide and human rather than academic, and as Bishop of Derby he was to show great interest in the social and material problems of his diocese.

## MEMORIES:1920–27

### Edward Upward, 1922

The passage leading to my first rooms could be reached in a few strides by anyone turning to the left after entering the College through the main entrance from the street. The room directly above mine was occupied by a, no doubt, very rich relative of the Aga Khan. Its ceiling was painted a night-sky blue with gold stars stuck at intervals all over it (I don't remember how I managed to get a glimpse into it). Whenever he descended the stairs he exuded a powerful scent which lingered on for quite a while after he'd gone. I was told that he was friendly with an old Reptonian named Gates who was also rich and owned an impressively large car.

*Charles Hugh Egerton Smyth, Fellow.*

My sitting-room led into a bedroom which had barred windows to prevent any occupant from getting out into the street. But the bars did not hinder me, when friends of mine were being rather noisily festive in my sitting-room, from carefully conveying a strong drink to a smiling policeman who stood on the pavement just outside. He had got to know me by coming upon me once in the street when I was not totally sober.

Among my newly-made friends was Halford White, who had rooms at the top of the same New Court building as mine. He, like myself, had a £60 scholarship. The school where he'd been educated was St Paul's in London. He was more sophisticated than I was, and he showed he was no novice when it came to picking up girls in the street. One evening he took me with him to hunt for them in the streets of Cambridge and before long we sighted two of them who, becoming aware of being followed, slowed their pace until we overtook them. I forget the name of the girl he chose – probably he thought she looked likely to be willing to go further than the other, whose name was Milly. I got no more than a kiss from her, but next morning I remembered it with joy.

Much of my time was spent playing card games, especially poker, in White's room at the top of the building. The other players and I, including Eric Woodward who became a friend of mine, were not studying history as we were supposed to be. Our lack of serious application so far to the study of this subject for which we had been given our scholarships had the unexpected consequence that we were before very long put through a test, and then we were told we would have to spend a large part of the summer vacation under the instruction of a tutor who would help us catch up on what we had missed.

White and I managed to spend our evenings very pleasantly during that summer vac. He thought of an ingenious way of getting back late into the College when the main gate was shut. At the rear of the College there was a narrow lane with a telegraph pole standing against a high wall and with two thick wire cables tautly attached to it. 'Follow me,' he said. He gripped the cable nearest to him with both hands, and by working his knees against the wall he brought himself to the top of it; and then, gripping another cable on the far side, he slid down out of sight. I managed to raise myself to the top of the wall but then to my horror saw nothing but trees below me. 'Get hold of the cable and slide down

*The Corpus party watching the 'Mays', June 1899.*

it,' he said. I did, and the thrashing trees seemed to do me no injury as I slid through them. I then followed him to an open window which led into the Corpus library. 'This morning I arranged with one of the College servants that he should leave the window open. Don't tell anyone else about this, or they'd spoil it for ever'. Years later I saw that barbed wire had been twisted round the cables.

Two events made my third year at Corpus very different from my first and second. One was the arrival of Christopher Isherwood with an £80 scholarship and the reputation of having scored higher marks than anyone in other Colleges who had taken the same exam. He wanted to read English, not History, but the Corpus authorities adamantly opposed this.

As for myself, my having won the Chancellor's Medal for English Verse persuaded them to allow me to stay on in the College for a third year, whereas my friend White had to leave his upstairs rooms and go out to an approved lodging in the town. I was given very attractive rooms in the Old Court. But I was also given a duty, which was to open the doors of the famous Parker Library at a certain hour in the morning, so that visitors could come in and admire the exhibits.

Isherwood was one of my visitors and both of us were especially fascinated by an exhibit which showed the wheel of fortune, under the rim of which was written: *rursus ad astra feror* (once again I am borne up to the stars).

Charles Smyth, a brilliant historian from Repton who had got to Corpus a year before us, and was strongly disliked by us because we regarded him as a poseur, asked me on the occasion when the first trade delegation from the Soviet Union were visiting England, to let him take over from me and show them round the famous library. I let him, and he wore a red tie.

However, he proposed both of us for membership of the second poshest club in the College (the poshest, for some reason, was the Chess Club and it had very few members). The second poshest was whimsically named the Young Visiter's Club after the title of Daisy Ashford's best-selling juvenile novel. Smyth told me I had qualities that would make me eligible – good looks (I possessed them then), a good public schooling, good football (I was in the College soccer team), and a history scholarship. He tactfully avoided alluding to my lack of good family connections. Isherwood had an advantage over me in this. His family regarded itself as 'County'.

We had to read the book, and before being initiated into the Club we had to answer correctly a number of questions about it. We also had to write a letter stating why we thought ourselves deserving of the privilege of being accepted by the Club. I can't remember what I wrote, but Isherwood told me he'd stated that he was very rich.

As for the activities of the Club, I don't think they consisted of anything except having occasional dinners at which I got pleasantly drunk; but after a while I became bored with them and ceased to attend. This, and perhaps a remark I made about the silly playfulness of the poshocracy, gave deep offence and led to the 'wrecking', as I called it, of my allotted rooms in the Old Court. These were beautiful rooms. The main door opened on to a large sitting-room with white-painted walls, and at the far end of this there was a small gilt-handled door behind which curving stairs went up to my bedroom where a still smaller door concealed a tiny cupboard-like windowless space. Isherwood and I called it the 'oubliette', and we thought that gramophone-playing, which was illicit in Corpus, wouldn't be heard there. Actually it would have been, because, as we discovered in good time, there was a don with rooms close by. So if we wanted to play records we went to my brother's rooms in Sidney Sussex College where record-playing was allowed.

Isherwood and I did not spend much time on the academic work we were expected to be doing. We had to write occasional essays for our supervisors and read them out aloud, and I think Isherwood's supervisor may have been critical of his work, which was not of the first-class quality he should have been capable of. My supervisor, Aubrey Attwater, who was a Pembroke not a Corpus don, because no don in Corpus taught English – thought that I might just possibly get a First.

There was a College Commemoration dinner at the end of term, and I was seated next to Kenneth Pickthorn, a young don liked by both Isherwood and myself. Before I left the table he told me that the only sexual relief Proust demanded was to see a rosy-cheeked butcher-boy killing rats.

After standing up rather unsteadily I invited several people I recognised to come and have drinks with me in my room. Not all came, but one who did was Boris Ord, a good musician and a very nice man. He stood quite still while I wrote in French on his evening-dress shirt

*Chess Club, 1900.*

front all four verses of a passionate love poem by Baudelaire. Meanwhile Isherwood kicked down the stairs an admirer who had compared the colour of his eyes to that of periwinkle flowers.

Suddenly in single file, so it seemed, poshocrats I recognised as having been members of The Young Visiter's Club came into my room without speaking to me. I soon noticed they were handling various objects in the room. Messiter had taken down one of my pictures from the wall and Harnett was looking into the drawer in my table, and Gedge was fetching things out from the cupboard where I kept food and crockery. Gedge went on to amuse himself by slicing my butter with my bread-knife and then flicking up bits of butter towards the ceiling, a game at which several others soon joined him, using more knives from my cupboard. I in my drunkenness was amused by this too – at first. Suddenly I became angry, I scented a plot. The poshocracy had come up to my rooms with the fixed intention of spoiling them, had very likely planned the whole thing before they got drunk. I saw my broom standing head uppermost against the mantelpiece where someone must have transported it from my other cupboard, and the sight of it suggested a method of revenge which I immediately put into practice. I smeared butter over its

*1st Lent boat, 1902.*

bristles which were soft, and then went quietly among the poshocrats and buttered the backs of their dinner jackets. None of them seemed to notice – they must have been too drunk or else the general crush in the room must have made them insensible to the soft contact of the broom. I was even able, to my considerable satisfaction, to butter Gedge himself. But there was one of the poshocrats who appeared to have escaped all this. His name was Agnell. He was sitting on my table under which there was a drawer. I kept boxes of matches besides other things in it. He had found the boxes and had begun hitting them with a hammer he'd got from somewhere. White smoke puffed out of them.

His face had an epicene look. People thought he was homosexual. I sensed that he resented this and that he was, in fact, quite philistinely anti-homosexual.

I said to him, 'When you've finished with my matches, perhaps you'd like to *bugger* the pictures'.

As I walked away from him I noticed a lump of butter on the floor. I picked it up and went towards the door.

When I got there I switched off the light and flung the butter as violently as I could into the darkness of the room. Then I switched on again and I saw a large circular yellow medallion stuck on to the satin lapel of George Padlow's jacket. I had known him in the Young Visiter's Club as a rugby player. He was a big man. Someone pointed me out to him as the thrower of the butter. He came towards me and I went for him head down, determined to hit him before he hit me, but he fended me off with one hand while with the other he removed the medallion from his lapel and rubbed it vigorously into my hair; then I managed to close with him and tried to hit him with all my strength, but two of the Club members pushed us apart, and soon afterwards, as though an authoritative voice had shouted, 'All members out!' they filed silently out of my room and not one of them looked at me.

However, within a quarter of an hour one of them returned – Gibson, who had been awarded a £60 scholarship to Corpus at the same time that White and I were. He helped me to clean up my room. 'You, at least, are a gentleman,' I said when we'd finished. (At that period I thought it complimentary to call someone a gentleman). 'Thanks,' he said expressionlessly.

But I felt angry with Isherwood, who had remained talking with Boris Ord and hadn't come to my help when the poshocrats were wrecking my room. I wrote him a letter breaking with him for ever, which I tore up in the morning. The thought came to me that our enemy –'the Authorities' – might not be displeased by a split between us. And next term was going to be crucial for us both.

I worked hard at revising for my English exams. I felt that if only I could see the kind of answers that were marked alpha plus I could imitate them and get a First. In reality I discovered on the day before the exams that I had mumps on one side of my face. I decided not to see a doctor because he would probably tell me not to sit for the exams, and I wouldn't get a degree at all. I did sit for them, and I got a Second. 'It was quite an ordinary Second,' Aubrey Attwater told me. 'Weren't you feeling well?' I didn't admit to him that he had guessed right.

As for Isherwood, he didn't need to do any revision. He knew he hadn't a hope of getting the First that was expected of him, and he decided he would rather fail altogether than get a Second. He would write comic answers to the questions. I encouraged him to carry out this plan. We both knew it would get him expelled, but he intended to make quite sure he would never become a don, which was what his mother wanted him to be. He would have to live off her, and she could afford it, until he began to be a success as a writer.

His name was struck off the College books, but when he became a well-known writer he returned to make his peace with the College, and his name was restored to the books.

As for myself, I would not wish this contribution from me to be printed without mention of three of the dons I much respected. Kenneth Pickthorn was one of them. Geoffrey Butler wore a high boot on one leg and was always amiable, (and modest too). Once, when I hadn't produced an essay that was due from me, he left in my room a piece of notepaper on which he had written the words, 'I'd value it.' And I did not realize until after 'going down' from Cambridge that he too, as an undergraduate, had won the Chancellor's Gold Medal for English Verse (when it really was gold and not base metal like mine) and I've heard tell that Rupert Brooke had been one of the unsuccessful contestants.

The third Corpus don to have made a lasting impression on me was Hoskyns. He gave performances of Schubert's *Lieder*. He was a good singer, and I think I shall never forget the convincing passion with which he sang, standing almost on the tips of his toes:

*Dann, Blümlein alle, heraus, heraus!*
*Der Mai ist kommen, der Winter ist aus.*

[The author of this contribution has given pseudonyms to some of the people he mentions.]

### André Marling, 1926

My first contact with Corpus was the interview granted me by the Tutor when I applied for admission to the College as an undergraduate. I was the son of Russian refugees, but had no social or other distinction. A piece of flotsam from the remote shipwreck of Imperial Russia, I happened to have washed up on the shore of sempiternal Cantabrigian stability.

Pointing to a chair facing the large desk between the windows of his office, the Tutor, Will Spens, invited me to be seated, his gesture, aloof rather than welcoming, matched the occasion. At that time, the golden promise of the Communist regime, close on ten years old and seemingly come to stay, had for most people, including university educators, dimmed to a tarnished memory the splendour of the overthrown Empire. For me, on the other hand, 1917 had put an end to a world that should have been mine, leaving behind it a formidable void.

The Tutor's business-like approach to the question of my possible future studies and college career was impressive. Here was someone who could fill the uncomfortable emptiness in which fate had left me. We spoke as man to man, launching together the vessel of my nascent manhood on its voyage through the world, free of the previously necessary but tiresome intervention of parents and school-masters.

It took the Tutor only a few minutes to dismiss my preliminary choice of Mathematics or Philosophy as the discipline of my university studies. After a brief review of the world economy, the labour market and unemployment, and my prospects as a future graduate looking for work, he advised me to take a degree in Economics.

My interview with the Tutor convinced me that he was a person of exceptional understanding, who had the further merit of understanding me. His advice was therefore worth heeding. Many other young students must have been of the same opinion. A Corpus graduate whom I met in Vienna in the 1990s spoke with profound gratitude of Spens as the man who, fifty years earlier, had given him the chance to choose a career in the media, which had brought him wealth and success.

Benefiting from the Tutor's wisdom in the ways of the world was not the same thing as integrating into a college society. The undergraduate population in the 1920s was still largely cast in the public-school mould and basically gregarious. My first few evenings in College I dined in Hall. Handicapped by chronic shyness, I found the undergraduate community of my contemporaries impermeable. The rattle of knives and forks, the continual flow of conversation, might have been the middle of the Sahara: they only deepened my feelings of solitude.

Individually, the undergraduates were friendship itself. I was quickly on intimate terms with my nearest neighbours. Within a week, one of these was consulting me on a personal matter, which had him perplexed. He wanted to be certain he would be doing the right thing if he were to marry a young lady from his hometown with whom he was deeply in love. What made him hesitate was that the lady was not only older than he was but the only thing they had in common was their love of horses. I cannot remember whether I was able to relieve his perplexity, but we remained friends and he invited me to visit him later at his parents' home in Sussex.

While the slightly aloof manner I had remarked in Spens was characteristic and increased the respect he commanded as Tutor, the impression he was also apt to give – that no one mattered more to him than the person he was talking to at the moment – must have helped many members of the College to feel that Corpus was a second home. In my own case, the College became indeed a second home when, visiting Cambridge a few months after going down, I broke my ankle and the Spenses [Spens was by then Master of Corpus] very kindly put me up while my leg was in plaster. I was still in bed when they asked my former supervisor to come and see me to relieve the monotony. It must have been then that I spoke of my ambition to be a poet and

sent the Master's wife a long juvenile poem I had written entitled *Cassandra*. Corpus was again a home from home for me when, returning to England on the outbreak of war in September 1939, I had rooms in College while I found somewhere I could wait until I could enlist in the Royal Navy as a volunteer.

It was only some time after I had left the University that, looking back on my years at Corpus and the friendships I had made there with undergraduates and Fellows, I came to see the College as a digest of British history whose pages were written in the lives of Corpus men themselves. Each of my contemporaries had his line or paragraph in this tome.

Shortly before I went down, when Spens was already Master of Corpus, I was invited to lunch at the Master's Lodge. The day of the invitation happened to coincide with the publication of the Tripos results. My modest Third, product of a month's swatting every night until three in the morning, was celebrated the more heartily by my friends, because wholly unexpected. Even my supervisor had warned that I might be failed. I sat down at the polished Sheraton table to be faced with a surprise hazard, a hard-boiled egg up-ended on a round of toast. A bedevilled knife and fork crossed each other on their way through the layer of mayonnaise separating egg and toast. Not an eyelid twitched to show the Master had noticed anything untoward.

> **CAMBRIDGE REVISITED**
>
> *Sometimes I wish that we could walk again*
> *Beside the river where, when we were young,*
> *The days drifted gently downstream among*
> *Hopes, perhaps fond, but surely never vain:*
> *Dreams, brighter than the sun, castles in Spain*
> *Far more than real, so square they stood and strong,*
> *And though the battle for them might be long,*
> *It was already won!…. The years remain…*
>
> *Yet Spring hopes (long since faded or fulfilled*
> *In shallow eddies, or a sluice to stay*
> *One moment an inexorable flow*
> *Of the same waters on their downward way)*
> *Remembered – leaves falling in autumn – gild*
> *The mists of memory with youth's afterglow.*

# MEMORIES:

Introduction by Betty Bury

## 1927–39 *The time of ever less certain peace*

*William Spens.*

The late 1920s were years of far-reaching and important reform in the University and colleges. The adoption in 1926 of new statutes created the faculty system, reformed much labyrinthine administration and defined conditions of employment for teaching staff; in this arduous reorganization Mr Spens, as a member of the Statutory Commission, had played an important part and he was the obvious candidate to succeed Dr Pearce when he resigned the Mastership.

William Spens, always known as Will, was unanimously pre-elected to succeed Dr Pearce as Master on 3 October 1927. In 1906 he had migrated from King's to become the College's first Director of Natural Sciences and a year later when Colonel Caldwell became Master, was elected a Fellow. As Steward he won the affection of undergraduates for his accessibility and his success in improving the quality of their meals and the general amenities of the College. From 1907 to 1927, apart from the years of the Great War, he served as joint and then sole tutor. His administrative ability and sound judgement meant that he quickly gained recognition in the University as a whole. He was elected to the Council of the Senate and the Financial Board and in 1923 became a member of the Statutory Commission which drafted the new statutes for the University and the colleges. A liberal Anglo-Catholic, he was also appointed in the early 1920s, together with two other Corpus men, to the Archbishops' Commission on Christian Doctrine. From 1930 to 1939 he served as Chairman of the University Appointments Board, and the Spens Report on secondary and technical education was published in 1938. He was knighted in 1939. The *Dictionary of National Biography* described his character as

having 'its fair share of paradoxes: ruthlessness and kindness, detachment and sentiment, shrewdness and sometimes blind loyalty, keen analysis and unshakeable religious devotion'.

In Corpus a number of major decisions had already been taken by the time of Mr Spens' election to the Mastership. The College was to remain small, candidates for pass degrees were no longer to be admitted, undergraduates were to dine together at one time, dons and undergraduates were to lunch together, and attendance at Chapel was no longer to be compulsory, although a good congregation was hoped for at Sung Eucharist on Sundays. Members of the small Fellowship were expected to be very good academically, to be practising Christians, to dine in hall at least three times a week, including Sundays, and to vote Conservative.

In these years there were two Conservative Members of Parliament among the Fellows. Sir Geoffrey Butler, a distinguished Fellow of the College from 1910, was elected Burgess for the University in 1923. Almost alone he developed the Conservative Association into 'a regular school for young Conservatives of ever growing value to the Party'. Dr Pickthorn, who succeeded Mr Spens as Tutor, was elected Junior Burgess for the University in 1935; in 1950, when University seats were abolished and he was still a Fellow of the College, he won the Carlton Division of Nottinghamshire for the Conservatives by a narrow majority. On the extreme Right *Granta* reported that F.H. Lawton of Corpus, sowing his political wild oats, presided over a small Fascist organization in 1933, the year in which the Union heard Oswald Mosley give a brilliant but unsuccessful performance on the motion that 'This House prefers

Fascism to Socialism'. On the far Left some of our contributors recall the Communists in Corpus putting their case, as happened in the University at large, with a stridency out of all proportion to their numbers. Did any members of the College fight for the Republicans in Spain, a cause which attracted great sympathy?

At a time when the University was increasingly permeated by the emotional evangelism of Buchman's Oxford Group movement and the tone of the theological school was predominantly liberal, Corpus took its own line. Sir Edwyn Hoskyns, the Dean of Chapel, became an increasingly severe critic of 'Liberalism'. He was, wrote Canon Smyth after his death in 1937, 'one of the two outstanding names in the history of Christian thought in the present century'. His lectures were unforgettable, his sermons (two of which were on the importance of the Parker MSS) by contrast 'curiously restrained', and his influence on the younger clergy unrivalled. His interests were wide and Dr Pickthorn recalled 'his almost unique awareness of the reality of other people... street cleaners or farm labourers or princes and prelates, the whole external diversity of human life'.

As a keen sportsman and Treasurer of the Amalgamated Clubs, Sir Edwyn would have welcomed the building of a squash court, first used in 1936, and the final turfing of the new larger playing field behind Grange Road which could be used simultaneously for games of rugby, soccer and hockey. Was it on the Corpus field or on their village greens that members of the College coached boys from Willingham and Over in cricket and football in response to a request from the Playing Fields Association? 'Matches have been arranged; and the boys are keen and promising.' It was, however, on the rugby field in 1937 that the College distinguished itself by reaching the semi-final in the 'cuppers' for the first time. Rowing had for many years been the most prestigious University sport and it was not surprising that, when the legendary coach Steve Fairbairn died in 1938, *The Times*' readers were reminded of his dictum that you should face your stretcher as honestly as you should face your God. The fortunes of the Corpus Boat Club had so greatly improved (after many years of decline) that in 1937 the College won the Michell Cup. This was awarded to the Club which had 'the best all-round record for the year'. In the 'Sportsman's Diary' in *Granta* for 8 June 1938 an

*'Cambridge students mocking Hitler' 1936.*

article on the Mays commented: 'Corpus is perhaps the most improved boat. Turner is a great asset to them and deserves the highest praise.' This was A.M. Turner, the Secretary of the Boat Club for 1938–9, who rowed in the same year for the University.

Patrick Bury describes the first twelve years of Mr Spens' reign (1927–39) as lying 'within the time of ever less certain peace between the two World Wars' and being 'concerned mainly with the development and strengthening of the high position now won by the College and with adaptation to growing economic insecurity'. By June 1931 unemployment figures had risen to nearly three million, and by August the financial and political crisis had resulted in the formation of a National Government. It was becoming increasingly clear that political and social problems could no longer be solved only by the League of Nations and that Fascism must be opposed by collective resistance or pacifism. Undergraduates in general were not greatly interested in politics in the early 1930s and attitudes changed comparatively slowly; there was, however, increasing concern about Fascism and the effects of long-term unemployment which some undergraduates saw for themselves in Jarrow. In 1933 a group of volunteers from Westcott House ran the first Cambridge Camp for the Unemployed – Canon Raven of Christ's served as Chairman of the Universities' Council for Unemployed Camps – and in 1936 the Hunger Marchers came to Cambridge and the Spanish Civil War began.

As the international scene darkened, some debates in the Union and political societies were on serious topics and, T.E.B. Howarth thinks, reflected University opinion more significantly than they had done for many years past. In 1932 and 1933 there were huge majorities in the Union in favour of disarmament, and in 1934 the Presidents of the Labour Club, the Anti-War Movement and the Christian Peace Society protested against 'the scandalous campaigns for a larger Air Force that are allowed to appear in the Press'. In May 1935, when Italy had invaded Abyssinia, *Granta* reported that the Union Jack and the Abyssinian tricolour were floating from the eastern pinnacles of King's Chapel; it also reported a vote in the Union against disarmament. In 1937 Frank Singleton, the President of the Union, incongruously wrote that their debates reflected 'the passionate belief of social democrats and everyone to the left of them that it was possible in Spain to stop the march of Fascism and that this would be a good thing'.

Before 1936 the balance of opinion in Cambridge had favoured the National Government and an undergraduate poll taken during the 1935 election resulted in the National Conservative candidate polling 650 votes, the Socialist 275 and the Liberal 171. Christopher Cornford, before his death in Spain in 1935, had, however, played an important part in increasing membership of the Socialist Club from 200 to 600 and ensuring that it was Marxist-dominated. By 1938 more than one in five undergraduates belonged to the Socialist Society, no doubt attracted in part by its lively reputation.

In May 1938 Mr V.A. Annett of Corpus, 'a *Times* editorial come to life', spoke in the Union against the motion 'That this House will reject any appeal from the present government for National Service', while Mr P. Astbury of Christ's refused to 'support a call to arms

from a government whose policy was not a peace policy but one of appeasement'. At the same time *Granta* reviewed a recent book entitled *Air Raid Protection: The Facts by Ten Cambridge Scientists* which found that 'far too little attention has so far been paid to ARP by undergraduates'.

The Munich Agreement was signed on 29 September 1938. The Vice-Chancellor, speaking on the following day at the beginning of the Michaelmas term, addressed the University as follows:

*To all during the last weeks of vacation who by wise counsel and hard work have made preparations to face the dangers with which we were threatened, I wish to express my most sincere gratitude. Yesterday, in common with the rest of the world, we awakened from the horrors of a dream to face the new day with thankfulness and courage. The University, freed from the threat of imminent war, looks forward today with hope and confidence, recently beyond expectation, to the peaceful and productive labours of another year.' And indeed the* Cambridge Review *was soon able to report that the University was running as smoothly as ever. Nevertheless, as John Roach points out, its members were encouraged to place their qualifications and experience on record, offers of service were classified and plans made for an emergency.*

There appeared in these last peace-time months to be no consensus of opinion. By the end of the Michaelmas term of 1938 the post-Munich euphoria was already waning and in November three members of Corpus spoke in a Union debate when, by 233 votes to 107, it was decided that the defence of Britain was unsafe in Mr Chamberlain's hands. In February 1939 the Bishop of Ely, the Mayor of Cambridge, the Chairman of the County Council and the Vice-Chancellor wrote a letter which, 'in a critical year in world history', was designed to draw its readers' attention to the increasing international momentum of Moral Rearmament. In May Winston Churchill came to Cambridge in order to counteract the Union vote against conscription and after a lively meeting was glad to find that a final show of hands indicated a 10 to 1 majority in its favour. In the same month Peter Studd, the Captain of University cricket and a future Lord Mayor of London, said that he hoped to God that Hitler would not declare war before the cricket season was over. As we know, he had his wish.

## MEMORIES:1927–39

### Eric Fielden, 1927

Life was obviously different then: more perhaps on the sexual side than on any other. Although I had a normal interest in and attraction to the opposite sex, I think I can say that in the whole of my three years at Corpus I never had occasion or indeed a fair chance of social contact with a member of the opposite sex. Any such experiences were strictly limited to vacation time.

In 1927 the majority of Corpus undergraduates came from public schools with a decent number of grammar school boys. There was no conscious exclusion of one set by another, but on the whole they settled in different camps and most of my friends were, like me, from grammar school, with an admixture of Americans.

Anything I lacked in social freedom was certainly balanced by almost total freedom in my studies. In my second and third years, I don't think I attended five lectures: this with no adverse comment from authority.

Certainly in my time, the basis of teaching in Cambridge lay in the weekly personal supervision. If any teacher helped me to a double First in Modern Languages it was Pat Charvet, who was elected to a Fellowship the same year I came to Corpus.

### Peter Curgenven, 1929

If, before I knew Corpus, I had been asked for my mental image of a don, I might well have replied that it was of someone immensely learned, who spent a large part of his time poring over books and manuscripts and so on, but who also, to help earn a living, had the less congenial task of giving lectures and tutorials to undergraduates in preparation for their university degrees. In short, there was a sense in which undergraduates were a tiresome extra. One of the things my time at Corpus was to teach me, in those distant days of 1929 to 1933, was drastically to revise my ideas on that subject – not, however, that the dons were less learned than I had supposed!

There were four dons in particular whom I came to know well and with whom I kept in touch, to a greater or lesser extent, long after I went down. All were of outstanding ability, men whose reputation extended far beyond the bounds of Corpus and Cambridge. One was [Sir Edwyn] Clement Hoskyns, Dean of Chapel, whose international standing as a theologian I came to realize fully only later. I was not one of his pupils, but that made no difference. I remember having lunch with him and Lady Hoskyns in their home on an occasion when we had a common interest in that I was reading German for my Tripos and he had been working on the translation of Karl Barth's *Römerbrief*. Alas, it was only four years later that he died at the early age of 54, a devastating loss to Anglican scholarship.

Then there was Kenneth Pickthorn, the Senior Tutor, who was one of my supervisors for the History Tripos Part I. Outwardly he could be somewhat intimidating and he was certainly not one who suffered fools gladly. But he was immensely kind and generous with his friendship. Constitutional History, the subject of his lectures, is not easily combined with hilarity, but he mercifully contrived, with his dry humour, to make us laugh.

Charles Smyth, like Kenneth Pickthorn, was in my time a lecturer and supervisor for the History Tripos. He became a lifelong friend, not only through our relationship as tutor and pupil, but through a shared experience as members of the University of Tübingen. He, as a young priest, had gone there to sit at the feet of famous German theologians, among them Kittel, a friend of Clement Hoskyns. In my fourth year and having to learn German from scratch to complete my Tripos, I had been granted two terms' absence by the College. My debt to the College for that leave of absence and consequent time at Tübingen can be realized when I was later to teach German, the main foreign language at Christ's Hospital, and when my knowledge of German led to a commission in the Intelligence Corps in the Second World War and service in North Africa, Italy and Greece.

My last memorable don must be Pat Charvet who was my supervisor for French; and it was the blend of English and French ancestry in him which gave him his particular brand of a lively wit and characteristic verve. I was to enjoy his hospitality in his home and at tennis on the Corpus courts in Sidgwick Avenue.

As an undergraduate I did not appreciate how lucky I was to come under the influence of such outstanding mentors. But, as I look back, the extent of my good fortune seems all the more noteworthy in that we were living in a far less egalitarian age. We would, for instance, never have dreamt of being on Christian-name terms. But, while the very real distinction between don and undergraduate was always respected, the difference itself posed no problem to the possibility of an equally real growth of a lasting friendship. That, at any rate, was my experience and the same, no doubt, applies today, in a vastly different social environment, to the family that is Corpus. *Floreat antiqua Domus*!

**Frederick Lawton, 1930**

I first came to know that Cambridge existed when I was six. Before her marriage my mother had kept an album of postcards she had received. In it were four that my father had sent her when he was courting her. They were coloured ones of the Backs. They showed young men punting. All wore white flannels and had girls with them carrying parasols. To me Cambridge seemed a dream place; but not one that I would ever be able to enter.

I thought no more about Cambridge until just before the end of my first term at grammar school. At assembly one morning the headmaster announced that a boy named Rose had been awarded a scholarship in foreign languages at Sidney Sussex College. He said that it was the first Cambridge scholarship any boy at the school had won but he hoped that more would follow. Towards the end of the first term of my second year, the second master, Mr H.G. Hall, asked my father to call on him, which he did. He told my father that I seemed to have the potential for gaining a Cambridge scholarship. He explained how, with the help of a London County Council major scholarship, which would be awarded on gaining a Cambridge open one, boys from my kind of financial and social background could go there.

I went into residence at the beginning of October 1930, having little idea of what to expect. When I received the telegram informing me of my award of an open exhibition I had not even known where Corpus was in Cambridge. The main entrance and the New Court were what I had expected – early nineteenth-century neo-Gothic. The College itself is like its Old Court: discreet, unobtrusive, yet at the very pinnacle of excellence.

By the 1930s Corpus was regarded as the centre of High Toryism in the University. The Master, Will Spens, was President of the University Conservative Association. At the general election in 1935 the Tutor, Kenneth Pickthorn, as a Conservative, was elected to represent the University in the House of Commons. He was to be the last to do so. As an undergraduate, I remember seeing leading Tory politicians dining at High Table quite regularly.

During my time at Corpus there were about 150 undergraduates, 50 in each year. There were a few from the families of the aristocracy and gentry. Most came from prosperous professional and commercial families and had been to the leading public schools. One was the son of a solicitor, another of a small local businessman. Two, of whom I was one, came from working-class families. I had arrived through the open-scholarship system; the other young man, who intended to become a parson, was financed by a church charity. In addition, there was the son of a leading Iraqi politician, a wealthy American and an Indian. The American and the Iraqi quickly fitted into College life: the Indian never did. This was probably because of the racism which was then endemic, particularly amongst the middle classes.

As soon as I arrived in Cambridge I had to learn how to budget. My income for the academic year totalled £230, which was £70 short of the £300 which at that time was the amount which the tutor at Corpus advised parents that their sons were likely to require. I knew that my parents would be unable to discharge my debts if they were of any size. When I went up they had dug into their meagre savings to fit me out as best they could with the clothes that they thought I would require during my three years in residence. My father's days in domestic service had given him a good idea of what I would need, and, during my time in Cambridge I never thought that I was shabbily dressed or below the standards of my fellows. They even bought me a dinner jacket, an article of clothing that in those days was unknown among the working class.

What was clear to me at once, however, was that I should avoid any activities that necessitated the outlay of money, such as joining clubs, which required subscriptions, and theatre – and cinema – going. Taking part in College athletic activities provided no financial problems because Corpus, like all other colleges, deducted a fixed amount each term from undergraduates' College accounts. This entitled them to take part in all forms of activity organised at College level. After much thought, I decided to join the Cambridge Union. I could not afford to pay the full subscription of £9 which would have made me a life member. I opted for a term's subscription of £1. I am glad I joined. I attended the weekly debates regularly and used the lending library which was then available. I fancied myself as a debater and from time to time tried to catch the President's eye. I only succeeded a few times. I was an indifferent performer.

In 1930 Cambridge still had a mediaeval flavour in the matter of sanitation. At the bedroom level in Corpus, chamber pots were still in use. In order to take advantage of a water closet, all living in College had to go to the facilities in the Old Court. They were alongside the bath-house which had been installed in the early 1920s. In it were about ten baths, separated from each other by wooden partitions. There were no showers. Before their installation, undergraduates had to make do with hip baths brought to their rooms by the College servants. The practice of having a daily bath was well established by 1930, as was that of taking a bath after vigorous physical exercise.

All colleges shut their outer gates at 10 pm. Anyone entering after that hour and before midnight had to pay a small fine. Returning after midnight or not at all before morning was regarded as a grave disciplinary offence. In Corpus an unpleasant interview with the Tutor invariably followed. There was one rule, common to all colleges, relating to the entertainment of young women, which nowadays seems bizarre. Young women were not allowed in College save between 4 pm and 6 pm – and there had to be two of them. Breaches of this rule were regarded as serious misdemeanours. Having a young woman in one's room overnight resulted in being sent down.

There were only two women's colleges, Girton and Newnham. Each had about 250 undergraduates. Few undergraduates established relationships with girls who worked in Cambridge. Having a 'girlfriend' and spending a lot of time with her was thought unmanly; 'soppy' was then the vogue word. We were naïve about sex. When in 1932 an undergraduate in Sidney Sussex College was found bound up and dead there was much discussion as to what had happened but it did not occur to me or to any of my friends that he could, with or without help, have been practising the sexual perversion of bondage. It was the same with homosexuality. During my time in Cambridge homosexuality was practised among some dons and undergraduates but I did not know it then. A well-known Fellow of King's paraded his homosexuality by his dress. My friends and I regarded him simply as a silly old man.

For me Cambridge provided the turning point in my life, as it did for my contemporaries who came from the same background as I did: it gave me social confidence. It prepared me for the world into which I was to move on going down.

*Edwyn Clement Hoskyns, Fellow 1916–1937.*

## John Burkinshaw, 1931

My first act on arrival at Cambridge was to buy myself a bicycle, a necessity of which I was very proud. One day it vanished from outside Kings. Having reported the loss to the police I went to the police station where I met the Bicycle Detective who, after one glance at me, led me straight to my bicycle which was parked with dozens of others in a big shed.

During my first two years I lived in F7 above the entrance to New Court. There were three rooms. The gyp room had a gas ring, sink, cold-water tap, cupboard and work surface. The bedroom's adequate furniture included a washstand equipped with basin, large water jug, soap dish, slop basin and chamber pot. The large sitting-room had a coal fire and the usual furniture, not forgetting a pipe rack and a metal box to hold a hundred cigarettes (ten for sixpence), which were the small change of hospitality in those days when 'everybody smoked'. All this was devotedly cared for by my dear bedmaker who treated me as one of her family. Breakfast one prepared oneself – usually a scrambled egg cooked on the coal fire. You could, if feeling extravagant, order breakfast, usually an omelette with tomato sauce, which was brought from the kitchen by a lad in his teens who ended up as Head Porter. Breakfast was also a social occasion of which Dr MacCurdy's breakfast parties were the prime example.

It was not uncommon to invite a friend before going off for a nine o'clock lecture. Before breakfast, if you looked out onto the street, you would see men in dressing gowns carrying towel and sponge bag on their way from their lodgings to the 'New Bathrooms' in Old Court. One was expected to dine in Hall wearing a gown. The food was very good. The wearing of Plus Fours in Hall was forbidden and one often saw people stuffing their Plus Four-ed legs into the Flannel Bags (trousers), which they had brought to Hall in compliance with this rule.

Another College rule forbade the playing of gramophones loudly enough to be heard outside one's room after dinner. The rule ended cryptically with 'Trumpets are gramophones'. Radiograms, as they were called, were the latest thing and were a great joy, enabling me to play my 78 rpm records of Beethoven and Mozart and, after my post-prandial study, to listen to the glorious music from the great dance bands which the BBC broadcast after the nine o'clock news, from the posh

London restaurants. My radiogram was my first venture into the Brave New World of hire-purchase. I told my Father about it in my weekly letter to him. Six weeks later (that was how long it took to get a reply from India) I received a letter saying how angry he was and telling me to pay off the debt at once and promise that I would on no account ever do it again. Excellent advice but, alas, too late. I did, however, save a little money by taking up an offer by *The Times* newspaper to supply me, if I signed up, with a daily copy for a penny instead of two pence a copy.

From time to time one received an invitation to dessert after dinner with Kenneth Pickthorn, the College Tutor. These gatherings of half a dozen students took place in his room in College. At nine o'clock precisely the phone would ring. He would hold the receiver to his ear for about five seconds and apologetically explain 'I'm afraid I have to go'. Very tactful and very sensible.

Tea at the Dorothy Café was a focal social event. The large room had many tables, with the proprietor Percy Cowell at the piano. Again I blush to report that quite often there were occasions when sugar lumps were flying through the air in profusion.

I must also mention Ruby's coffee stall in Market Square. Ruby was a most attractive creature and, in those monastic and sex-starved days, it was not surprising that she did a very brisk trade in cups of coffee.

University medical lectures started at 9 am. The lecture theatre was always full. At one minute to nine the only three female medical students would enter together and make their way to the front row, where there were three vacant places, to the accompaniment of a slow handclap. How brave, and how times have changed.

The Boat Club was great fun. At that time, there was much debate as to the relative merits of two rowing styles. The orthodox style used fixed rowlocks – like those in sea-going boats, and a straight back. The new style used 'swivel' rowlocks and a round-shouldered rowing technique introduced by Steve Fairbairn, the great Australian rowing coach. My first year was with 'orthodox'; the second with Fairbairn. The Corpus second boat won their oars with each.

The Long Vac term was a delightful experience. For medical students there was 'bugs and drugs', a course of lectures in those subjects which took place in the holiday atmosphere which pervaded Cambridge during August. Only a few students were up in College and the

river in those days was not crowded. There were not many tourists but I did once see half a dozen in Old Court, earnestly reading a notice beneath a bundle of laundry placed on a vacant lamp bracket. The notice read 'This is the laundry bundle left in the College by the poet Christopher Marlowe before he went to London in 1590.'

I blush when I recall the first and last triennial dinner of the Medical Societies of Oxford and Cambridge. This took place at the Dorothy Café in 1934 after a rugby match between the two Societies organized by Charles Dick, our President and a rugger Blue who later played for Scotland. The big mistake was to open the bar a full hour before the advertised time of the dinner. The guests included the Professors and Heads of the various Medical Departments of both Universities. As Honorary Treasurer of the 'Med. Soc.' I was placed at High Table next to one of them and we struggled to converse amid the uproar which had developed by the time we took our seats. But when a roll of bread splashed into the Professor's soup all verbal communication ceased. The dinner went no further than the meat course and I am haunted by the vision of the President standing on the table trying to restore order. A week later I received a bill for sixty pounds from Percy Cowell accompanied by a letter ending 'you will note that we are not charging for the flooding of the lavatories'.

I remember also spending a few days at the College's Mission in Walworth. This existed to try to bridge the gap between rich and poor. I did not enjoy it. There was an embarrassing air of false heartiness, which must have made the Walworth lads feel that they were being patronized by the 'toffs,' which in truth was actually the case. I have to admit that although the country at that time was in the throes of the Great Depression, my years at Corpus and later the London Hospital were among the happiest of my life. Lucky privileged me!

### Jack (W.J.H.) Earl, 1931

My overall recollection of Corpus in the early 1930s is of a warm and supportive society whose members were forever arguing about world politics and their probable future course but still managed to enjoy themselves. I would like to place on record my deep gratitude to two senior members in particular: Kenneth Pickthorn, whose weekly assaults on loose thinking or careless writing in my essays both terrified and inspired me, and

*The Dorothy Café, c. 1929.*

Edwyn Hoskyns, whose sermons and conversation opened my eyes to the depth and richness of the Christian faith. He also left me with impossibly high standards for kippers. I have never yet managed to find a kipper to equal those he provided at his breakfast table.

### William Harding, 1931
Even in the 1930s the variety of the students was impressive, but it was a very friendly place. We tended to form into 'sets'. The members of my own set were all totally different but we got on very well together.

### The Hon. Hugh Lawson Johnston, 1931
Following a serious illness in my second year at Eton I was sent to a 'crammers' in Switzerland. It must have been a good crammers for, after only three terms, I had exceptionally good results in School Certificate. This resulted in my going up to Cambridge too young. I came up to Corpus in October 1931 at the age of seventeen and totally naïve. I didn't know anybody at Corpus

at that time but soon made some friends, in particular Peter Carter, who became my mentor. Being eighteen months older than me he was a man of the world and educated me.

My rooms were brand new to the College: Y and Z staircases over the National Westminster Bank with a wonderful view of King's College Chapel. This was luxury accommodation with a bathroom on each floor saving the necessity of going with the crowd to Old Court. There was a bedroom and a sitting-room with a gas fire. My furniture, which was purchased for me, included table and chairs that I still use. There was also a gas ring on which we could cook snack meals, but it was still very, very cold in winter.

Besides Peter Carter, there were a number of others such as Ambler Thomas, Marcus Sieff and Graeme Lawton. Coming from an almost teetotal family I had not smoked and was plummeted into drinking and smoking at the University. I smoked cigarettes the first year and hated them, the second year I tried pipes until I found I was merely smoking matches, so I gave all that up. I can't remember what I drank but I'm sure it was not beer and equally sure that sometimes I had too much. The Master was Will Spens, though I never exchanged words with him but once – in my parents' presence. The Senior Tutor was Kenneth Pickthorn who, being an historian, was my tutor. I used to be terrified of tutorials. He never gave me a word of encouragement and my essays were all trash. In my third year Patrick Bury took over the history tutorials. That was a great relief. Humphrey Mynors was Junior Tutor, and other dons included Terence Sanders, a great oarsman, Patrice Charvet and, of course, Dr John MacCurdy. I was still not allowed to join in any athletic occupations. I used to walk long distances and I played golf in my first year at the Gogs. The second year, when I had a car at Royston, I used to go in winter to a rough shoot we had in Bedfordshire. In my third year I had riding lessons and took to hunting after Christmas.

### Maurice Maling, 1931
During the three years I was up there were sixteen resident Fellows (fourteen at any one time). Apart from my Director of Studies (Terence Sanders) relations were distinctly formal during ordinary terms. I did, however, spend the Long Vacation terms of 1932 and 1933 in Cambridge, when it was much easier to get to know the

dons since a lot of the rules were relaxed. Those whom I did get to know better were Pat Charvet, Humphrey Mynors, Sir Edwyn Hoskyns, in my last year Desmond Lee and Professor Lennard-Jones. On the other hand, the porters and Buttery staff became real friends, in particular Albert Jaggard and Bert Lawrence.

One of the less conventional members of the College whom I got to know well in my last year was Patrick Baird. He had come up in 1930 but had failed his exam in 1933 and so came up for the Long Vac term. Since all his old friends had gone down he joined our little set. He and I came from opposite sides of the River Tweed, and found we knew quite a few common friends. I have three distinct memories of him:

Cricket – In the Long Vac term a side called the Pelicans played very friendly (incompetent) cricket. Getting out eleven players was often difficult and once Patrick was persuaded to play. His fielding was even worse than most others, he was obviously thinking about other things. He was at mid-wicket when the batsman sliced a ball above his head. 'Catch it' shouted the Captain. Patrick turned his back on the pitch, held out one hand, and the ball stuck.

Climbing – I knew that Patrick had done some mountaineering in the Alps but little else. One very warm evening in the Long Vac term, many of us were gathered in the Old Court chatting and drinking in the evening cloud. It was almost dark, I was chatting to Pat Charvet (then Dean of College) outside O staircase when I observed a shadowy figure traversing the north face of the tower which connects the Old Court to the New Court: he was only using his hands. I had visions of appearing at an inquest. I managed not to react to the notice of Pat Charvet and in due course Pat B went round the North East corner of the tower and disappeared in the gloom.

Patrick's final departure – In early May 1934 Pat announced that he would be going down on the following Monday for good, since he had been offered a place on an expedition to Greenland. He threw a very alcoholic party on the Saturday night. On Monday morning as I walked towards the bicycle shed he shouted 'Come and push'. On the Cats side of the road was an ancient Morris Cowley filled to bursting point with luggage. It wouldn't start. Four or five of us pushed and, opposite Bene't Street, it fired. Pat waved his hand and disappeared along King's Parade. I never heard of him again except that he had settled in Canada and died many years ago.

**Charles Selwyn, 1931**  *N1, Old Ct, 1934.*

My Corpus career (October 1931 to December 1933) was entirely lacking in distinction. Such interest as there is, is entirely subsequent.

On getting married in December 1933 I went (not sent) down. The motivation was almost entirely romantic but perhaps not without calculation. Jobs were hard to come by in the slump. I was continuously employed, albeit modestly, in the city from January 1934 until the war. When I had passed Part I of the Tripos (II.ii), Kenneth Pickthorn said 'Quite right, you have a second class brain.' The only time in my life I have been asked about a degree was in 1940 when I came up for a commission. Asked about my university qualification I replied, knowing the Brigadier had not been to university 'Passed with honours History Tripos Part I, of course', as if only clots took Part II.

When, soon after, I arrived at a regiment the Colonel said, 'I see you were at Cambridge; presumably you can write a letter which my adjutant can't. You're assistant adjutant'.

In about 1941 Corpus very kindly got me a degree under some wartime regulation. This came in handy when I arrived on our Isle of Wight County Council and was the only member with a degree (there were several heavy-weights, but products of Sandhurst or

Devonport). A degree was overvalued, a fact on which the senior officers traded. I was able to stand up to them. I subsequently enjoyed an entirely unwarranted reputation as an intellectual (which, by usually keeping my mouth shut, I did little to change) and got made chairman!

### Graham Charlton, 1932

Corpus at that time (1932–1935) was a small college and as such was very friendly and cohesive. Most of the British undergraduates came from a similar background i.e. public school. Very few were madly rich but some including Marcus Sieff and Frances Sandilands did extremely well in later life. There were a small number of members from overseas (USA, India and Sri Lanka), notably Senanayake who became President of Sri Lanka.

Academic standards were high and covered a wide spectrum. We had a first class Master (Will Spens) who took a real interest in all aspects of College life. I can personally remember a number of times, being invited for dinner in the Master's Lodge, followed by a duplicate bridge match when the students were thrashed by a team of Master and Fellows.

*Colonel. Shamsher Singh.*

We had a very good team of senior active Fellows, particularly outstanding was Kenneth Pickthorn, who subsequently became a Conservative MP. He was a small waspish man who called a spade a spade. I learnt one always-remembered lesson from him, namely how to discourage and frighten interviewees. This took the form of seating an individual on the sofa in his room and then marching around behind them firing questions so that the effect of the answers could not be seen on his face! I survived this ordeal and came up with an Exhibition.

Another outstanding character was Pat Charvet who spent his career helping the College in all ways. I was and still am a great friend of Robert Beldam, the College benefactor par excellence. A strong lively character who did not at that time hint at his future activities on behalf of the College.

### Shamsher Singh, 1933

The trepidation I felt in standing at the gates of Cambridge, for admission to Corpus in 1933, was greatly softened by my friends from India who now occupied positions of consequence in town; Field Marshal Lord William Birdwood, who once commanded the Indian Army, had assumed charge of Peterhouse; Sir Geoffrey de Montmorency, Governor of the Punjab, was an Honorary Fellow of Pembroke; R.B. Whitehead, ICS Administrator of the Raj in a Northern District, functioned as the Advisor to Indian students at Cambridge, appointed by Whitehall; my cousin, the Honourable Justice T.J. Bedi who had preceded me at College a little earlier, had left behind favourable comment with Sir Will Spens and Tutor Pickthorn, who took kindly to me on arrival.

Personal social accord was later made with the Charvets, Bury, Thomson and H.D.P. Lee who went to Clifton as Headmaster, where I had studied in the mid-1920s.

I rowed a little. Knowles was Captain of the Boat Club. I joined the Chess Club where no one knew the game. Hot Burgundy sitting round the fireplace, brought much amusement communicating with friendly spirits through planchette.

In 1935 I was married and the following year brought us a son, born at the Brunswick Nursing Home. It was a rare sight those days to see an undergraduate wheeling a perambulator down King's Parade, duly attired in his regulation gown.

41

Marriage obliged me to move out of my rooms (YI, Old Court), to rented accommodation in Eltisley Avenue, subject to approval of the University, requiring my wife to function as landlady, to ensure adherence to the Porter's Lodge rules for students. She was assisted by our Indian staff which replaced my excellent gyp at College.

In 1936, King George V passed away at Sandringham. His body was taken by a special train, in mourning black, to London. On the platform, we stood in solemn reverence to pay our last respects to the departed monarch. Naval guards, with reversed arms and bent heads, added their salutes.

Sir Will, at my urgent request, granted me leave to travel overnight by car to witness the historical pageant in London when Edward VIII addressed the Nation over the radio, abdicating the throne to his brother 'For the woman he loved'.

### Gordon B. Robinson, 1934

I arrived at Corpus for the Michaelmas term of 1934 with a falconer friend reading Medicine at Trinity. He brought with him two fine peregrine falcons, which he had arranged to lodge in a disused greenhouse at Cherry Hinton. I agreed to help with their management according to our respective lectures; the daily bicycle ride to feed and exercise them was irksome. For £6.10s we bought a 1923 bull-nosed Morris Oxford, which our irate parents confiscated on discovering that motorcars were forbidden to freshmen. Later, my own hawks,

housed over a nearby boathouse, made occasional forays into College; my bedder removed evidence of their visits with equanimity.

### Philip Yarrow, 1935

I arrived in Cambridge by train from Newcastle upon Tyne early in October 1935, the first boy from a brand-new secondary school to go to one of the older universities. I was not quite eighteen. I had a College exhibition (£40), a state scholarship (fees and £80), £60 from the City of Newcastle, and a Kitchener scholarship (£10). In my final year, when the exhibition had become a foundation scholarship, I had £250 besides my fees. Over sixty years later, this does not sound much; but the starting salary of a schoolmaster on the Burnham scale was then £240.

I remember visiting Bowes and Bowes that first morning, and buying the *Maximes* of La Rochefoucauld. I must also have arranged a bank account, bought a gown and a square, and ordered some visiting cards (then an essential part of an undergraduate's equipment). I remember shopping – chiefly at Woolworth's – for other necessaries, such as cutlery, a kettle, a teapot, a saucepan, cups, saucers and plates, a milk jug, a water jug, a toasting fork, and so forth. I must also have bought stationery and ink (no ball-point pens in 1935).

I was in C5, a staircase in New Court with rooms looking into Old Court. In those days, we had two rooms, a study and a bedroom. The study, of course, had neither telephone nor computer, and the bedroom no

Left: '*Passengers and members of the railway staff standing bareheaded as the train bearing the late King and the Royal mourners passed slowly through the station.*'

*The present Master with three generations of Yarrow men.*

*Sidney Street, with F.W. Woolworth in the foreground, after improvements, 1936.*

running water, only a ewer and basin. As the College had recently installed a splendid bathhouse in Old Court, this did not matter. As a scholar, I enjoyed the privilege of living in College for all three years, and I kept the same rooms all that time. They were *my* rooms, and I could leave my belongings in them during the vacations.

I had a gyp, Pilsworth, and a bedder, Mrs Mansfield. The gyp brought over the daily bread and milk, carried up the coals, tended the fire, and dealt with the laundry; the bedder made the bed, and cleaned the rooms: such, I think, was the division of duties. A bootboy ran round every morning, cleaning the shoes.

The Tutor (H.D.P. Lee) addressed the first-year students one morning, there was a matriculation ceremony, one bought a copy of the *C.U. Reporter* containing the University lecture list and called on one's Director of Studies, and work began. My Director of Studies and French supervisor, Pat Charvet, was a good supervisor, and I enjoyed his supervisions. The one I enjoyed most was one afternoon when he arrived very late in hunting costume, sent for tea and toast, and just chatted. Every

year, before the Tripos or Mays, he would give us good advice (which I never followed), always ending: '*Et surtout purgez-vous bien*'. People in the 1930s felt strongly about constipation and laxatives.

In those days, the Butler library was very ill-stocked, at least as regards modern languages. Its chief attraction, as far as I recall, was Muret-Sanders' German dictionary.

All my life, I have been bookish and nothing else, no sportsman or athlete or handyman, so – unlike my son and my grandson – I contributed nothing to College life. At least, for a very brief period, I belonged to a choir. We met once or twice in someone's room and practised *Oh! Who will o'er the downs so free*? My exercise came chiefly from walks, to Grantchester or along the Coton footpath. Two fellow modern linguists, Lansdowne and Tatham, used regularly after Hall to walk a mile or two along Trumpington Street and back, and sometimes I joined them. I played a little squash, and occasionally went punting. During the Long Vacation terms (the College gave me a grant of £10 to keep them), I played tennis early in the morning with a medical student of my year called Howarth. He once showed me a bookmark he was making from a strip of human skin.

Miss Dorothy Joy of Newnham, now my wife, and I went to two May Balls. The price was £2.2s for a double ticket. We began the evening with a Fellows' dinner sent up to my room.

So far as I recall, on my staircase in my first year were Archdall and Campbell on the ground floor, Bamber, Professor Lennard-Jones, myself, Donald Forbes, and Graeme Chivers. Archdall I have completely forgotten. Campbell was a second-year modern linguist, whom I came to know during my first Long Vac term. Bamber was a fresh-faced, youthful-looking CICCU man. Professor Lennard-Jones, of course, I never knew personally; but he was a good-looking, urbane gentleman who looked like the quintessence of ripe donnishness. Donald Forbes, a gaunt, emaciated Old Pauline reading Classics, was the hardest worker I have ever known; he transferred to Law after Part I. Graeme Chivers, a first-year modern linguist, was a rabid communist; we did not get on.

My chief friends in the College, apart from Lansdowne and Tatham, were Jack Eaton and Robin McCoy. Jack Eaton, a Manchester Grammar School boy, a fellow modern linguist and a rowing man, was a close friend. In 1938 he took me home with him, on the pillion of his motorcycle. We once took a vow not to talk about things of which we knew nothing; I have, I think, kept it pretty well. Robin McCoy was an American reading History, who, nevertheless, aiming at broad scholarship, read Hebrew, Greek, Latin, French, Italian, and German each for quarter of an hour every day. At one time, Jack Eaton and I used to meet in his room every day for breakfast. Some of us also used to foregather there after Hall to listen to gramophone records.

In those days, too, we wore sports jackets and trousers (mainly grey), ties, and shoes. Outside, a College scarf and an umbrella were the standard uniform. We wore gowns for lectures, supervisions, Chapel, Hall, and outside after Hall (with squares) on pain of a fine if one were caught by the Proctor and his bulldogs.

On the subject of discipline, if I remember aright, we were fined 2d if not back in College by 10 pm, 4d if out after 11 pm, and 1/- if not back by midnight – in which case, I believe (but I don't think it ever happened to me), one also had an unpleasant interview next morning with the Tutor or Dean.

### Leslie Hill, 1936

My Director of Studies and French tutor was Pat Charvet, a very polished, witty, elegant and charming man, who was also Domestic Bursar of the College. Throughout my three years, he was a stimulating and interesting tutor, and became one of my few real friends. But a few weeks after I started being tutored by him, he told me that I did not seem to be interested in what he was saying, and that if I wanted, I could find another tutor. I hastily and truthfully disclaimed that I was bored, and henceforth made efforts to drop my mask and allow my face to show the interest I really felt in the questions we discussed. At Canford, thanks to Hodgson, I had developed a very effective poker face, which I could don at will, but this volatile man with the French blood could not stand it.

*Leslie Hill, collecting money for the Poppy Day 'Mile of Pennies', 1937.*

On November 11th we always made a big effort to collect money for Poppy Day. My contribution was to provide people with change for our 'mile of pennies'. I used to start off with five pounds' worth of pennies from the bank, and go back for more as I accumulated larger coins and notes in return for the pennies I gave out. I had a big sign with CHANGE written on it in as many languages as I could manage to find the word for.

[From: *A Bit of an Outsider Really* by Major Leslie Hill.]

### John Broadhead, 1937

My work at Cambridge had been concentrated but it covered a wide field that included Arable and Grassland Farming, Building Construction, Law, Business Management and Animal Husbandry. I found that I was in a minority at Corpus in that this was a relatively new area of studies, but I soon discovered what a blessing it was to be a member of a small College with a limited number of students from a wide variety of faculties. That rubbing of shoulders did, without a doubt, give me a wider experience and approach to life than I would otherwise have experienced. The result was that my Cambridge friends were mainly from the College and, although I spent one summer vacation on a large farm in Suffolk, my others were spent travelling with future lawyers, clerics, and doctors from Corpus – and that was of great benefit to me as a person.

My main exercise was on a bicycle when I cycled to the University Farm opposite Girton College – and once I cycled home 100 miles away because I did not seem to have the train fare. Then there was hockey and tennis and running and swinging across the upper reaches of the Cam on a rope precariously tied to the upper branch of a tree. One day, Arthur Turner – a Blue who, because he mistook me for someone else, but mainly because of my weight – asked me if I would like to go boating – as a cox! I seemed to pass all the necessary tests and I spent many happy and rewarding hours on and off the Cam – and we made visits to Putney, Marlow and Henley. There are, of course, stories about each outing and my family tell me that this is when I learnt to shout. It was with the second boat that we won our oars or, for me, a beautifully emblazoned tiller, which I only returned to the College, together with my blazer and cap, a few years ago.

It was my background that made me register as a conscientious objector in 1939. I was blessed with understanding parents and family but, as matters became more tense and ominous, I felt that I should play my part in preventing the spread of Nazism. I enrolled for service with the Royal Engineers – to follow my father's example in the First Great War – but, because I had disrupted normal proceedings, I received calling-up papers to my home address after I had already been accepted by the REs – providing I finished my last year's learning and joined the University's OTC. That was a serious problem and I shall always be grateful to Desmond Lee for sorting the problem out to my advantage.

*Kenneth Pickthorn, Fellow 1914–1975.*

## Desmond Fitzgerald, 1937

In January 1937 I was commissioned as Second Lieutenant in the Royal Engineers, joining the School of Military Engineers at Chatham, Kent. The young officers' course lasted 32 months and included two academic years studying for the Mechanical Sciences Tripos at Cambridge University. So it was that in October 1937 seventeen of us pitched up at Cambridge.

There were about 70 of us there at any one time. The powers-that-be reckoned, wrongly, that we had done the equivalent of the Tripos first year at the 'Shop' (RMA). We were paid ten shillings a day but our allowances bumped it up to fourteen because we were living in Cambridge, designated by the War Office as an 'Isolated Fort.' The Army paid our tuition fees; we found all our living and other expenses ourselves.

We were distributed at random to various colleges. My best friend, Michael Wilkinson was one of about eight in Peterhouse. I was lodged, the only sapper in the even smaller Corpus, in New Court.

Work-wise I had no connection whatever with Corpus. It was lectures and practicals in the labs of the Engineering Schools and my tutor was a don in Sidney Sussex. We went to other specialists: one I particularly remember – in 'Emma' – was a metallurgy man, who for a few bob would sell you the exam questions (not on paper mind you, he would advise you on what to revise).

I was given two inestimable privileges at Corpus: to live in College both years, and to be spared the indignity of being 'gated', so that I never had to climb into College after hours. Most of my military mates were less lucky. One, climbing over the wall of Trinity Hall landed at the feet of a don taking a late night stroll.

*Union Cinema in 1936.*

> FROM KENNETH PICKTHORN'S OBITUARY FOR SIR EDWYN HOSKYNS:
>
> *In a society like the Corpus High Table in the post-war years, where almost everyone was young, where conversation was unrestrained and almost wholly disrespectful and frequently ribald, he always, without effort and without the least itch to correct, preserved his personal and priestly dignity; he was always intimate with every colleague, and entertained by all of them, without ever allowing it to be conceivable that his merriment had any tinge of that offence into which parsons often slip when their collars are unbuttoned.*

'Really, Mr Ronaldson, you must be more careful where you land,' he remarked, as he passed on his way. Pat's landing had taken place within feet of the open ground-level entrance to an underground cellar. My colleagues mostly had to spend a year in 'digs.'

We needed cars when we were studying to be soldiers at Chatham during the Long Vacation, so it was tiresome to be banned from running one at Cambridge. I garaged mine near the railway station unbeknownst to the proctors.

I was up during the Mastership of Sir Will Spens, and was entertained once in the Lodge. The Dean of College, Mr Bury, asked me more than once to breakfast. Socializing at breakfast seemed to me positively outlandish. I tended to think in terms of breakfast as my father used to, telling of his days as a subaltern in the officers' mess of the King's African Rifles in Nairobi. There it was a heinous offence not only to utter, but even to make the smallest, noise.

Mr Patrice Charvet was the Domestic Bursar. I remember him as a kind, helpful character, and of corresponding with him, I believe, in the 1950s, after he had stopped being Bursar. He was the person who made one feel part of the College when one was actually an out-sider; and this feeling of belonging surged back suddenly when, in January 1997, I received a card for my 80th birthday. I was surprised and charmed.

My rooms were on the right as one entered New Court on the first floor overlooking St Botolph's Churchyard. Above me lodged a music scholar, who later, I was told, directed King's College Music. He practised endlessly on the piano.

I usually took breakfast in my rooms and lunch and dinner in Hall. One had to eat a number of dinners in a term, a way of making sure you were in residence. The food was pretty good; but eating under the grim surveillance of that terrifying judge, Mr Justice Avory, whose picture frowned down upon the assemblage, could ruin one's appetite. Lunch was *à la carte* and very good indeed. I often had friends as guests. The wines from the Buttery were first class, and rivalled those from the Headquarters RE mess at Chatham. At dinner I regularly sat next to half a dozen or so fellow students, who became not very close acquaintances. There was a sprinkling of Law students but the majority were either aspiring Anglican parsons or musicians.

We all learnt ballroom dancing at the feet of Sheila Mitchell, John Elton's eventual wife, who had a studio over Millers, the music shop in, I think, Regent Street. We attended the Med. Soc. Ball. There was ordinary cinema at several picture palaces, and extraordinary (Marx Brothers and French films) at a fleapit off the market place where the projector was behind the screen. There was good theatre and occasional ballet (I entertained Margot Fonteyn) at the Arts, and excellent repertory at the Festival Theatre (Shaw, Ibsen, etc.). There was a good cheap eating-place in St Edmunds Passage, and we drank at many pubs including the Eagle, the haunt of flamboyant homosexuals (The East Anglian beer was, we thought, inferior – Greene King and Tollemache, pah!). Occasionally we went racing at Newmarket. Although there was wonderful choral music at King's and other colleges (including Corpus), there was no concert hall in Cambridge. After Hitler invaded Czechoslovakia there was a symphony concert with an eminent Czech conductor where feelings ran high. It took place in one of the cinemas.

On the very first day of residence I was beset with politicians soliciting my support. The Socialists, the Fabians, the Independent Labourites, the Communists and the Conservatives (no British Union of Fascists) all beat on my door. I said to all of them: 'I am an Army officer and am not encouraged to indulge in politics.' That was sufficiently pompous for them to leave me alone forever. Privately, I would have liked to join the Fabians. It was difficult not to be left-wing inclined in the days of the Great Depression (shades of Jarrow and Ellen Wilkinson).

The clouds were gathering in 1939, and the menacing shadow of imminent war enveloped us in gloom. With an imported girlfriend I attended the May Ball but I did not attend the Senate House degree ceremony. I was at Chatham putting the finishing touches to my military expertise.

### John Jeffries, 1937
When I first came up to Corpus in 1937, I was given rooms on G staircase with a fine view of the Chapel and another window overlooking the cycle shop in Trumpington Street. I envied my friends who lived in the Old Court, with its ancient stones and temple-haunting martlets. Years later, I was invited to a MacCurdy Dinner and was given a room in Old Court. My great joy, however, was marred by nocturnal footsteps along Free School Lane, right next to my bed. How glad then I was, that my student years had been passed in the New Court!

### Harold Last, 1935
The year 1937, Coronation year, was probably the last in which most undergraduates were able still to disregard the threat of war and to continue enjoying their Cambridge days single-mindedly. An amusing incident took place in Corpus towards the end of the summer term, which probably deserves to be recorded. It involved the Head Porter, Beasley. Beasley had been in office for 37 years, and was one of the most senior and respected Head Porters in Cambridge. In Corpus he was a veritable institution, a large and imposing figure, always appearing in a subfusc suit and sporting a fine top hat. One warm afternoon he decided to take a stroll round the New Court without his 'topper'. As he was passing the Master's Lodge at a leisurely pace, a lad on the roof-top, armed with a peashooter espied an irresistible target, and scored an immediate bull's-eye on Beasley's unprotected pate! This was a heinous offence! Luckily for its perpetrator (who shall be nameless) the

Master was not in residence at the time. It took all Lady Spens' diplomacy, tact and charm to appease the wrath of an outraged Beasley. The following day at a tea party in her sitting-room she was heard to say 'I hope Bill never learns anything of this'. He never did.

Shortly after the end of this happy summer term, tragedy overtook the College. Sir Edwyn Hoskyns became seriously ill and died. He was only 54 years of age. Members of the College Choir and the Organ Scholar were summoned back to Cambridge for the services that followed, in the Chapel and at Grantchester. It was a saddening experience for all concerned. Eventually Noel Davey succeeded Sir Edwyn as College supervisor in Theology and sponsor of the Bene't Club; Charles Smyth became Dean of Chapel and Mr Bury was appointed College Librarian. It took the undergraduates involved some time to come to terms with these changes.

The two years that now followed (1938–1939) were increasingly overshadowed by war clouds. Nevertheless, the routines of academic and social life went on much as usual. By a curious irony the last foreign visitors to the College during this period were Germans. In 1938 two theologians from Tübingen University were guests of the College, a Professor Fehzer and a Dr Stumpf. One evening while the Professor was elsewhere the good Doctor was being entertained by Noel Davey and a coterie of Corpus 'theologs'. A friendly atmosphere was engendered and before the party ended, the Doctor confided to all present his detestation of Hitler and the Nazi movement, sadly opining that the Führer was a threat not only to other countries but to the Fatherland itself. He asked us to treat his remarks as confidential, and to say nothing to the Professor who apparently was a keen 'party man'. A third German visitor arrived during the summer term of 1939, only two or three months before war broke out! This was a young Lutheran pastor, a very personable and friendly man, but full of enthusiasm for Hitler and the Third Reich. This made him rather less acceptable.

The Name Day Feast that final year (1939) was as splendid a celebration as ever. There was a distinguished company. The weather was perfect and everything went well. Perhaps the magic of the Lodge garden in the 'cool of the eve', after the splendid feast and the customary ceremonies were over, lingers most happily in the memory of those who were there and can recall the occasion as a fitting finale to the twenty years that had gone before.

## John Press, 1938

Although most of my friends were first-year historians I often sat in Hall next to three men, all of whom were reading other subjects and all of whom came from richer and more sophisticated backgrounds than I: the Raja of Khetri, who ruled a small state in Jaipur, John Coatman, whose father was a senior officer in the ICS; and John Reid-Dick, the son of a well-known sculptor. After Hall we often went to Khetri's rooms, which were on the ground floor of New Court next to the Butler Library. There we would drink port and discuss various topics, mainly politics, although John Reid-Dick, whose knowledge of politics was rudimentary, usually remained silent. John Coatman and Khetri would wrangle amicably about ending British rule in India or about Khetri's dictum: 'Honest, Intelligent, Conservative. A man may be any two of these but not all three'. One evening he put a record on his gramophone, saying that we were about to hear the finest piece of music in the world. It was a wordless version of the Internationale. John Reid-Dick was delighted. 'That's a pretty good tune', he said, 'what show does it come from?'

I made the acquaintance of Mr Bicknell, Keeper of the Lewis Collection of gems and other precious objects, which was housed in the Parker Library. In addition to holding this sinecure he gave six annual University lectures on the reign of the Emperor Hadrian.

His views on race, politics and society were fearsome. He greatly regretted his failure to witness a public execution. Early in the 1920s, when on holiday in France, he read in a newspaper that the Greek generals who were held responsible for the military disaster in Asia Minor were to be executed in Athens in Constitution Square. He raced across Europe, hoping to be present at the spectacle; but, to his chagrin, arrived too late.

He was fond of gazing at the readers in the Butler Library and, after due observation, would confidentially predict how they would perform in the Tripos. He informed me that, if I worked hard, I should get a II.i.

One day he expressed the hope that I should not follow in the footsteps of Bradshaw-Isherwood, who would have secured a First had he not played the fool. Knowing from *Lions and Shadows* that its author had, in the Tripos, answered a question on the foreign policy of Charles II by composing a sonnet, I asked Mr Bicknell if he was referring to Christopher Isherwood. 'He is', came the reply, 'on the College Books as Bradshaw-Isherwood, whatever you may choose to call him. After going down from Corpus, he went to the bad and ended up in Hollywood'.

A few days after the outbreak of war on 3 September 1939 Desmond Lee, the Tutor, despatched a circular letter and an enclosed form asking gentlemen to complete it and return it to him if they wished to volunteer for National Service. A few days later a second letter arrived, stating that the government wanted gentlemen who had completed their first year to return and take their Tripos. They should, therefore, present themselves at the College for the Michaelmas term.

The Government appointed Regional Commissioners who would be granted emergency powers if a German invasion made this necessary. The Regional Commissioner for East Anglia was the Master of Corpus, whose Headquarters was a large house, St Regis, in Chesterton. This inspired Charles Smyth to tell the story of the faithful bedmaker (for the authenticity of which I cannot vouch). A Corpus bedmaker who kept a lodging-house with her husband in Chesterton was sworn to secrecy about the nature of the house opposite hers. One of her lodgers was a German postgraduate, who began asking her awkward questions, which she parried. 'It's just an ordinary house, sir, nothing particular about it.' The lodger persisted: 'That cannot be. The Master of Corpus often goes there. So do other Heads of Houses, Professors, and senior Army and RAF officers'. The faithful bedmaker thought for a moment before replying: 'You are right, sir. The house is a VD treatment clinic'.

The Ministry of Information occupied certain rooms in the College. Among its officers was the novelist R.H. Mottram, with whose son I had been at school, and who greatly enjoyed his life at Corpus, especially his membership of High Table. Mottram became friendly with a Fellow of the College, Dr Bueno de Mesquita, who spoke English with a very slight foreign accent or intonation. When Mottram asked him how long his family had been in England, Mesquita answered, with a slow smile: 'About three hundred years'. Mesquita was my supervisor. Impassive and courteous, he seldom made more than a brief comment on my essays. One day, however, he paused after I had finished reading and said: 'I sometimes think you may have a talent, but I am not sure that it is for history'.

The evacuation of the LSE to Cambridge brought in its wake a number of attractive young women, including the famous LSE blonde. Since this is not an autobiography it is enough to note that I lay beneath the spell of an LSE brunette from the spring of 1940 to the summer of 1941.

One of the first-year men was T.E. (Peter) Utley who had been blind from the age of five. Desmond Lee had been doubtful about admitting him, despite his high intellectual standard, but all worked out better than anybody could have hoped. First-year men took Peter to lectures, where he jotted down notes on his braille typewriter. Second-year historians read to him or summarized books and articles from periodicals that were too long or too dreary to read *in toto*. He often went out in the evenings with a variety of friends; and on Tuesdays he and I attended the Union, where he soon became an eloquent speaker.

Reluctant to tear ourselves away from Corpus, several of us stayed on for some days after the end of the summer term. When we were drinking on the lawn of the Old Court before Hall, Matthews approached and said: 'Gentlemen, the Master orders you to pack your belongings and leave the College by twelve noon tomorrow'. He refused to divulge the reason for this order; but we learned, soon after our departure, that the College had been requisitioned to house troops retreating from Dunkirk.

I was called up on 30 September 1940 and commissioned on 21 December 1941. I was posted to the RAF station at Duxford, that was guarded by six Bofors anti-aircraft guns of my Battery.

In May 1942 my Battery sailed for Kenya, where I remained until the end of September 1945, when I was granted a Class B release and returned to Corpus. I found there about twenty men of my year, all of us now BAs, having been granted wartime degrees. John Roach was not among them, not being strong enough to return until after the beginning of the Lent term, after recovering from four years' incarceration in loathsome Japanese POW camps. He then accomplished the remarkable feat of getting a First in Part II of the History Tripos.

A score of men had come up straight from school. The food in Hall was execrable: an affliction borne fairly philosophically by the BAs. The first-year men watched with anger the delicious food carried from the kitchen past them to High Table. They were particularly incensed because they suspected that a portion of their butter and sugar rations had been diverted into the luscious puddings relished by the Fellows. I did not believe that any Fellow would stoop to such a manoeuvre; but I had my doubts about one or two of the senior kitchen staff. One evening in mid-October, after grace had been said, the entire body of first-year men walked out of Hall. Shocked by this unprecedented act, the Domestic Bursar received a delegation of first-year men. Thereafter, the food improved noticeably, though not spectacularly.

Edward Thompson, whom I had not met before, sometimes discussed with me the paper in Part II of the History Tripos on the Theory of the Modern State, for which he had an almost unmitigated contempt. 'I saw Mussolini hanging upside down in a Milan square, and after that it is clear that Bosanquet and the Victorian Idealists are talking academic piffle'.

It was not easy to concentrate on academic studies when so much of one's time and energy was devoted to looking for a job. My wish to join the British Council did not commend itself to Desmond Lee. 'No Corpus man has ever joined the Council, so it is probably not worth joining'.

'There are', he remarked, 'vacancies for a history master at two good public-schools. You and Roach would be strong candidates'. Alternatively, I might well be acceptable to the Foreign Office. When he saw that I was intent upon the Council he was immensely helpful, guiding me in tortuous negotiations and steering me away from undesirable appointments. I can still see his look of incredulous disdain when I was offered the post of housemaster at an Egyptian school in an oasis 80 miles from Cairo: 'Really, a Corpus man should do better than that'. When I finally accepted the post of lecturer at the Institute of English Studies in Athens, Desmond Lee expressed his approval: 'I'd rather like a year in Athens, myself. And if the Council turns out to be no good you can resign at the end of the year and look for something better'.

### John Roach, 1938

There were three Wolvesey exhibitions given in 1938, and the other two men both became friends. Edmund Randall was the only one of us who was eventually ordained. He finally became head of a theological college in Adelaide, South Australia, and has stayed in Australia in his retirement. The third man, W.R. (Billy)

*John Roach.*

Behrendt, was a charming mathematician who was very sadly drowned in an accident at the University bathing place at the end of our first year.

When I came up, there was one Fellow still surviving, C.A.E. Pollock, who had been elected in 1881 in the old Low Church days. I never knew him personally, but he dined in Hall and said grace regularly. He died in 1944. As an undergraduate I saw nothing of the Master, Will Spens. My tutor Desmond Lee, who was a classical philosopher, was about 30 and as a young man was shy and difficult to get to know. We freshmen were all invited to tutorial wine parties after dinner, and I can still remember at my first such party the ignominy of trying to pass the port the wrong way, and being in consequence reprimanded by my host and tutor!

Apart from some teaching by Kenneth Pickthorn in the first year, I was taught during my first two years very largely by Charles Smyth, and I saw a good deal of him through the Chapel as well. I think that Charles was an excellent supervisor for an able man, and I certainly enjoyed my supervisions with him. At the personal level he and his wife were friendly and hospitable, and he tried, when he could, to introduce us to interesting people who were visiting the College. I remember being invited among a group of people to meet T.S. Eliot who was giving the Boutwood lectures, which were later published as *The Idea of a Christian Society*. I vividly recall Eliot's dark handsome head and rather beak-like profile, but I don't think that talking to the young was his forte, and I can't remember that anybody said anything. But that was not Charles's fault.

My undergraduate career, until I joined the Army in July 1940, was dominated by the threat of war and then by war itself. Pacifist feeling was strong in the 1930s through the influence of bodies like the Peace Pledge Union. I was influenced by the pacifist case, but never convinced by it. When the threat of war was averted by the Munich agreement, I was as relieved as everyone else, and didn't look much beyond that point. In the end, the Michaelmas term of 1938 began about three weeks late, though after that the remainder of the academic year went pretty normally.

From the time I went up to Corpus I had been a member, though not a particularly active one, of the Officers' Training Corps, and within a few days after the declaration of war on 3 September 1939 I had gone up to Cambridge and volunteered for service. Conscription had already been introduced, and some young men had been called up, though I was still too young to be affected.

It was not clear at first whether ordinands would be exempted, though eventually they were, and I was not at all sure what I should do if exemption were offered. I went to talk to Desmond Lee, my tutor, and he gave me the excellent advice that, if I took exemption, I should be cutting myself off from what would be the major experience in the lives of the men of my own age. I was very impressed by what he said, and decided not to claim exemption when it was offered. I have always thought that for me this was the right decision, and nothing that happened afterwards changed my mind. I think that my fellow ordinands in Corpus split just about half and half. Some of us went into the services. Others, like my friends Rex Hartley and Kenneth Skelton, who eventually became bishop of Lichfield, went on to theological colleges and were ordained in the latter part of the war.

The History Tripos Part I in May 1940 was a strangely unreal experience. One just got on with it, since it had to be done, and we twenty-year-olds probably had less imaginative grasp of the real horror of what was happening in Europe than had we been older. There were none of the usual May Week celebrations that year. Very wisely they had been cancelled because, at the time when they would have been held, Cambridge was full of troops who had been evacuated from Dunkirk. Two Scotties slept in my rooms on T staircase, Hostle Yard. One of them was a Glasgow tram-driver who showed me with great pride a copy of Burns' poems which had been presented to him by the city transport department when he joined the forces.

So far as the lighter side of life was concerned, I was rather restricted by the fact that I had very little money. My grant covered fees and expenses during term, and I even made an effort to save a little, reckoning that I would need a little capital behind me when I started work. It never occurred to me to think that I could attend a May Ball or anything of that kind. Such things were out of my financial reach and I never thought about them. I certainly didn't envy those who were socially and financially 'better off' than me. My impression is that in the College in the first year there was still quite a sharp division between a small group of quite well-to-do young men and the rest of us. It is interesting to remember that there was still a 'gyp' who, for a fee, would look after young men's clothes and clean their shoes and no doubt wait at lunch and dinner parties. After 1939 these distinctions disappeared as we all sank into the grey anonymity of war.

Most of my friends in College came from grammar schools or small public schools. Some of them were ordinands, others were not, like my fellow historian John Press from Norwich, who eventually spent his working life with the British Council. Some of my contemporaries were killed in action. Our general pattern of social life was to entertain one another to tea in the afternoons or to meet and talk in the evenings after dinner.

I rowed for a short while, though I gave this up because I found it difficult to combine with my work, and I gave some, though not very much, time to the OTC. The best thing I remember about that was a very enjoyable camp near Mettingham in Norfolk at the home of the CO of the Engineer Company, Donald Portway of St Catharine's. For exercise after I gave up rowing, I used, like nineteenth-century undergraduates, to walk. The 'Grantchester grind' was a favourite, and Rex Hartley and I used sometimes to walk out to Matins on Sunday mornings at Grantchester church, which is a College living.

I reported at the Royal Fusiliers depot on 18 July 1940. Five years later and by the end of the war I had abandoned the idea of ordination. I decided to teach and for that purpose thought that I needed a full degree and not the war degree which I had earned on my two years of study before 1940. I had about three weeks in Cambridge before Christmas 1945, worked through the Lent and May terms, and took Part II of the Tripos at the end of May 1946. I worked hard and was lucky enough to get a First and to win a second Bishop Green Cup. As I look back, it is remarkable that I and many thousands of servicemen moved from war service straight to a life of study without any real break. Even in the case of people like me who had suffered the harsh experiences of prisoner-of-war camps, there was no suggestion of rehabilitation or counselling. One just jumped in and got on with it. Provided that one was reasonably healthy and well-balanced, as I was, this rather rough treatment was probably the best course. One just had no time to worry about whether one could cope or not, since coping was the only available course.

Most of 1945–6 I was taught by Patrick Bury, and it was at this time that there grew up what was to become one of the strongest and most important of my friendships. He had married in January 1944, and his wife, Betty, soon became a good friend too. Not only did I pick up old friendships, but it was at this time that I got to know Geoffrey Woodhead, later for so many years a colleague, and Michael McCrum and John Barry, who had come up in autumn 1946 after service in the navy and who took their degrees in 1948.

Both the undergraduate body and the High Table were small, so that we knew one another pretty well. Nor must the College servants be forgotten. Many of them were very fine people, experienced and long-serving, and they formed a strong strand in the general pattern. In May 1952 Will Spens, not long before he retired from the Mastership, gave an address in Chapel, and I noted in my diary (11 May 1952) that he

'talked about the College as he had known it, about the change in our traditions in the early part of the century, about Fanshawe, Geoffrey Butler and so on. It can't be said that this sort of thing is much in my line, but I was impressed by the Master's emphasis on friendliness, on our all seeing the best in one another and on the importance of the different undergraduate sets mixing up together.'

*Sundial in Old Court in snow.*

# MEMORIES:

Introduction by Betty Bury

## 1939–45 *Wartime conditions*

At the end of August 1939 Fellows of the College laboured against time to fill tea-chests with the Parker manuscripts and early printed books which, loaded on a large lorry and accompanied by a car carrying fire-fighting appliances, were then hurried off to a safe place belonging to the National Library of Wales.

War was declared on 3 September and for the second time in a generation the normal course of academic life was interrupted. However, despite the rapid disappearance of many academics into the armed forces or the civil service, Patrick Bury writes: 'The interruption was less rude' than in 1914 'because the authorities were in some ways better prepared to meet it and there was no intention that University life should cease'.

The *Association Letter* for 1939 describes the College adapting itself to the first weeks of war as follows:

'The delay in the appearance of this *Letter* is due, like so many other delays, to the outbreak of war. As we go to press the College is rapidly adapting itself to wartime conditions. A new term finds the Master hard at work in his new headquarters as Regional Commissioner and a part of the College occupied by Government offices. Mr Sanders is commanding a battery of the RFA, and two other Fellows, Professor Vincent and Mr Bury, have been called away on national service. A large number of undergraduates have been up before the Recruiting Board, but, as the War Office has decided to postpone calling up young men of 18 and 19, between eighty and ninety are expected to be in residence, that is slightly more than half our normal complement. There has been little time so far to make detailed arrangements, but undergraduate life in wartime is likely to be very different from undergraduate life in peacetime.

Military activity will be to the fore, as it is expected that most people will want to join the OTC. Outings and entertainments will be curtailed by rationing of food and petrol. The hard life of the Proctors will be made still harder by the 'blackout', and they are at the moment trying to devise a means of dealing with this new problem.

Apart from the invasion by Government offices, war has in several ways affected the appearance of the College. The bicycle sheds and garage have been transformed into shelters. Trenches have been dug in the New Court and the little garden adjoining Free School Lane and fitted with shelters, the excavations in the New Court incidentally disclosing a brick, vaulted and empty cellar, which probably belonged to the old Dolphin Inn. Staircase windows have been painted blue; Hall is being shrouded with red curtains, and an army of bedmakers has been busy cutting up black material to darken rooms.'

Dr Carter, the Praelector, had the difficult task of organising an Air Raid Precautions service, the College plate was secreted below ground, and air-raid shelters and a large static water tank disfigured the New Court.

Some years before the second war it had been decided that Cambridge should be the Regional Headquarters for the Eastern Counties in time of need and as the East Anglian section of the coast would be highly vulnerable in the event of invasion, the Master's post as Regional Commissioner was a particularly responsible one. He was joined in his headquarters in Chesterton by Mr Lee, the Tutor, whose work in College Dr Carter and Mr Roberts took over until 1944. In the dreadful year of 1940 the Master asked all heads of colleges to disperse the University immediately the June examinations finished. Only medical students, signallers of the Senior Training Corps, gunners and sappers and any others who could help to defend the town were to stay in Cambridge. The Deputy Regional Commissioner, the Earl of Cranbrook, and the Regional Air Liaison Officer, Air Vice-Marshal Sir Norman MacEwen, lived in College for most of the war and they and other senior members of the services who came to consult the Regional Commissioner and his staff, became most welcome members of the depleted High Table.

Also in 1940, an evening meal of a very different kind was prepared for more than a hundred weary troops who had been evacuated from Dunkirk. A telephone call had been received about 9 pm by one of the seven Fellows still resident in College asking for beds and a meal. In the words of Mr Roberts: 'Their improvised meal, following exploration of the kitchens and with the final and more professional assistance of one or two hastily collected members of the kitchen staff, was regarded as something of a triumph, being consumed to the last crumb some time towards midnight, to the sounds of the first bombs dropped upon the town'. The town mercifully suffered very little during the war and no college or University building was damaged.

The Christmas 1941 report from the College Mission in Camberwell, London, naturally told a much gloomier story. 'The Mission District has suffered badly. About half the houses have been destroyed or damaged too badly for occupation'. The clergy house was fitted up as a temporary church and the congregation scattered all over the country. However, 'in spite of the depopulation of the neighbourhood Sunday morning usually finds the temporary church (which holds about 65) full and sometimes the congregation overflows into the adjoining room'.

We cannot guess how many victims of these raids came to Cambridge, but we do know that some 2000 students from colleges and institutions of the University of London remained in the town until the end of the war, although in 1943 medical students from the London Hospital returned home. Government departments were housed in Trinity, Caius and Sidney as well as Corpus, and the RAF took billets in no fewer than nine colleges. A considerable number of cadets from the signal corps and the navy had also to be housed and taught on short courses before joining the forces.

*Taking the stained glass in King's Chapel to a place of safety, 1939.*

In Corpus, after two years of war, 'the Chapel has now been permanently blacked out and the wearing of surplices has been intermitted for the duration. Undergraduates are frequently seen about the College in uniform as well as civilian or academic dress; there are obviously fewer of them – about half the usual number and they are here for a shorter time. Medical students and technicians naturally predominate... The Master continues as Regional Commissioner... and the College is fortunate that his official duties, responsible and exacting as they are, do not prevent him from continuing to preside at College meetings, to keep the threads of College policy in his hands, to dine frequently in Hall and to be in his stall in Chapel every Sunday'.

Most of the Fellows remaining in Corpus took their weekly turns at fire-watching and Mr Charvet and two others were members of the Home Guard. Dr Clark-Kennedy became second-in-command of the 7th Cambridgeshire Mobile Battalion and combined this with his academic work and his duties as Dean and physician to the London Hospital. Dr Carter, assisted by the Head Porter, remained in charge of Air Raid Precautions, Mr Lee was designated Alarm Offi-

*Pat Charvet,
Fellow 1928–62.*

cer for the Eastern Civil Defence Region and Mr Roberts, one of the members of the Home Guard, also instructed members of the University Air Squadron in deflection shooting.

For the 143 lecturers and demonstrators out of a peacetime total of 370 who remained to teach in Cambridge life was difficult, especially when unfamiliar syllabuses had to be combined with civil defence duties. The Vice-Chancellor, in his review for 1943, pointed out that there were now at least twelve categories of student ranging from 'Cadets (five types), State Bursars, ex-service applicants, the medically unfit and conscientious objectors to the more normal members of the different age groups who must in their turn be split up into the various wartime courses of study, many of which are subject to rigid limitation'.

In common with the rest of the country, members of the University experienced increasing shortages of food, fuel and clothing and of domestic staff as the enrolment of women proceeded. The feeding of hundreds of hungry young men and, to a lesser extent, of young women who also 'dug for victory' in their college gardens must have been a complicated task. At the beginning of 1944 A.S.F. Gow described seeing young men at an age when the ration was really insufficient carrying loaves, which were not rationed, under their arms. Corpus must at least have been well supplied with vegetables, as the *Association Letter* for 1942 and 1943 reported that the unturfed corner of the new sports ground and the adjoining field provided the College with some seven acres of market garden. Less importantly, clothing coupons were not needed for gowns or hoods, which counted as hats, and when mortar boards became unobtainable the proctors were reported to have reduced to half price the fine for not wearing one.

Much more serious was the severe shortage of paper and worries about the supply of textbooks for the small number of undergraduates in residence. They did, however, find time to field rugger and hockey teams and the cricket eleven, in the words of an *Association Letter*, 'added an enterprising number of Long Vacation fixtures to their list, mainly with RAF stations in the neighbourhood'. In 1942 and 1943 the College gave a dance for men who were soon going into the services, 'the domestic staff in particular and those who were responsible for the organisation' reaching 'an astonishing standard of achievement'. In the spring of 1944 the

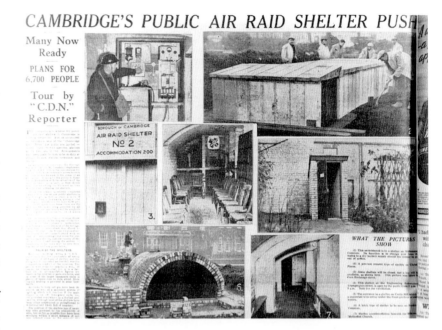

*Various air raid shelters, 1939.*

Hall was used for a very different purpose when senior officers who had taken part in a conference at the Union on preparations for the landings in Europe were entertained to dinner by the Master and Fellows.

On 12 May 1945 the Editorial in the *Cambridge Review* described the Mayor addressing a vast crowd on Market Hill on VE Day: 'a close packed crowd which filled every corner of the market-place and overflowed into Rose Crescent and on to the roofs... one remembered the men of the Cambridgeshire regiment... who were still in prison camps in the East; and one remembered those men, both Town and Gown, who had loved Cambridge and its beautiful ways, who had so often crossed Market Hill on their way to shops and offices, to lectures, to Hall, or to the river, and will never come back from the war to cross it again'.

In Corpus, Patrick Bury writes that the fatal casualties were particularly severe amongst those members who were in residence or who had come up about the time of the outbreak of war. No fewer than 128 pre-war members of the Cambridge University Air Squadron were killed in action and the *Association Letter* for 1946 lists 29 members of the RAF, 1 member of the Royal Canadian Airforce, and three members of the Fleet Air Arm on its Roll of Honour. Three men were awarded the DFC and one the DFM. The names of all the 93 Corpus men who died are commemorated in a memorial tablet on the south side of the Chapel.

*John Bolton-Maggs, right with T.E. Utley.*

## MEMORIES:1939–45

### Edmund Randall, 1938

One evening in the Michaelmas Term in 1939 I was rushing from the JCR to get to Hall, and collided with one of the buttresses of the oriel window. I must have been a bit stunned as it was not till after grace that I realized from the way that my fellow diners were looking at me that something was wrong: apparently my face was covered with blood and half of my left eyebrow was missing. After dinner I found I was not the only casualty of the blackout that night; it must have been moonless and particularly cloudy. So three of us piled into a taxi and went to one of the 'sports doctors' in Grange Road, who patched up our various wounds, putting a sticking plaster above my eye and telling me my eyebrow was gone for ever.

Next day the College maintenance staff, to prevent further casualties of my kind, put a white board up on the offending buttress; and soon after the end of the academic year I went off to five years in the Army.

In August 1945 I found myself kicking my heels at Woolwich Barracks as the result of the Pickford Scheme that arranged for the exchange of officers from the European theatre with those in the East. I was awaiting a passage to India, VJ Day came and our draft was still to go, but on the very day we were to sail I was told I had a Class B Release to enable me to resume my studies. As a result I was one of the first students to return to Cambridge, and in time for the beginning of the new academic year.

A few weeks later the maintenance staff began to dismantle the remnants of wartime precautions, and I noticed they were taking down the little white board from the buttress in the New Court. After they had finished, I went to inspect the scene of my accident. Round the area where the board had been there were chalk lines presumably put there originally to show where to affix the board, but in the middle of the area were some short stiff hairs and some very small particles of skin which I carefully removed. As, however, despite the doctor's warning, nature had long since restored my eyebrow, I decently disposed of these remains. So I cannot, alas, send you any memorabilia with this recollection.

### Peter Barrett, 1939

My two years at Corpus (1939–41) meant a great deal to me, and I look back on them with gratitude.

I was fortunate in my friends – one in particular who was on the same staircase – Peter Utley who, like me, was reading History. He was blind and it was my 'privilege' to escort him to lectures and suffer the chatter of his portable braille machine as he took down his notes. His was a brilliant intellect and I became a devoted disciple to his strong Conservatism which soon replaced any left-wing proclivities that remained in me. Charles Smyth, our Tutor, discreetly reinforced our Tory sympathies. I remember with amusement the horror of some of my old King's friends that I had become a Tory convert.

The war having just started, and although in its 'phoney' stage for my first year at Corpus, there was naturally a feeling in many of us to make the most of life while the going was still good. Most of us joined the STC and played at soldiering in order to get a Certificate B which would qualify us to go straight to OCTU rather than through the ranks.

*Bomb damage in 1940.*

There was of course a certain amount of rationing. I particularly remember with some distaste arriving in Hall for lunch to find an unappetising slab of whale meat on my plate and we were invited to make our comments on a piece of paper provided with it! It wasn't too bad in fact, though rather fishy. I don't think it appeared again in my time at Corpus.

I don't remember many air-raid alerts, though I do remember hurrying down to the College shelter to find I was sharing it with the Master, Will Spens, and his guest Herbert Morrison.

College Audit Ale was still available and there was no shortage of wine, beer and spirits in shops and bars.

I also seem to remember there being very few choral services in Chapel compared to those our skeleton choir sang in St Bene't's.

### John Bolton-Maggs, 1939

In 1939 the town was shrouded in the darkness of the blackout. At nightfall there were no more bustling crowds on brightly lit streets – only shadowy groups passing in the gloom.

Although New Court had been desecrated to accommodate an air-raid shelter, food rationing had not yet reached the low levels of later years and the Corpus cuisine maintained its high standards under the direction of the incomparable Matthews. Audit Ale was still brewed, and Balkan Sobranie tobacco was still on sale at the Buttery. But this was the era of the 'phoney war' when Britain was virtually untouched by hostilities until the drama of Dunkirk. So student life carried on much in its traditional ways. Desmond Lee held his customary gatherings for incoming freshmen but our combined shyness made these slightly embarrassing occasions. As I had decided to read History I was put in the care of Pat Bury. I could not have wished for a kindlier introduction to the tutorial system. The following term I came under the rigorous tutelage of Charles Smyth whose unvaried routine was: 'Good evening, Maggs. How are you? Please sit down and read your essay." Then he lit his pipe, sat back and turned a critical ear to my naïve reflections on the Tudors and Stuarts.

I struck up an early friendship with two fellow historians – T.E. 'Peter' Utley, later to have a distinguished political and journalistic career and reputedly the only person permitted to smoke in Margaret Thatcher's prime ministerial office, and Bill Bates who achieved ambassadorial rank in the Diplomatic Service and whom I was to meet up with during the 1966 civil war in Nigeria. As Peter was blind, Bill and I used to take him to Hall, lectures and other activities.

Student life carried on with minimal disturbance from wartime diversions. In College the Gravediggers Club met regularly for play-reading and there were ample opportunities for sporting activities. The Arts Theatre provided a feast of good shows, the cinemas thrived and the tradition of morning coffee at the Dorothy or the KP was made more pleasurable by an influx of evacuees – the young ladies of Queen Mary's College, London. Peter Utley and I regularly attended Union debates. The then President of the Union was Gervase Steward, whom I was later to meet again at the Royal Naval Air Station in Trinidad where, sadly, he was killed in a flying accident.

Despite these signs of normality, thoughts of war were never far away. The three services all had their recruiting agencies and training schemes in the University. Many of us signed up in that first term and in December I was invited to attend a Fleet Air Arm medical exam at Portsmouth. Shortly afterwards I received notification that I was fit for aircrew training and should report to HMS St Vincent in Gosport on 1 July 1940. My final memory of my first year at Corpus was sitting on Old Court lawn after Hall with a group, most of whom would shortly be in uniform.

The squadron in which I was serving was on the brink of departure for the Far East when the atom bomb brought the war to a dramatic and devastating end. Suddenly there was a future to contemplate and decisions to be made. By this time I was married with a small son. My naval pay had been adequate to support the family but could we survive on a student grant if I returned to complete my degree at Cambridge? Or should I seek immediate employment? Eventually I chose the student option and was back in residence at Corpus by March 1946. For that term I had a room in New Court but for the next year I was a guest of Miss Badcock and Peggy at 2 Silver Street.

Returning to Cambridge after six years' absence was a curious experience. Most of the undergraduates were ex-service, a number were married, and enough had small children to warrant the establishment of a University crèche. Family accommodation was hard to come by in Cambridge, particularly for those of us who had a child. My searches led me to the door of Professor Bruce Dickins in Selwyn Gardens. I was met by the formidable figure of Mrs Dickins. 'Do you have a child?' she demanded. I reluctantly said, 'yes'. 'Good,' she replied. 'The flat is yours.'

The usual aspects of student life soon returned to normal. Societies revived, the arts began to flourish anew and sporting activities thrived. I do not recall that the usual restrictions of being *in statu pupillari* were enforced very strictly on ex-service students. But the town and its populace seemed dowdy and war-weary. There was still strict rationing of food and clothing, beer was weak and in short supply, the Buttery shelves were bare and the Corpus cuisine was an insipid caricature of its past delight. When Corpus boldly decided to hold a May Ball in 1947, it seemed to symbolize that the years of austerity were past and a more certain future lay ahead.

*The Eagle in 1937.*

## James Cable, 1939

My two years at Corpus (1939–1941) are still a vivid splash of sunlight in my memory, after the darkness of school, before the drab routines of my nomadic existence in the Army. Cambridge contemporaries will remember how the aftermath of the first, and worst, crisis of the war in 1940 heightened our enjoyment of the University's ancient magic. Being allowed to live freely and without distracting responsibilities among hundreds of intelligent and equally untrammelled people of one's own age is always a lifetime privilege, but I think we felt it more keenly then.

The Corpus I knew was a smaller College and the existence led by its undergraduates a strange blend of privilege and discomfort. My rooms comprised a large sitting-room overlooking Trumpington Street (which I was expected to furnish) and a small, unheated bedroom, for which the College had generously provided a range of equipment, including ewer (its water occasionally freezing on a winter night), basin, slop-pail and chamber pot. For lavatories, baths from which uncounted generations had worn the enamel, wash basins with taps and copious running water, one had to resort to the public baths of the College. These I could reach down some stairs and through corridors with only a few yards' exposure to the elements in the Old Court. Many undergraduates had two open courts to traverse through rain and snow, in dressing-gown and pyjamas, before they could cleanse their bodies or ease their bladders.

My supervisor at Corpus, Pat Charvet, was young, clever, thoroughly agreeable and a brilliant teacher. He was also half French, bilingual and a perfectionist. I grew accustomed to hearing that what I had written was entirely correct, simply 'not French'. The polish he imparted helped me to a First in French in Part I of the Modern Languages Tripos. German, however, was as alien to Corpus as it was abhorrent to Pat, who ranked it with Descartes, Galsworthy and other *bêtes noires*, usefully discussed whenever the pressure of life's diversions had prevented completion of the weekly essay. So for German I went to an uninspired Welshman in another college.

I made more friends in my two years at Cambridge than anywhere else, ranging widely in the University, but the first, and the only one I kept to the day of his sadly premature death, was Claude Barry. His rooms were immediately above mine on staircase X. He later became a barrister and we would foregather whenever we were both in London, but the chronic ill health that crippled his career limited the frequency of our meetings. He had a natural kindness and – a quality often lacking in the kind – an instinctive tact and delicacy which made it impossible to quarrel with him or his sometimes eccentric opinions. At Corpus he could still lead an active life and his two years there may have been his happiest.

Even in Corpus I was constantly reminded of another potent influence of those years: the war. Recalled to Cambridge for Home Guard duties in the Long Vacation of 1940, I discovered that the College had just provided temporary shelter for soldiers evacuated from Dunkirk. Its buttresses were particularly bruising in the blackout and it was up an endless ladder that, under instruction as an auxiliary fireman, I dragged a hose to the crenellations of the New Court. My hearty guffaw when our mentor from the Fire Brigade explained that hoses had male and female couplings – I had never heard the expression and thought he was making a bawdy joke – drew a frown of disapproval from our solemn Senior Tutor.

Relations with him had never recovered from his decision, in the aftermath of our initial interview in 1939, to write to my father, who believed him, that my failure to win a Corpus scholarship must seriously diminish my chances of passing the Diplomatic Service Examination. Eight years later, when I emerged from the Army and did manage to get into the Foreign Office in 1947, the Tutor wrote another letter, not to me, but to the Editor of *The Times*. Ostensibly he was defending the new selection processes introduced after the war, but his main purpose was to proclaim that every post-war candidate who had studied at Corpus had so far been successful. Not long afterwards he decided on a career change and became a headmaster, an occupation for which he was temperamentally better suited and in which he achieved considerable success.

The most insistent reminder of war came from the University Officers Training Corps, where the need to obtain first Certificate A, then Certificate B, gave its archaic rituals an urgency and a relevance that quite outshone Part II of the Tripos. But the noise of distant battles, which we followed in the media and which, privately among friends at Corpus (Claude, a disciple of Liddell

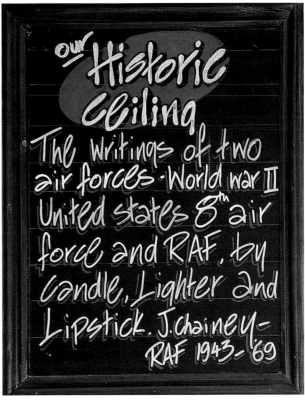

Above: *US 8th Air Force and RAF writings: The Eagle.*

Far right: *Sign advertising the writings.*

Hart, was a particularly keen strategist) or openly in the Union, we debated, was always a drum-beat background to the rich variety of our diversions. Nor was Cambridge immune from some of the neuroses that afflicted the nation during those early years of anxious and uncertain struggle, when men in authority and reserved occupations could sometimes be over-eager to exhibit their patriotic zeal. In 1941, for instance, the Union was closed down to forestall a debate on the motion (which I was to oppose) that this House would welcome the end of the world. Somebody, we imagined, had remembered the uproar over that notorious Oxford Union debate in 1933 and had been assailed by nightmare visions of Defence Regulation 18B and the Isle of Man.

Such irritations did not disturb us unduly. When I look back on my time at Corpus and try to compare my memories with the little I have gathered of undergraduate life today, I find few obvious reasons to envy the twenty- first century student. Much the most important reason is that today's students are drawn from both sexes. The residual monasticism of my era was an unnatural way of living and an education that positively discouraged learning from the opposite sex was necessarily incomplete. This was not a view the College could have been expected to take in my time or that the conventional wisdom of the day would have tolerated. The nation had to change first and other aspects of that change have been unfortunate. But I envy the mixed couples I see nowadays descending the steps into Trumpington Street.

### James Speight, 1937

Most of the air-raid precautions within the College bounds were the responsibility of the College staff but, initially, members of the College were invited to assist with fire-watching in the event of a raid. Elementary instruction was given in the use of stirrup pumps, foam extinguishers, and other simple equipment. I well remember being required to carry a reel of hose and a standard brass nozzle up a far-from-stable ladder leaning against a three-storey wall in New Court. It was an experience not to be repeated – what it would have been like in the dark, I shudder to think. Fortunately by the time of the first 'Alert' in June 1940, the staff had completely taken over these duties.

Air-raid precautions were, however, not the only things to introduce changes into our lives. Food rationing was another area which was to affect College life markedly. Hitherto it had been compulsory for members to dine in Hall at least five nights a week. For other meals, students could either prepare their own or have dishes sent to them from the Buttery. That was to change, and three meals a day, and these alone, were henceforth to be served in Hall. Additionally, small amounts of tea and milk together with some non-rationed goods were available from the Buttery.

Life in College proceeded relatively smoothly, punctuated only from time to time by intimation on the notice board that members of the College had been killed in action – a stark reminder of the fact that we were at war. One of the first of these – if not the first – was Pilot Officer D.G. Glennie (1937–1939) who as a member of the University Air Squadron had been called up as a part of the RAFVR at the very outset of war. Glennie and I had shared supervisors in Mineralogy and Crystallography and in Physics and I greatly respected him. Otherwise such was the normality of academic life that by the beginning of the Lent term I had more or less completed arrangements to return to Cambridge in July and undertake a research project under Dr G.B.B.M. Sutherland of the Department of Physical Chemistry towards a PhD.

This, however, was not to be. On returning for the Easter term, I learned that, with the worsening war situation, only those who had already started a research course would be allowed to stay up to complete it. Then, later on in the term, when the threat of invasion became apparent, Sir Will Spens, in his capacity as Regional Commissioner for East Anglia, gave instructions that students should not complete the termly residence but go down as soon as they had finished their examinations unless there were good reasons to the contrary. In my own case, I was allowed to stay up a further ten days in order to complete negotiations for a post and, if that was not possible, to seek further advice from the University Appointments Board. Because of this, I had my first experiences of an air raid and a real fiasco it turned out to be. As was my habit, it was nearly midnight before I went to bed. I dropped asleep straightway and was later roused by the air-raid siren. I quickly donned some clothes over my pyjamas and went down to the shelter, to find it empty apart from the College Air-raid Warden – I had slept through the 'Alert' and had only wakened on the 'All-Clear' sounding, whilst the Warden had overlooked the fact that I was still in residence! There was no such mistake on the next night when the Warden, on the pretext of checking my blackout, was actually passing the time of day when the 'Alert' sounded.

As it turned out, so ended my residence in Corpus. Within a few days I learned that I had achieved a first-class degree and later I received a letter from the College congratulating me and informing me that I had been awarded the Bishop Green Cup for 1940. The letter went on to say how sorry the College was that I would not be returning to do a PhD and promised that, if, at the end of the war I wished to return, there would be a place for me. In the event I was not able to avail myself of that offer though in subsequent years I often wondered what might have happened had I done so.

## Alan Cook, 1940

When I came up as a major scholar in October 1940 France had collapsed, the Battle of Britain had been fought and the RAF had survived. Cambridge had changed from pre-war times, but those of us who had never known it before the war cannot have appreciated how great the changes were. Some came about because two London colleges, Queen Mary College and the London School of Economics, were moved to Cambridge. That brought many female undergraduates to Cambridge, who shared lectures with Cambridge students, while members of the faculties of the London colleges gave some lectures in Cambridge courses. Nurses from the military hospital set up in the Leys School also augmented the female population.

Many undergraduates were allowed only a first year at Cambridge before going off to the forces or other service. Consequently there were few members in residence in their second or third years, members who would otherwise have been, for example, officers of college societies. The undergraduate population was changing too rapidly for active corporate life. Those of us who, as scientists, were directed to take Part I or even Part II of the Tripos had to take additional courses to fit us for technical posts in the forces or related activities, and everyone, in whatever year, had to be a member of the Senior Training Corps, which, for non-scientists was the preliminary to officer training. Those of us who were directed to take Part II with a view to doing research and development for the forces continued in the STC and were made members of the Home Guard. At the end of my second year I was interviewed by C.P. Snow and his colleague Henry Hoff, directed to take Part II of the Natural Sciences Tripos in Physics, and then to join the Admiralty Signal Establishment for radar research. For those reasons far more of my time was spent outside College than would otherwise have been the case, and so my recollections of College life are rather imprecise.

As in other colleges, some senior members were away at the war, most notably the Master, Will Spens, who was Regional Commissioner for East Anglia, and Desmond Lee, the Tutor, who was his deputy at St Regis. Kenneth Pickthorn, the President, was sometimes in College, but often in London as he was the Member of Parliament for the University. Sir John Lennard-Jones, a Professorial Fellow, was head of the explosives research establishment at Fort Halstead in Kent. George Carter was acting Tutor, and also Director of Studies in Natural Sciences. Charles Smyth was Dean of Chapel, and persuaded some of us to make up a rather scratch choir in Chapel, where I learnt the Merbecke settings of the mass in English. The College was host to at least one senior military man, an Air Vice-Marshal who had some liaison post with the Regional Commissioner's Office. He was a member of the High Table and sometimes entertained undergraduates. I well remember an occasion when he spoke of his time in the Royal Flying Corps with Allenby in Palestine in the First World War.

Corpus was not notably scientific in those days, and I was the only one in my year reading Physics for Part II. When I was elected to the Royal Society in 1969, I was only the third member of the College who had been an undergraduate there to be elected to the Society, the others being Stephen Hales and the meteorologist Dines. My supervisors were accordingly from outside the College.

When the war ended I came back to Cambridge as a graduate student in the Department of Geodesy and Geophysics. We had rooms in the Geography building on the Downing site and a laboratory out at Madingley Rise near the Observatory, and there I spent most of my time, or away from Cambridge on fieldwork. Of course in those days there were no special provisions as there now are for graduate students, yet I came to know more junior and senior members than in my undergraduate years. I think that with the end of the war life felt much more relaxed, and we had futures to look forward to. I had a room in the Eagle and came often into College, especially after I had taken my MA in 1947 and had dining rights at High Table. Many junior members were completing degrees that they had started but had been obliged to suspend in wartime. Michael McCrum was one such, others were Robert Baird, later a master at Eton, and David Ritchie. Geoffrey Woodhead, who came up as a scholar in the same year as I did, was back. I also came to know some of the Fellowship: George

Carter again, John Harley-Mason, and Geoffrey Styler, Dean of Chapel. Roland Walls, a colourful priest who has been for many years now at Roslin Chapel near Edinburgh, came to Corpus at that time.

As a graduate student I supervised Physics undergraduates for the College, among them Tony Horsfield who later joined my Division at the National Physical Laboratory and whom we continue to see at Old Members' functions.

## Derek Hill, 1940

I was at Corpus for one year in the early part of the last war, finishing my degree after it was over and going on to do my teacher training at the Cambridge Institute of Education.

By the time I returned after the war I was married and lived mainly outside Cambridge. Amongst tutors and lecturers two stand out for me: Pat Charvet was, as far as I am concerned, the outstanding model of a University tutor: interested in his students, concerned for their welfare and sensitively supportive of their progress in their studies. He championed me in my vegetarianism (very eccentric in those days!), and when the College could or would not supply vegetarian meals during the war he negotiated my escape from having to attend Hall. I ended up purchasing my own food and eating mainly doorstep salad sandwiches and drinking soups boiled up on a gas ring.

Dear Professor Eliza Butler was an inspiring lecturer, alight with enthusiasm for her subject, somewhat eccentric at times in her spoken German, but always worth listening to even on subjects outside my own curriculum. I still have her excellent little book *Daylight in a Dream*.

I rowed in the College eight in my first year. We were not particularly successful! I do remember being incensed, as were the rest of the crew when we bumped a preceding crew who then obstructed our boat, leading to our being bumped in our turn. Our appeal was disallowed.

That year we took part in a major Army exercise towards Ely. We were a 'reconnaissance unit' mounted on heavy bone-shaker bicycles! I remember lazing in a farmyard stretched out on a dyke, drinking lemonade kindly supplied by the farmer's wife. Then a night in the open trying to sleep on a ground sheet. The next morning we were holed up in a copse from which we watched paratroops pouring out of a large lumbering bomber – a fascinating sight. We 'opened fire' on them, but we were soon told by a self-important judge with flashy armband that we had all been 'wiped out'.

Soon after that I joined up, went to Sandhurst, became an Intelligence Officer and was back in Cambridge within a few months on an Interrogation Course. I was not selected but was put in command of a Wireless Intelligence Unit. I served in Northern France and in India and returned on demob as a Captain, ready to complete my degree.

### Kenneth Leech, 1940

I matriculated in September 1939 but because of illness and the uncertainty due to the declaration of war I did not go up until January 1940. The war had then become the 'phoney war' and my health was restored.

I had rooms over the Copper Kettle in King's Parade and shared a lavatory and washbasin with H.B. Harral, walking into College for a bath. The rooms looked right down into King's and the views were stunningly romantic. Mr Jaggard looked after us and, I think, locked us in at night. College was all bustle and activity and Hall a pleasurable daily ritual. I knew a few men from school and got to know my fellow medics fairly soon, though I was hampered by a bad speech impediment. A bout of flu and then German measles held me up a bit my first term also.

The summer term started as if there were no war and no worries except exams, and then came the blitzkrieg. Everything suddenly changed. There was an air of *Carpe Diem*. Exams were taken but uncertainty was everywhere. The pleasant German who had sat opposite one in Hall was interned in the Isle of Man. No one knew what would happen next. Our course was reduced to two years without a Tripos. A Long Vacation course was organized for medics and so we came up in July and had College more or less to ourselves. I had volunteered for the forces but wasn't wanted and went back to my studies with a clear conscience. Meanwhile, everyone waited for the invasion and the air raids to begin.

In September we came up as usual. Cambridge had changed. Students were either for reserved occupations, medics or in one way or another unfit for service. The blackout was strictly enforced. I had moved into O staircase in the Old Court. On moonless nights it was important to keep on the paving as it was common to bump into the buttresses if one was in a hurry or a little disorientated. The Battle of Britain was on in the air. There were numerous air-raid alarms but no bombs. Only once did I go to a shelter and that was in the daytime in the Yard. There were long periods of Alarm at night and, when they were on, the Old Court gate was left open and one could go in and out at night freely. I cannot remember the shelter in New Court ever being used.

Mr Cator was the Head Porter who had some influence on our behaviour. On the whole we were well behaved. Drink was not allowed to be brought into the College without permission. Once some man, I think from Jesus, brought in several crates of beer and wine and there was some outrageous behaviour. Our nice bedder was heard to remark the next morning 'I don't mind clearing up my own gentleman's sick but I do dislike clearing up the sick of gentlemen from other colleges.' A wonderful example of College loyalty.

Mr Matthews was the Butler. There was no nonsense from him. His son was killed on a bombing raid over Germany. By an unlucky coincidence B.A.J.C. Gregory and I called that day at his house, having been given the wrong address, looking for a borrowed bicycle. He and his wife were so grateful we had come from Corpus with our condolences. We felt terribly embarrassed but managed to cope with the situation. He was always easy with me afterwards even when I turned up once in Hall wearing a Caius gown.

We worked pretty hard with lectures, demonstrations and dissection at the Anatomy and Physiology Schools and later at the Pathology School. There was very little teaching at tutorials in College because Archie Clark-Kennedy was Dean of the London Hospital and had to spend much of his time there with all the problems of bombing and dispersal of patients. I also had to complete my Organic Chemistry from the first MB exams and start on Biochemistry with Dr Parsons, who had a pipe which continually went out, and a beautiful daughter Pauline who also went out a lot.

We seemed to be a cheerful lot. No very organized games, though we played some tennis and occasionally bicycled out to the Gogs for a round with our hickory shafts on our backs. There was morning coffee at the Dot with Percy at the keys with his trio playing light music for sedate dancing. The clocks chimed from the College chapels and towers but there were, of course, no bells. In the spring and summer the weather seemed to have been good as we punted and canoed quite often. The invasion became less and less expected. The war in North Africa seemed far away and the U-boat campaign

*A picnic by the river.*

*Norman Tapp, Anthony Craven and Bill Dixon on Graduation Day, 18th June 1947.*

was only starting to become severe. We made the most of our good fortune. In summer 1941 we took our second MB exams and then did another Long Vac term to get us ready for clinical work. In September I went to Bart's with B.A.J.C. Gregory and George Yerbury. Initially we were at the evacuated wards at St Albans. I was homesick for Corpus and quite often hitchhiked to Cambridge and spent a Saturday night in Corpus until I was discovered and asked not to do so.

In June 1944, after three years' clinical work I went up for my Finals. I remember lying on the grass in Old Court one lunchtime when the exams were over with a tankard of cool shandy. The war had become intense with D Day but surely the end was in sight. I felt happy and at home. Then the papers, which we hadn't seen earlier, arrived. London was under fire again; this time it was the buzz bombs or doodlebugs coming to spoil things.

### Geoffrey Woodhead, 1940

John Chadwick begins his 1945–1952 memoir by saying that, on demobilization, he went straight up to Cambridge. It was on 8 October 1945 and we literally began again where we had left off in 1939. We had corresponded intermittently during the war, but it was only in the course of a long conversation that evening that I really learned how things stood between him and Joan Hill, and how he was able to contemplate a job in Oxford after he finished the Tripos. Thereafter we were regular companions. Food and fuel were alike in short supply, and in the chill days that followed we worked out a system of sharing both. We took it in turns – on one day we would use his rooms for work and for sharing our tea and for welcoming any friend who came by, and on the next day we would use mine. A note on the door redirected anyone who came to the wrong place. In this way we eked out our meagre ration of coal, which we supplemented by collecting wood in the course of the cycle expeditions we made into the country when the afternoon was fine and we felt in need of exercise. I have the record of afternoons on the Gogs or out in the direction of Barton or Coton. Our last and longest venture came in the summer of 1947, when we went to Ely and back. The A10 was a quieter prospect in those days. A particular memory remains of my mending a puncture on a windy day somewhere in the neighbourhood of Hardwick, while John regaled me with a blow-by-blow description of his latest session with Professor Jopson.

But the main occasion of socializing was at teatime. We pooled our meagre rations (a substantial part of which was retained by the College kitchens) and other resources we were lucky enough to acquire, and our friends would quite regularly drop in, either by invitation or 'on spec'. If they had been able to get hold of buns or a cake, not easily come by, they were additionally welcome. The main *pabulum* was toast, done on a toasting fork in front of the coal fire. We had little butter to put on it when done, but there was margarine to help out, and someone had usually come by some jam. With the return of more friends the venue rotated, but throughout the winter the pattern remained pretty consistent. The demands of a supervision or any essay to be turned in on the morrow usually had the effect of setting a time limit to these very enjoyable gatherings.

There was one element of our week, developed in the course of time, in which John did not participate. On Saturday afternoons and evenings the returned veterans broke loose, with improvised games of hockey or rugby or attendance at Grange Road, followed later by lengthy and often noisy sessions in someone's rooms or at the Bath, the Lion, the Anchor or the Little Rose. (This last has, I think, always been regarded as a Peterhouse pub, but at that juncture it was much favoured by Corpus.) I am sure that it did us good and kept us sane.

### Douglas Eves, 1940

The previous occupant of my handsome rooms in the Old Court was a peer, called from his estate and College to serve his country. I inherited his large and handsome desk, topped with burgundy red morocco leather with gold inlay. He was expected to send for it but happily found storage in College more convenient. My bedmaker, Mrs Hunt, was kindness itself, brought shaving water in a jug, laid my breakfast of cornflakes, bread and coffee-percolator, cleared and washed plates and cutlery with despatch and made my bed.

I wished to read English and later did so, but I am glad that I first had the discipline of Classics and, much later, of Law. When I came, years after leaving Cambridge, to learn Italian and to re-educate myself in French, I was aware intensely of the debt I owed to Latin and no-one interested to the smallest extent in thought can help but feel the stimulus and astringency of Greek.

For the Lent term, when the Marlowe production took place, I was out of College, having rooms in 8a King's Parade over an antiques shop. It was almost exactly

opposite King's, which was most convenient for calling on Dadie Rylands. My attempt to establish a routine of working was slightly handicapped by Arnold's choosing punctually at 11 o'clock to arrive for a talk on Marlowe matters, English matters, or any matters which would consume precious time and include a suggestion for lunching somewhere. Yet he had a heart as true as oak, a gay sense of humour and offered so many instances of hospitality in the house he and Letty, his wife and a former nurse, had bought along Huntingdon Road. No one did more to support and nurture his friendships than Arnold who had an outstretched hand for all, Marlowe companions, rowing friends, and all he had encountered and liked along the highways and byways of life.

A centre of entertainment in College, especially before dinner, was the Buttery, an alcove and small bar in a corner of the Old Court presided over by Lawrence, a genial barman who dispensed ale, admirable sherry, and gin for the hardier spirits. There was a cramped but friendly intimacy generating bonhomie and resolution to confront the rather meagre meal, enforced by postwar stringency, in the Hall above.

There was a Long Vac production by the Marlowe Society of *The Tempest* and, in the next spring, of *Bartholomew Fair* by Ben Jonson. For intellectual stimulus there was a course of lectures by Bertrand Russell. The Clark Lectures, elegant and eloquent, were given by the poet Cecil Day-Lewis, a man, as a poet should be, said Wordsworth, speaking to men.

There was at Corpus, in the rooms once occupied by Sandy Wilson, an undergraduate named Geoffrey Drayton who had an unusual gift for cooking and for entertaining, and who made many welcome at his parties. I met there a nursing colleague of Letty, with raven dark hair and a face of classic beauty. She came with me more than once to dinner and partnered me at dances and, as I look back over the unforgiving years, I wonder that I could bear to part from her.

[From: *Reflections at Random – The Story of a Life* by Douglas Eves]

### Anthony Craven, 1941

In September 1941 I went up to read Law and one of the first duties I performed was to take Kenneth Pickthorn, a Fellow of the College and MP for Cambridge University, to Gallyon's shooting school and assist him to hit clays!

*The static water tank on the New Court grass. Sketch by W.A. Cooper, 1943.*

On 11 November I attended an aircrew selection board and I joined the Cambridge University Air Squadron, being recommended for training as pilot/observer. On 9 December 1941, I and others went to RAF Cardington (No. 2 Reception Centre) where we were sworn in or 'attested' to the RAF Volunteer Reserve and I was given my 'other' rank number (1621523) as an aircraftsman. I was then put on deferred service as were all other volunteers until such time as the service could accommodate them, and this enabled me to complete my academic year reading for and taking my Law Tripos Part I.

A rather sad occurrence happened during the first term of my return in autumn 1946 when my Law tutor, Robin Roberts, in College shot himself with his shotgun in his rooms. He had been my tutor in my first year and I had seen him from time to time at the College when I was in the RAF. I think that he was probably what would now be described as a 'closet gay'. Our impression was that he had found the return of students as mature men too much for him and sadly his life was terminated in this way.

## John Blundell, 1941

There was much to remind us that the war was going on: blackout regulations with no chinks of light allowed around curtains after dark, a very large circular static water tank in the New Court, Home Guard parades and training once or twice a week, and distant sounds of aircraft leaving, some evenings, for night bombing excursions to German-occupied Europe. East Anglia had many wartime airfields. During those two years there were no enemy air raids on Cambridge, at least not in term time, and this came as a relief, for my own public school had not escaped German airforce attention. Both College and University authorities were well aware of the potential disasters, particularly from the possibility of large numbers of small incendiary bombs landing on old Cambridge buildings. Rows of buckets of sand stood waiting in strategic spots. We had practice sessions with a trailer pump and hoses, drawing our supply from the New Court static water tank. We practised with water buckets and stirrup pumps. 'Fire-watching' duties on a rota duty basis were organised, both at College, and at the University Library where my own Home Guard unit was based. The idea was that you smothered each bomb with sand, quickly, at the early smouldering stage, before it burst into flames, so speed was of the essence. Fortunately these lessons never had to be put into practice.

After nine years of silent endurance of boarding school cookery where innovation, enterprise, herbs or spices never entered the kitchens, it was a delight to find that these considerations, and more, were all alive and well at Corpus. I remember actually looking forward to the three main meals daily in Hall which were part of our daily routine. It was a time in life for vast appetites, brought on most likely by growth, much physical exercise, rowing, bicycling, and much hurrying out and back for lectures. Food was rationed. We drew our miniscule butter ration, of course, from the Buttery hatch on Mondays. So by Wednesday it had all gone. For the remainder of the week other spreads or fillings had to be found for the seven 1 lb white loaves I ate every week. Sausage meat was 'off the ration' at a local butchers and could be fried in thin slices to make useful sandwiches. Maltesers could be put in a mug with boiling water, stirred, and you had a nourishing hot drink. Eggs could be had at farmhouses a few miles out of town. The baker's shop was a good stand-by, not far from the Porter's Lodge, turn left and on the left, with a good choice of cakes, scones and other joys. A notice and cartoon on the counter reminded customers, please, to bring their own bags, which became rather travel-worn by the end of term. Keeping those appetites satisfied took some organising.

Rowing provided a good deal of the regular exercise and the College deployed three eights upon the river, in which we practised regularly. When eight crew could not be mustered, the small single sliding seat craft, we called them 'toothpicks', were fast and fun, and you could travel a long way in an afternoon, remembering some small change in a pocket for the lock-keeper's toll. I helped furnish the third boat and the eight of us treated this activity with a good deal of levity. But we consistently beat the second boat on speed, so authority declared we must exchange titles. We took it more seriously thereafter.

My own Home Guard unit was based at the University Library. We did little drill or marching, concentrating on weapons training, live firing at the rifle range and other matters. The rifles in use appeared to be First World War vintage or earlier. We dug slit trenches in the immaculate mown turf close to the great building. But no-one had investigated what lay below that turf.

*E8, as seen in 1942, drawn by Tony Merriam.*

Suddenly there was a bright flash as someone's pick went into a major underground electric main cable. No-one was hurt, but it put much of the town without a supply for longer than was convenient. We also set up miles of private Home Guard phone lines, so the 'Captain Mainwarings' of the area could talk to each other. These were stretched above the traffic below from trees to lamp posts to electric or telephone poles, with cheerful abandon, and quickly, for we did not expect the war to last as long as it did. No doubt within two or three years they needed much maintenance. We found good reasons to take the lift to the top of the Library tower where the view over the town was impressive, and much

more beyond on a clear day. In sunlight the lead roofs of Ely Cathedral stood out brightly.

At weekends I spent much time outside the town cycling on my own or with others, taking a look at wildlife or archaeology. On one morning, a little south of Willingham, a single Lancaster bomber came over, quite low, evidently returning from a continental bombing mission. It had clear damage to the wings and only one of the four engines was working. We watched in some horror as it continued to lose height, and it went below the tree line on the flat horizon. Then there was a dull thud and a great column of black smoke blowing away on the wind towards Hemingford Grey.

## William Cooper, 1941-43 and 1946-48

At the suggestion of my Headmaster, who was himself later to become Principal of Jesus College, Oxford, I applied to Corpus and was accepted for autumn 1941. After three years of disruption and uncertainty I was captivated by Cambridge and felt immediately that I was embarking on a period of stability; indeed at the very first dinner in Hall (with grace and formal dress) I sensed that there was something special about this College: this was endorsed by the genuine warmth of the welcome from the Master, Fellows, porters, 'bedders', and other staff.

It was wartime with blackout, rationing and other restrictions but there was a feeling that everybody was in it together and that life would go on as near to normally as possible. The winter of 1941-2 was bitterly cold like the two which preceded it and a back-aching memory is the carrying of the coal ration (one cwt sacks!) up three flights of stairs to the top floor of Staircase D, New Court. We helped each other! My room was in the corner with a splendid view of King's Parade and if the room was cold the adjacent company was not. Geoffrey Woodhead, a future Fellow, was next door and nearby Sam Scorer who was reading architecture. He and I were both aspiring artists and his room quickly became something of a studio for us and his friend, another prospective architect, Sandy Wilson (now Sir Colin St J. Wilson, a Fellow and Royal Academician). Here in Sam's room, with Sandy as the driving force, we prepared to mount what was to prove the only current art exhibition in Cambridge. Heffers Gallery remained open and had just hosted the first exhibition in England of Oscar Kokoschka who was then an unknown Austrian refugee. We did not pretend to be in his class but Sandy persuaded the Director of the Fitzwilliam Museum to sponsor an exhibition of 'Three Corpus Undergraduates'. The *Cambridge Review* gave the exhibition an encouraging write-up and posed the question as to where our artistic talents might take us – 60 years later one of the three is a Royal Academician and another an Academician of the Royal West of England Academy! It was at this time that I received my first commission from the College to paint a picture of Corpus New Court in wartime, where a rather basic air-raid shelter had been dug into the northeast corner of the lawn, a round static water tank and hose dominated the centre of the court, and an ugly wooden shed hous-

ing Ministry of Defence equipment had been erected on one side. So far as I remember these items were only ever used during fire drills. The painting, a student effort with no particular artistic pretensions, does, however, show the sadly disfigured New Court which took some years to renovate after the war. Although I am uncertain as to the fate of this picture I am flattered that it is reproduced in Patrick Bury's official history of the College and also in *Some Artistic Impressions* – a small pictorial history of Corpus.

These two wartime years at Corpus were amazingly fulfilling after the school years of evacuation. We all worked hard and appreciated the privileges of the life, education, and successful continuation of College sport, especially in the circumstances. I captained both the cricket and soccer XI's and also enjoyed play-readings with the Gravediggers. In these years of austerity, the camaraderie and Corpus experience culminated in a remarkable May Ball in 1943.

Now it was immediately into the Army. I left Corpus immensely grateful for what the College had done for me and for what I had achieved. I anticipated that I would only be returning for dinners or similar reunions. But fate had other ideas. Within eighteen months I found myself in the North West Frontier of India and then on a lengthy train journey back south to Bangalore where I was due to be trained to take a unit for action in Burma. However, it is likely that it was on that train journey that I contracted poliomyelitis, and ultimately, after being invalided out of the Army, this was to prove the reason for an unexpected return to Corpus. At a crossroads in my life, when I realized that a change of career was inevitable, and badly needed help and advice, a visit to a sympathetic Desmond Lee, still Tutor, encouraged me to return to Corpus for two more years to read Geography. So October 1946 found me back in Cambridge, no longer on the top floor of A staircase, but on the ground floor looking onto the now-cleared debris of New Court lawn. It is no exaggeration to say that Corpus came to my rescue as I felt my shattered confidence being restored and I settled to the study of a new subject with a view to becoming a schoolmaster.

The peacetime years were a different experience but the College had adapted and understood the new needs. Many undergraduates returning from the war were older, more mature and some were married. War was hardly mentioned. Unhappy or traumatic experiences were put aside. There was a renewed commitment about work and life. Wartime studies had been stimulated by the pressure and uncertainty of the future; now there was a relaxed seriousness as careers and the prospect of jobs were being put back on track. Above all the College continued to work its magic and by 1948 I was a different person. I remain grateful for the vital and integral part which Corpus played in my life during the roller-coaster decade from 1938–48, and I like to think that my wartime painting is a small tribute.

### John Fitch, 1941

I came up to Corpus in October 1941 and, for my first year, kept in M5, in the attic under the Old Court roof at the top of M staircase. Its dormer windows looked out onto the Old Court on one side and onto Free School Lane and the Cavendish Laboratory on the other.

T.E. (Peter) Utley, who also lived on M staircase and whom I came to know very well, smoked like a chimney and, after socializing over coffee after Hall, kept very late hours. He was a brilliant conversationalist and, to me at least, pretty uninhibited. As he had been totally blind since childhood, he used braille both for reading and writing. The National Institute for the Blind was very good to him and 'brailled' most of the highly specialist books he required specially for him. Peter had thin, tapering tobacco-stained fingers, which were extremely sensitive, as was his hearing, to compensate for loss of sight. He formed a kind of visual impression of people, particularly of attractive girls, by feeling the contours of faces. We used to have coffee together at odd hours of the night, and I would read to him sometimes, and occasionally take him to lectures.

At the beginning of my second year, in 1942, I moved to N1 at the foot of the N staircase and there I remained until I went down in 1945.

M and N staircases shared the same bedmakers throughout my time, Mrs Hunt and Mrs Bell, the tall and the short of it, both from the King Street area of Cambridge, like most of their kind. Their loud voices and clatter of mops and pails still echo in my memory. The Head Porter in my time was Cator and his assistant, Chapman, both excellent at their job. The Porter's Lodge was a friendly place. The Butler in Hall was Matthews, whose resounding bang on the High Table was the invariable sign to stand for grace. Only one dish stands out in my memory from those days; it was jugged hare, often on Sunday evenings. I don't think I ever tasted it before or since. It was delicious. One other College servant I particularly recall throughout my time was the Fellows' Man, as he was called, the saturnine and tactful Lewis. He it was, I believe, to whom it fell to discover the dead body of Robin Roberts, a Law don, who committed suicide in 1946. The Buttery was presided over by the suave and super-efficient Miller (or Müller – I have an idea he was Swiss).

In my own year as an historian was Richard Feilden, still going strong and still living in Sussex. Another historian in my first year, and an altogether outstanding personality, was the late Edward Thompson. Edward was even then, in this strongly (then) Tory College, a red-hot socialist and leading light of CUSC (Cambridge University Socialist Club), in which he tried to interest me. I still think I have somewhere a card from Kenneth Pickthorn (poles apart from him politically) to E.P. Thompson summoning him to a supervision and overwritten in EPT's characteristic handwriting, 'I bloody well can't go. Can you?' Thompson went down in 1942 to do his military service – he approved of the war after Hitler attacked Stalin's USSR!

Another historian of the time, a year ahead of me, was Stuart Hetley Price, who, like me, changed over from History to Theology after taking History Part I. We quickly became and remained close friends. Hetley too had an excellent all-round brain and a keen sense of humour. He later became Bishop of Ripon. He too, like me, was not called up for military service. Another good friend of my first year was Derek Bowen, who was destined for Holy Orders. He joined up in 1942 and was badly wounded near Capua and invalided out of the Army with severely impaired hearing. He returned to Corpus to go on reading Theology and we resumed our friendship. Derek later worked for the Cambridge University Press, where he helped see the New English Bible through the Press.

Peter Utley's circle of close friends was a remarkable group, which included Campbell Adamson, an economist who later became Secretary General of the Confederation of British Industry and, by an unguarded remark, helped unintentionally, to lose the Conservatives a general election. He had a girlfriend, Gilfran, even in those days and later married her. Another outstanding friend was 'Sandy' (Colin St John) Wilson, son of the Bishop of Chelmsford (also a Corpuscle). Sandy was a notable artist – his full-length portrait of his father in his robes was exhibited with others and with paintings by, I think, another Corpus contemporary, at the Fitzwilliam in my time, thanks to Louis Clarke, then Director, and one time inhabitant/lessee of Leckhampton. Also in that circle was Norman Methven, reading Law, a gentle courteous soul.

In different disciplines to mine I knew and liked Alan Cook, a scientist, again of distinction, who was an active member with Hetley Price of a College SCM (Student Christian Movement) group. Oscar (or Owen) Watson, a charming linguist, now and for long past, residing in France, Jim Butler, a shy, kindly scientist, Norman Robson, an Irish economist of great ability and good sense, Geoffrey Winter, another linguist and Allan Swan, an engineer, both of whom I was delighted to meet again recently at a Corpus lunch. Also Michael Drayton from Barbados whose ready hospitality and wartime supply of rum and molasses made him especially popular, "Bobby" (R.D.) Baird, a jovial extrovert who, I believe, later became a master at Harrow and was later still ordained, and C.D.E. Jones, my neighbour at the foot of N staircase. A whole group of delightful medicos: Mike Corfield, Johnny Sloper and Ian Mackichan. And finally, junior to me, Johnny Blundell, an agriculturalist with a particularly healthy appetite, his friend Richard Lenfestey and George Bennet, a scientist, later a master at Clifton and later still ordained.

Two 'foreigners' much senior to me were the Dane, Dr (later Professor) Paul Christophersen, and Antonio Orbaneja, a Spanish economist and liberal, who had, however, fought on the Nationalist (i.e. Franco) side in the Spanish Civil War. Both were also friends of Peter's.

It is a fact that in the whole of my four years there, the last two as a foundation scholar and indeed the senior scholar, I had not a single conversation with the Master, nor did I ever so much as cross the threshold of the Master's Lodge. I was, of course, admitted by him in Chapel as a scholar, his hands placed over mine as I knelt before him and he uttered the Latin formula of admission. That was all. But, of course, he was throughout the war Regional Commissioner for East Anglia, with his offices at St Regis in Chesterton Road and in the event of an invasion, his powers would have been quasi-dictatorial. He was immensely devout, as befitted the author of a respected contribution to *Essays Catholic and Critical on the Theology of the Eucharist*. He seldom, if ever, missed attendance at Chapel with Lady Spens and the invariable prelude to their appearance from the

*J.P.T. Bury and Will Spens in Corpus during the war years.*

adjacent Master's Lodge was the very audible flushing of the WC in the Lodge. He was always the first to come up to receive the sacrament, followed by the other Fellows present in order of precedence.

The Master's two deputies in his office as Regional Commissioner were the Earl of Cranbrook and Air Vice-Marshal MacEwen, both of whom were often seen about the College and at High Table where they enjoyed dining rights. The Master often had distinguished guests at High Table. One of them, soon after I came up, was Herbert Morrison, Labour Home Secretary in Churchill's Wartime Coalition Government. I was totally new to the College and was alarmed one evening in New Court to be accosted by the well-known figure of Morrison, who asked me the way to the Master's Lodge. To my deep embarrassment I had to confess that I didn't know!

The Tutor is supposed to be *in loco parentis* to the undergraduates, but my relations with the commanding figure of Desmond Lee did not go far beyond formality. I was very much in awe of him. Later Dr George Carter, an altogether more benign and approachable character, took over the Tutorship from Lee. I have happy memories of many agreeable and relaxed conversations with George Carter, a zoologist specializing in invertebrates. He was the quietest and most unassuming of men, an inveterate pipe-smoker and a parson's son, who was seldom seen outside College but who astonished everyone by going off on a sabbatical to the remotest parts of Amazonia in search of rare invertebrates.

Kenneth Pickthorn was my History supervisor in my first year and as well as attending his (excellent) lectures on Constitutional History, it was my duty to see him in his rooms in New Court once a week to read an essay on a subject prescribed by him. He had a formidable reputation as the rudest man in Cambridge. It was to this man that I had to read my essays week by week. Pickthorn would sit playing with his pince nez on its black cord, or shredding (cut plug?) tobacco into a bowl. On one occasion I was stupid enough to write of a 'central bulwark'. 'Stop,' said he, 'have you ever seen a bulwark?' I hope I learnt something from that! Though I retained my awe of him, I came increasingly to like,

*George Carter, Fellow 1930–69.*

respect and even admire him. I found his politics totally congenial and soon perceived that, behind a bleak exterior, there was a kind heart.

With my friend Richard Feilden, I got involved in the University Conservative Association and there saw another side of Kenneth, who invited various luminaries of the Party to speak at meetings. One such was R.A. Butler, then President of the Board of Education in the wartime government and a former Fellow of Corpus.

The most impressively devout of all the dons was the Canadian psychologist Dr J.T. MacCurdy, the benefactor who later in his will, provided so munificently for the annual old members' feasts bearing his name. A fine figure of a man, bald, with a black patch over one eye, he swept a profound genuflection to the altar. He had a rich Canadian brogue and was always very civil.

Mr C.D. Bicknell was an extraordinary man. He was, or had formerly been Keeper of the Museum of Classical Archaeology in Little St Mary's Lane, but was employed by Corpus, as keeper of the classical antiquities in the Collection bequeathed to the College by the Revd S.S. (Satan) Lewis, a nineteenth-century Fellow. He was also effectively in charge of the Parker Library in the absence at that time of the Librarian Fellow, Patrick Bury.

When working in the Butler Library, one was apt to hear his footsteps creaking on the floor above. He had a red face and a shock of ginger hair and a bristly ginger moustache and wore his shapeless trousers at half-mast. He had the most extraordinary laugh I have ever encountered. Hetley Price (I think it was) and I were sufficiently approved of to be invited to tea in the Bicknell's extraordinary home in King Street. Part of the tea ritual was to go to a cupboard with the privilege of selecting one's own cup and saucer from a diverse collection there. One was advised, surreptitiously to use a handkerchief to dust the chosen vessels, which were invariably thick with dust, as was much else. The shabby ambience was one of semi-genteel indigence.

## John Neild, 1941

The main gate was shut at 10 pm and ladies were not allowed to enter after that time. However, lady guests already in could remain until 11 pm. Undergraduates could not leave College after 10 pm but could return to College up to midnight without a late pass. To overcome these rules I used to call on my cousin John Sloper at 10.55 pm and escort his future wife Sue, also a medic, to the front gate. In the meantime, John had climbed out of College through the Library and then took Sue back to Newnham.

Soon after the war ended, the then Dean Robin Roberts, arranged for the last easy exit through the Library to be closed up. Consequently members of the JCR, of which I was then Curator, were highly indignant. *The Wooden Horse* and *The Great Escape* had just been published encouraging us to light-heartedly plot the digging of a tunnel out of College. At that time there were still two underground air-raid shelters in the middle of New Court where, it was suggested, we could dispose of spoil from the tunnel. Shortly afterwards these shelters were flattened, New Court lawn being returned to its pristine self. About that time, matters came to a head at a successful Rugby Club Dinner after plenty of alcohol had been consumed. After dinner we complained to Robin about his closing of the last easy exit and said that we had been forced to start digging a tunnel. We explained that we hadn't proceeded very far before the roof collapsed, but we had left the project on hold pending the return of ex-prisoners of war who, no doubt, would be able to complete the project. At first Robin refused to believe us, but at that moment another undergraduate joined our group who could not have heard what we were talking about. Robin asked him if he knew anything about the tunnel. Fortuitously, he had been involved in the initial planning and was able to confirm all the details including the dumping of spoil in the shelters which had now been cleared. This really set the cat among the pigeons; for the next fortnight builders were seen around the College tapping on the floors, examining the walls for cracks, etc. The conspirators were all being pressurized into revealing the secrets of the tunnel location, before Robin and George Carter, the Dean, realized it had all been a hoax.

Another memorable occasion was 8 May 1945. We had been expecting all day to hear the announcement of Germany's surrender. Sometime in the evening the BBC reported that this would not happen until the following day. So about 8 pm I went to a film and on my late return I discovered that the official announcement had now been made. College appeared to be very quiet, so I decided to celebrate by climbing on to the Hall roof and ringing the Chapel bell which had been silent since 1940. The only response was George Carter waking

from a deep sleep ringing the Porter's Lodge wanting to know what the noise was. At that moment the ringing stopped and the Porter who had also been celebrating replied in a slurred voice that he couldn't hear anything.

---

*EASTERN REGION MONTHLY REPORT ON MORALE*
SIR WILL SPENS – MARCH 1941

*During the past month, the Region has again escaped any very serious attack, and there is, in consequence, little to be said in regard to the effect of bombing on morale, whether of the Services or of the general public. Such attacks as there have been have certainly not harmed morale, and the response of the Services has been good.*

*The present proposals for voluntary evacuation from the coastal towns and from Ipswich and Colchester, have been badly received by the officials concerned, who, without exception, consider that no substantial results will be achieved. The proposals have not yet been published, and, in consequence, it is not possible to make any statement as to the reaction of the public.*

*Three further points deserve comment. The first two concern the arrangements for communal feeding. Information has come from more than one source that it is of real importance to pursue the policy of allowing local inhabitants, as well as evacuees, to use the facilities provided. The local people feel, with some justice, that there is no reason why evacuees should be alone in securing the advantage from the point of view of rationing which communal feeding affords. It appears no less important to insist that the principle of self help should be applied to communal feeding centres. There appears to be no doubt that, in a number of cases, evacuees are refusing to do anything for themselves, and are coming to regard as a right that voluntary labour should do both the waiting and the washing up. The attitude which is engendered in such cases is clearly bad for morale at the moment. It may be no less bad having regard to the future, by inculcating the attitude that the community must provide.*

*The remaining point for comment is that careless talk, especially, but not only, in public houses, is apparently wide-spread. It is not necessary to emphasise the very special danger of such talk in a Region which, on the one hand, is a possible invasion area, and, on the other hand, contains an exceptionally large number of operational aerodromes. There appears to be little doubt that both members of the forces and civilians are to blame.*

*St Bene't's Church with Corpus Christi College beyond. Photo by Dr R.F. Griffin.*

I led a fairly blameless life, but there was one regrettable incident when we shot a duck by the boathouse. My friend had a walking-stick gun, which he was anxious to try, and he fired it at this bird. Trying to hide the poor duck we hurried back to College and gave it to the kitchen. However, the police discovered where the duck had been taken: my friend was duly fined and the Cambridge newspaper had the headline – 'Undergraduate gets the bird!'

### Maurice Richardson, 1942

I remember wandering round the shops on my first day trying to buy one or two things which were needed but which I had failed to bring with me. This was a time of great shortages, and it was a fairly miserable experience. I shall forever be grateful to the kind lady assistant in one of the shops who took pity on me and found a tin kettle – normally unavailable – for me.

The following day I cheered up considerably when I met two chaps who became my friends: Peter Sugden and Frank Bailey. We have always kept in touch and still meet from time to time.

The College looked very drab in those days: the Library side of the New Court was given over to some forces Short-Course students. The cycle stores under S staircase were bomb shelters. I was in S2, so wouldn't have had far to go. Most people had all meals in Hall, encouraged to do so by the sheer difficulty of doing anything else in those days of shortages. The College kitchens certainly had a good way with dried egg, from which they turned out an appetising savoury toast. We were allowed to keep a microscopic amount of the already small standard rations of such items as sugar and butter. We collected our entitlement at the Buttery and did our best with it for tea with our friends.

I went to see Pat Charvet, who was my Director of Studies and my French supervisor. As there was no expert in the College in German, my other subject, I was sent to see Dr Garland at Emmanuel. I had a great regard for Pat Charvet, whose strong royalist views added zest to our discussions on the life, literature and thought of France. I stayed in touch with him, and visited him in his retirement in Gloucestershire. He would have been so pleased to know that one of my two sons, Tristan, would, 45 years later, come to Corpus (to read Maths and Computing), but sadly he died without knowing that.

### Tony Appleby, 1942

A benevolent government sent me to Corpus in 1942 on an RAF University Short Course. The hope was to provide a suitable training for future Commissioned Officers. Half the time was spent in the role of ATC cadets, and the rest as bona fide undergraduates. We duly matriculated and attended lectures such as Meteorology and the British Constitution. I think we were promised some sort of Certificate on completion of the course, but this did not materialize.

Much of the College was occupied by the Ministry of Food. The New Court had two large Emergency Water Tanks – plus ducks! We lugged heavy sacks of coal up ninety stairs to the top of E Staircase, where we had the luxury of two rooms, which I shared with another lad from Cornwall, who was later killed in the war. The Hall was dingy, without its treasures and William Morris wallpaper, but Corpus was still a very special place.

I rowed at number seven in the first boat. Potential rowers were scarce, no doubt, but I think we had some success in the Bumps. Anyway, we had a party afterwards. I reported in the Corpus Letter the ghost we discovered in the Old Court, and made several attempts to persuade it to revisit us.

*Patrick Bury, Fellow
1933–1987.*

There was a less enjoyable part of our days in Cambridge: we were required to join the Senior Training Corps and to give up some evenings, weekends and at least a week or so of the vacation to readying ourselves for eventual service in the forces. Having an interest in radio, I opted for the Signals unit, and eventually joined the Royal Corps of Signals. At no time in the regular army was my training tougher than it was in the STC – ten mile route marches, crossing streams hanging down from a wire, scrambling over brick walls and so on. I know I was one of the least successful, but it stood me in good stead a year or two later, when after wireless operating for Bletchley Park during the campaign against Germany, they decided to toughen us up to meet the Japanese. Such was my STC training that I now shone amongst my fellow softies. I had done it all before!

At the end of our first year we did not have a May Ball, but the College provided a substitute in the form of a Farewell Ball which ended at 3 am, rather than going on all night. I spent some happy hours with Victor Sylvester's *Ballroom Dancing* manual preparing myself for this event under the expert tuition of Frank Bailey, who also helped to find me a partner by chatting up a London School of Economics student called Audrey in the Copper Kettle (LSE had been evacuated to Cambridge).

Three years later things were very different. Cambridge was so busy, over-full with people returning from war service, some already married, and all realizing that it was now a serious business of preparing to earn one's living. It was known to be one of the hardest-working and most serious generations of students. In many ways the shortages were even greater, with the ending of US help to this country. I will just mention that my last year was made much more enjoyable by having a room, as did three of my close friends, at the newly refurbished Newnham House, which was in the charge of the very likeable Lawrences – Mr Lawrence was also the Buttery manager. The only problem was that of reaching the Hall in time for breakfast, where a tall and sour-faced 'head waiter' (at least I think that was his title) stood with his pocket watch waiting for his greatest pleasure of the day, which was to shut the door in our faces on the stroke of time as we panted up the stairs. As rations were short, the option of breakfast in our rooms was not open to us, and the usual alternative was to go round to Petty Cury and see what the Joe Lyons café had to offer.

## Roland Saunders, 1942

I came up in 1942 on a state bursary to read Mechanical Sciences. (As far as I am aware I was the first person to go straight to Cambridge from my East London grammar school.) The normal three-year course had been crammed into two years but we did extra lectures and our surveying on Coe Fen during the Long Vac. We were also expected to find time during the Long Vac to obtain some practical experience: I went with other Corpus men to Stothert and Pitt's in Bath.

The student body in my time comprised 90–95 people. About half of this number were service cadets spending six months at the University; men taking arts courses were generally allowed to stay for only one year, scientists and engineers were able to stay for a second year, and a handful of people, who were unfit for one reason or other, to complete a third. Because I had been ill I had missed what should have been my last term and the Tripos exams, and was fortunate to be allowed back for a third year to complete the course.

The bursaries awarded at that time for engineering and science courses seem generous by modern standards, for they covered all fees, maintenance in term times and subsistence whilst on the practical periods. We used to eat breakfast, lunch and dinner communally in Hall, and afternoon tea, if we wanted it, in our rooms for which we drew 'commons' (part of our wartime food rations) from the Buttery. If one hoped to buy a cake for afternoon refreshment from Fitzbillies along Trumpington Street, it was necessary to have one of their paper bags with their name printed on it!

I had done very little sport at school and, looking for some form of exercise, took up rowing. I discovered that my lack of experience was no bar to my being appointed Hon. Sec. of the boat club, and in due course, as only a few of us proceeded to a second year, I became Captain of Boats. I regret to say that this was when rowing at Corpus was at a low ebb: we could not get enough men together to practise and row in the Lents, and had to share a boat with Queens'. In my third year, being unfit to row, I was a very bad cox with results which I shall not detail.

I was delighted to find that I could indulge my interest in music and I sang with CUMS in King's College Chapel and at the Corn Exchange (there were 'three Corpus tenors' before a better known three), in College Chapel, at occasional Bene't concerts and, as far as studies

*Hostel Yard.*

allowed, at other places by invitation. Most Bene't evenings were spent listening to gramophone records.

In the New Court was a static water tank and periodically students would drill with a mobile pump in case we should have to deal with fires. There were many American servicemen and women about and Flying Fortresses overhead. 'Passion wagons' used to pick up the girls outside the Bull Hotel and take them to the air stations for their dances. After Cambridge, war work. Most of my contemporaries seemed to land in REME. I went to Armaments Design Dept (Ministry of Supply).

### V.W. Brown, 1943
Does the sound of dying quacks still haunt T4? I was a Navy Short Course Undergraduate, the occupant of those rooms immediately after the assassin had gone down. When I entered the main room for the first time I was intrigued to find a pair of mallard wings lying on the window sill. The feathers were stirring gently, aided by a draught from around the window frame. The history of the duck shoot, which I very soon heard, lost nothing in the telling, and helped to put in high relief my time at Corpus.

### Jack Hains, 1943
The first thing I remember on entering the College was the trailer pump behind the gate beside the Fellows' cycle rack, and the large static water tank in the middle of New Court lawn. Within a few days I had been recruited to the trailer pump crew and we practised every week after lunch, spraying any suitable target! We were never needed! The lawn still bore the scars of the water pump when I returned to College in 1948.

My room on the top floor of Old Court was heated by a coal fire, as were many others in those days. We had to collect the coal from the heap beside the Master's garage at lunchtime on Tuesdays. Gowns were worn when carrying sacks of coal.

Those of us not on Service Short Courses were required to undergo some form of military training. The choices were the Naval Division, the Air Squadron, the OTC or the Home Guard. Those who chose the latter had to decide whether to join the 5th or the 7th battalion. I, together with several of my friends, opted for the 7th, in particular 'A' Company. The Company headquarters was at Ferry Cottage on Midsummer Common, next door to the Fort St George. Parades were held one evening each week at Milton Road School and on Sunday mornings on Midsummer Common. The Sunday parade finished at 12 noon, coincidentally the opening time of the Fort St George. 'A' Company was a cycle company whose commander was Pat Charvet. For possessing a bicycle, we were paid an allowance of half a crown a week (12½p).

A lasting memory of those days is the sound of marching feet along Trumpington Street as members of the RAF billeted in Pembroke College went past the College to their appointed task, then back again at lunchtime, with a repeat in the afternoon.

On returning in 1948, the changes most noticeable were the increase in undergraduate population, occupying all the College plus hostels; the government officers had returned to London; gas fires had replaced coal and we had Sunday mornings free to do as we pleased.

### John Yencken, 1943

Another about-to-be occupant of Marlowe's rooms in the Old Court, I arrived at Cambridge in 1943, from school and life on the land in Australia, and tutoring by a Jesuit mathematician in Spain. It was very strange and exciting. My early days were helped so much by the kindness and hospitality of Dorothy, Lady Spens. Will Spens had been my father's tutor at the College. These were the days of the Home Guard, and heavily damaged Flying Fortresses arriving back from their bombing raids. The gaps in the formations showed the ones that did not get back and there were many. Rumour had it that the Cambridge University Home Guard had the only tanks north of the Thames at the time of the Normandy landings. Luckily there was no German diversionary raid! Not all happenings were well regarded by the College. After a Rowing Club dinner, a bath appeared in the churchyard next door. Unfortunately, an outside cleric rang the Master to tell him that there was a body in a bath in St Botolph's churchyard. Obviously a lack of foresight. Some members, as an unfortunate result, were gated.

### Richard Holmes, 1943

I went up in September 1943 on a Potential Officers course for the Royal Engineers. I was accepted by Corpus by favour of Robin Roberts, as my brother Nigel (R.N.B. Holmes) had come up to Corpus in 1938, as a regular sapper officer.

The war years were special, rigorous but exciting with rationing, blackout and sandbagging round the treasures in various buildings. Cambridge was invaded by Bedford Ladies College, London School of Economics and other institutions, including some government departments. There were lots of undergrads on similar courses for RAF aircrew, and for RN dock officers, engineers and aircrew. We were a light-hearted bunch then, as the fortunes of war were starting to favour the Allies. American servicemen mingled with town and gown, and the Thunderbolt pilots favoured the Eagle, generally considered our 'local'.

Academically, we were busy with first-year Mechanical Sciences Tripos, which we did in six months, no vacs, just a week at Christmas. We had parades and training at the STC(?) grounds, about three times a week. We also did the required survey course for Tripos. All this kept us too busy to get into too much trouble, and we had to pass to get a commission later. Extra-curricular activities included rugby for Corpus, (and once for LX Club), Arts Theatre, concerts, etc.

Friends I remember from that time are Robin Roberts, Dean of College, and Pat Charvet among the senior members; and Tony Gordon, my room-mate (and later my Best Man), Mike Leslie, Andy Cleland, Bill Cargey, Bill Bricknell and Darcy Hallam; Norman Frizzel joined the RN Air Arm; Bob Ritchie, Hon. Sec. Rugby and member of the Kitchen Committee, was famous for introducing 'Croute Ritchie' to the College dinner menu!

We went down in March 1944, and joined our respective units for full-time service.

I came up to Corpus again for the Michaelmas term 1947. Sir Will Spens was Master, Paul Spens was my Director of Studies and Domestic Bursar. George Carter was Dean, John Harley-Mason directed Natural Science studies. Pat Charvet was still there. Rationing was still with us and electricity power cuts were common. Other friends were back: Tony Gordon and Mike Leslie. Angus Fawcett was back out of the RAF and Arthur Hill from the RN. Studies did not come so easily after three and a half years away. Rugby in the winter and tennis in the summer, plus Chess Club weekly, kept me busy.

In May week 1949 I met Joan Jopling, a newly qualified radiographer from South Africa. We 'hit it off' and saw a lot of each other. In December we attended the Ox-Cam ski meeting in Sestriere and announced our engagement on 1 January 1950. Sir Will and Lady

Spens suggested a marriage service and offered to host a reception at the Master's Lodge. This very generous offer was gratefully accepted. As Joan's father was unable to travel due to ill health, Sir Will kindly offered to give Joan away.

We were married on 10 June in St Bene't's. We had wonderful weather, with the College flag flying (the only thing that brought tears to my bride's eyes). That was the second wedding from the Master's Lodge, as Peter Boissier and his bride had enjoyed the same generous hospitality in 1948.

In 1952 we returned from Pakistan to find an invitation to the sexcentenary celebrations. Again Lady Spens excelled in hospitality by providing a crèche for infants so that mothers of baby Corpuscles could enjoy the festivities. Joan was among those mothers who were able to enjoy the party.

### David Kinnersley, 1944

Coming first to Corpus in 1944, when the course of the war had clearly turned but not yet reached its end, and coming back in 1948 after national service, was almost like coming to two different colleges.

The first was fairly empty, with only a few friendly medics and the Short Course people, such as myself, from all three services, but for six months only. Sir Will Spens was still in the Master's Lodge, I think as some sort of Regional Commissioner. Among the few Fellows who were around was Dr MacCurdy, rather dapper in his bow-tie, who endowed the dinners that bear his name. Making up College teams from these reduced numbers was not easy: they even asked me to play the occasional game of rugger, for which I had little aptitude. I remember also being asked to appear in the team photo for this season, as someone was missing with a severe hangover. As it happens, Richard Stuart-Prince who was captain then, now lives in the next village to me. The war did not seem all that far away, when we could see occasional flying bombs over Cambridge, but they did not fall near any of its treasures.

The arrangement with the services was that we spent two days a week on cadet training, and they paid our fees. The arrangement with the University was that they laid on courses of lectures and indeed exams and results within the six months. Elderly but distinguished dons gave remarkably fresh lectures outside their own usual subjects. Reading Law, I had the legendary Winfield

covering criminal law instead of tort on which he had made his reputation. For supervision, I was farmed out to Pembroke College.

Even under blackout conditions, all sorts of evening activities continued. College gates closed at 10 pm but they would be opened on request until midnight. I recall a turbulent evening on fireworks night and another night, with peace in the air, a meeting about the United Nations, as it began to be planned, with Gilbert Murray from Oxford, Bertrand Russell and G.M. Trevelyan, then Master of Trinity, all together on one platform.

Coming back in 1948, Corpus was, like other colleges, as full as it could be. I was lucky to get rooms in the Old Court for my first year, and in the Eagle Yard for my second, having been in New Court on the Short Course. As I recall, the Buttery still had to cope with things like butter rationing and the kitchens with ingredients such as whale meat, but most people still dined in most nights. Corpus was said to be the only college where everyone could sit down together at one sitting. High Table operated every evening, and was most popular on Sundays. Fellows who wanted lunch could usually find places on the undergraduate tables, which made for an agreeable sociability. Pat Charvet was President at that time and Geoffrey Styler and George Carter were tutors.

I was persuaded to change to Economics on the grounds that the College did not like teaching first-year Law. I was lucky to have a young research student, Norman Macrae, as my first-year supervisor. He had a great gift for making a sometimes heavy subject amusing and memorable, as shown by his years spent writing and editing much of the weekly *Economist*. This was not a good period for the Economics Faculty – Keynes had died in 1946 and bitter divisions followed. Ronald Henderson, the Economics Fellow, became fed up and went to Australia where he followed a distinguished career advising the Government.

Of the Short Course people, some came back and others did not, few seeing much serious action. John Holmes, on a Navy Short Course in 1944, came back to read Agriculture. Stanley Ellis did not: he made a good academic career at Leeds University instead, perhaps because Corpus was said not to be sympathetic to people reading English. But as a small college, it retained much welcome diversity.

One friend I had, who on his Short Course read Maths at New College, Oxford, later came to Corpus and gained a distinguished First in History. Uncertain about school mastering as a career, he declared he was going to ask the Master's advice about it, as he was said to be so good on such matters, even after two decades in the Lodge. I urged my friend to come to tea to give me a report after what might have been a doubtful interview. On the contrary, my friend said he now realized how well-founded Sir Will's reputation was. In about thirty minutes, the Master had given no direct advice, but asked a series of questions, such that my friend now realized he was clear in his own mind what he should do. After teaching at Tonbridge and Uppingham Schools, he became headmaster, first at Southwell and then at King's School Rochester. Sir Will's afternoon had been well spent.

I came to Corpus from a state school whose headmaster had been to Corpus, but I felt quite welcome there. As Corpus is occasionally spoken of as a stiff or starchy college, I hope these notes convey what a friendly college it was at both times I was there. I think this was helped by its small size, even at its most crowded in 1948, as well as by its diversity. Even Sir Kenneth Pickthorn, after the abolition of University seats in Parliament, still managed to win a mining constituency and spend much time away from the College. Geoffrey Styler was the most accessible of tutors and indeed came all the way to Cheshire to take part in my wedding soon after I came down. Although there have generally been shorter Masterships since the days of Sir Will, I hope the College has kept much of its early post-war virtues and attractions as a small friendly college. With the excellent Leckhampton hostel and the Henry Moore sculpture which Sir Frank Lee added to its years of history, the old and the new have been combined imaginatively. This now includes women students, hardly acknowledged as members of the University in 1948.

### Alec Loten, 1944

I was first at Corpus in 1944 on a six months Royal Navy Engineering Short Course as initial training to become an Air Engineer Officer in the Fleet Air Arm. The course was basically the first year of the Mechanical Sciences Tripos with a very strong bias to Aeronautical Engineering. In addition to the engineering study, those on the course were enlisted as members of the Cambridge University Naval Division and were kitted out in regulation Ordinary Seaman's rig for attendance at the Division. The headquarters of the Division was at a Nissen hut in the grounds of Downing College, where we had to attend, I think, twice a week.

We had training in navigation, morse code audible transmission, aircraft recognition, naval semaphore flag signalling, tying knots (!) and most importantly acquiring a knowledge and understanding of the unique vocabulary of the Royal Navy.

There was little or no rowing on the Cam at that time. However, the Naval Division had two whalers for use there. The whalers were (probably still are) what landlubbers would call an ordinary rowing boat; but as required by the Navy for service from the Arctic to the Equator were more or less indestructible and consequently extremely heavy. The efforts of a completely inexperienced crew to manage these craft on the Cam varied from the frantically desperate to the utterly hilarious.

The second experience was marching and arms drill carried out on the Downing College quadrangle. Our instructor, whose name I think I can still recall, was Chief Petty Officer Bortram. He had a very ruddy complexion and his voice was a rasping croak, both probably achieved from years of rum and salt air. If you were unfortunate enough to do something wrong, such as turning right instead of left or dropping your rifle, he would point an accusing finger at you and roar, 'At the double,' and you had to run round the perimeter of the entire quadrangle holding the rifle above your head. If, when you returned he thought you had not run fast enough or held the rifle high enough, you would be told to go round again. It was the most dire punishment.

### Michael Hamilton, 1944

My memories of my time at Corpus have faded, but I do recall:

Coming up in the autumn of 1945 to do a six month naval Short Course designed to instil into us 'officer-like qualities'.

Coming up again in 1947, after naval service, and reading Law. I remember having supervisions with Mr Roberts in his lovely rooms adjoining St Bene't's Church and later being shocked to hear of his suicide.

Collecting my rations from the Buttery – a few slices of bacon, some sugar and a minuscule amount of butter. Luckily meals in Hall supplemented this!

Rowing in the second Corpus boat that was so incompetent we even ran aground in a bumps race.

# MEMORIES:

## Introduction by Betty Bury

## 1945–52 *Problems of adjustment*

It was clear that in the post-war years of Sir Will Spens' Mastership he and the reassembled Fellowship would encounter very difficult problems of readjustment and administration. The Ministry of Food vacated the College in the autumn of 1945 and in 1946 the Ministry of Information relinquished the rooms which it still occupied. The air-raid shelters and the static water-tank were removed from the New Court and the kitchens, which eventually had to feed more than two hundred men, were enlarged and reconstructed. Much-needed bathrooms and lavatories were gradually provided for most staircases in the New Court and a new Junior Combination Room, I6, was made available for meetings and social gatherings. A matron and a nurse were appointed, room being found for a sick-bay, and the manuscripts and printed books were returned to the Library in excellent condition after an exile which had lasted six and a half years.

In 1946 the Ministry of Labour and National Service decreed that 90% of University places were to be filled by ex-servicemen who, over many months, returned in great numbers either as freshmen or to complete interrupted courses. The problems of accommodating them, increasing numbers of research students and graduate staff of the University were to remain acute for many years. Between 1938 and 1954 the number of teaching staff increased by 82%. Many pre-war lodgings had ceased to exist, the development of Cambridge as a regional administrative centre had obliged a number of civil servants to continue to live in the town and some undergraduates now needed married quarters. One obvious remedy adopted by Corpus was to reduce many sets to single rooms, and to convert 6 Selwyn Gardens, temporarily, and Newnham House, permanently, into College hostels.

The majority of post-war undergraduates worked strenuously in order to qualify as soon and as well as possible before entering the job market and there was little of the rowdiness which was noticeable after the First World War. There was a marked interest in religion and larger congregations in the churches, and John Roach points out that the increased number of grants and state scholarships meant that there were fewer extremes of wealth and poverty than there had been before the war.

In College, an enlarged society now had to make do without a variety of services which, Patrick Bury writes, had previously 'been regarded as indispensable'. Bedmakers no longer attended their young gentlemen three times a day, no longer could cooked breakfasts and sometimes lunch be carried to the more affluent from the kitchens, and no longer would coal fires be laid to

*Corpus Bedmakers, May 1947. From left to right:*

*Back row: Miss Chapman, Mrs Summerlin, Mrs Stanley, Miss Teversham, Mrs Firman, Mrs Jaggard*
*Middle row: Mrs Chapman, Mrs Whitehead, Mr P. Spens (Domestic Bursar), Mrs Odell, Mrs Bell, Mrs Mayes*
*Front row: Mrs Mansfield, Mrs Howley (Steward of the College), Mrs Sykes-Davies (College nurse), Mrs Holmes, Mrs Wright*

await the touch of a match. Rationing meant that all main meals had to be eaten in Hall and that gas fires replaced coal.

Nevertheless, in September 1945 the Committee of the Corpus Association reassembled 'after almost complete inactivity during the war' and 'took stock of the situation' and, in College, the May Week Ball, the Bene't Musical Club, the Chess Club and the Gravediggers, the Commemoration Feast and the Corpus Christi Dinner were all enthusiastically revived. Dr MacCurdy's and Lord Queenborough's handsome benefactions also made it possible for the College to entertain generously despite the difficulties of the time. The first Queenborough Feast was held in 1949 and, in accordance with the wishes of its founder, the principal guests were representatives of the Corporation and citizens of Cambridge as they are today. There was also a general revival of interest in drama and in May Week 1951 *Love's Labour's Lost* was successfully played in the Old Court – the first play to be put on in public in College since 1911! And in the same year Corpus artists, several of whom had exhibited in other places, aroused considerable interest when they showed their work in College. In sport J.M. Mills (1946) was captain of University cricket and A.G. Donald (1945) and S.Y. Dawbarn (1946) represented Cambridge against Oxford in athletics and boxing.

By 1947 the shortage of paper had become so severe that Heads of Houses made an appeal in *The Times* for text books that would be useful to undergraduates and I have in my possession a *Cambridge Pocket Diary* for 1942 to 1943 that even then had shrunk to rather less than half its peacetime size. Corpus men taking their Triposes nevertheless in 1947 achieved no less than 22 Firsts, or 25% of those entered for the examinations, an astonishing feat for those who had scarcely seen a book for many years. Eight men were also awarded Firsts in the Preliminary Examinations. Less happily, in 1948 the College sold the Sidgwick Avenue playing field and the adjoining Fellows' Garden to the University for much-needed building purposes which, however satisfactory financially, meant that Corpus was virtually the only college in the University to be without a Fellows' Garden or indeed any real garden space. On 15 July 1950 the Old Members' dinner was revived for the first time since the war and the *Association Letter* for that year published an interesting note on *Entry to the Col-*

*lege.* 'The Tutor would like to point out that pressure for entry to the College is now very great and shows no sign of decrease… He would therefore like to ask that, if any old member has a son or other relation who wishes to come to the College, some notification of this should be given to him not later than the time that the boy reaches the age of sixteen. In several cases recently he has heard of old members' sons only a short time before they wished to come to the College, and he has had great difficulty in finding places for them'. In some ways the life of some Old Member parents must have been easier 52 years ago than it is today.

In 1952 as Sir Will Spens was the first Master to be compelled, under the new statutes, to retire after reaching the age of 70, the College arranged for the main sexcentenary celebrations to take place before he did so. I leave our readers to enjoy Sir Peter Marshall's wholly delightful description of the Old Members' Party on 21 June.

| MY COLLEGE ACCOUNT FOR XMAS TERM 1945 AND LENT TERM 1946: | | |
|---|---|---|
| | | Credits. |
| Scholarship | | 20.0.0 |
| | | |
| **College a/c.** | | |
| Xmas Term 1945 | 82. 18. 5 | |
| Amount Paid | | 16.1.5 |
| | | |
| **College a/c.** | | |
| Lent Term 1946 | 71. 1. 8 | |
| Scholarship | | 20.0.0 |
| Amount paid | | 16.6.8 |
| | ——— | ——— |
| **Total** | **154. 0. 1** | **72. 8.1** |
| | ——— | ——— |
| | | |
| Fees claimed from Manchester Ed. Committee | | 68.15.0 |
| | | ——— |
| **Amount now due** | **12.17.0** | |
| | ——— | |

## MEMORIES:1945–52

### John Battersby, 1945

In October 1945 only two months after the surrender of Japan, most things were rationed, including coal (one cwt per week), which had to be carried on stretchers and tipped into bunkers on our landing. On bitterly cold November days I kept the fire going all day. Food rations (2 oz butter, a little tea, a little sugar) were distributed from the Buttery, supplemented occasionally by such treats as a tin of sardines, a bag of cocoa or a couple of oranges. Sugar and butter or margarine rations had to be taken into Hall at breakfast time to liven up the College porridge and toast. Corpus food in general had a high reputation, though the appearance of jugged hare on the menu led many to seek sustenance elsewhere.

Those of us who came up to Corpus straight from school – our national service having been deferred – were joined by older men whose degree courses had been interrupted or postponed by the war. Although members of both groups were to be found in the choir, the College eight, the soccer team and so on, at a more informal, social level the two tended to remain separate. There was no question of animosity, but a callow sixth-former had little in common with a veteran who had lived through several years of active service, and friendships were made, by and large, within one group or the other.

Money, or the lack of it, helped to determine priorities. In my own case, a £60 Mawson scholarship from the College was supplemented by a Manchester Education Committee award of £115 plus fees. The Tutor, Mr H.D.P. Lee, assured me that this 'would be adequate' – and so it proved. Membership of the more expensive University clubs was beyond my means, and I never joined the more affluent at the Buttery for pre-dinner drinks, but I don't remember feeling deprived. There was so much to see and do. In the first few weeks alone my diary of the time mentions a lecture by Bertrand Russell, a French Society talk by Harold Nicholson with G.M. Trevelyan in the chair, *Citizen Kane* at the Film Society and no end of sporting and social activities. My first major purchase was a Corpus scarf for 18/- but a second-hand gown cost only 12/6. The requirement of a suit for matriculation at the Senate House caused me some concern, as a suit was something I had never owned, but I was able to borrow one from a friend.

Looking back at the academic side of things, I find it hard to give a fair assessment. There was certainly a great variety of courses on offer. Some lecturers in my faculty (Modern Languages) were unquestionably on top of their subject, some covered the ground without demanding too much from their audience, and some were, regrettably, so inept that they soon found themselves with no audience at all. I suspect that the University at that time was not firing on all cylinders.

Teaching staff must have been greatly depleted during the war, and those remaining had extra, non-academic responsibilities thrust upon them. On the whole, we could not complain, though it came as a surprise to me that nearly all lectures were given in English, not in French or German. (Pat Charvet at Corpus and Erich Heller at Peterhouse were honourable exceptions to this.) One aspect of rationing that caused us some problems in our pursuit of learning was the shortage of paper for printing and publishing. Only in my final year did it seem to become easier to find copies of standard texts, either in the bookshops or the faculty library. My abiding memory of the Corpus libraries is not the glories of the Parker but the sight of Mr Bicknell, the curator of the Lewis Collection, padding about New Court in his slippers, with no socks.

Perhaps he was short of clothing coupons. It was a time of scarcity in some things and abundance in others. Amid all the political and social changes, not to mention the transformation in our own lives, we settled down into our new surroundings and were made welcome.

### Ian Collin, 1945

I was one of Patrick Bury's pupils in my years (1946–1949) and retain great affection and respect for that charming, gentle man.

One of the half-forgotten features of the immediate post-war period is the high proportion of married undergraduates in the ex-service intake in the years 1945–1947, and the cartoon caricatures the plight of some of them with delicious period detail. I myself was in fact able to maintain a closer resemblance to the 1937 vintage student!

The provenance bound into the framed cartoon reads as follows:
*This is the artist's original drawing of a cartoon published in the Summer Number of Punch on June 23rd 1947. It was*

*'University Life',*
*1937, top and 1947,*
*bottom.*

*one of a series of 'then and now' sketches illustrating changes in social life brought about by the Second World War. This cartoon was inspired by a visit by the artist, Norman Mansbridge, to his cousin Ian Collin during the latter's first year as an undergraduate at Corpus Christi College, Cambridge. It was the era of the ex-servicemen resuming their studies after war service, some of them by then married with children, and constrained to lead a rather less frivolous and hedonistic life than their pre-war counterparts. Mansbridge presented this original to his cousin, an unmarried ex-RAF pilot, with the inscription 'To Ian, who is still in the happy position of being able to choose between the two.'*

### David Sergeant, 1945

Life as an undergraduate was quite routine, and as a scholar I lived in rooms for three consecutive years all in the Old Court, same staircase. George Carter was my tutor. For one year (1946–47) David Attenborough was my fellow-pupil there and we established a friendship, but he was not cut out for an academic life and went back to the roving life of a field-naturalist. I was also a (not very successful) choral exhibitioner, so sang a few times solo and more often in chorus at the Bene't Club. I also learned the rudiments of bell-ringing with a University Club, mostly at St Bene't's Church with the clapper fortunately tied up. I rowed in Corpus II for two years (one year was successful, one not), but after that scientific courses were too demanding. I stayed on to do a PhD in Zoology, and Corpus gave me accommodation for one year of these three. I was supported by the Department of Scientific and Industrial Research, but after some training in Fisheries Research at Lowestoft, turned down a position there and went out to Newfoundland.

### Philip Allen, 1946

We came up by train and caught a bus to the Market Place. Our trunks had already been delivered to the Porters' Lodge. Rationing was pretty comprehensive – no bulging waistlines then. Our wardrobes were limited too; it was quite normal to wear the same jacket and corduroys throughout the term. The rooms were cold – no doors at the staircase entrances – and the furniture was sparse. There was no paving in the courts so the gravel made for dust or mud, depending on the weather. There were no flowerboxes, but plenty of peeling paint. The Hall was whitewashed above the panelling and we

sat on heavy oak benches. There was an all-pervading fragrance of furniture polish. But it was a great experience to be up at Corpus after the war years spent at school. I was one of the so-called 'schoolboys' (how we hated that term). Most places had been granted to ex-servicemen and no grumbles there.

There were some giants on the Corpus stage: Will Spens, Kenneth Pickthorn (our very own MP), Pat Charvet, Dr MacCurdy, Bruce Dickins, Garth Moore, Geoffrey Styler, Harley Mason and Desmond Lee. Michael McCrum was in his first year in the Marlowe rooms. I was lucky enough to come under the spell of dear Archie Clark Kennedy and saw much more of him at the London Hospital later.

There was no petrol – no cars – no tourists and no security. Gowns (very old) were compulsory after dark and the Proctor and his bulldogs could spot an incorrectly dressed undergraduate at 100 paces even on a pitch black night.

The Head Porter was a terrifying gentleman especially when he wore his top hat. Albert Jaggard was the junior in the lodge. The head butler even wore tails sometimes. After the bedders left at about 11 am the only woman left in College was Miss Higgs who worked in the tutor's office. Leckhampton was not even a glint in anyone's eye.

### Tony Merriam, 1946

I was a reluctant undergraduate. Coming up to Cambridge seemed like returning to school and I resented the rules and the quiet complacency of the place. As I sought my rooms, a well-meaning don remarked, 'Oh! you will be in Marlowe's room', to which I replied that I was expecting a room to myself. How was I to know that he was referring to Christopher Marlowe, the poet who died in 1593? On the first evening all the new arrivals, most of them, like me, returned from the services, were assembled in the library to be briefed by the Tutor and hear him say that he was to be *in loco parentis*. After five years' commanding troops through India, Burma and Malaya, I hardly felt in need of such parental control. I was told that, if I went out after dark, I must wear a gown to identify me as an undergraduate. A few days later, I came out of a cinema with my gown over my shoulder and was approached by a bulldog who told me that the Proctor wished to speak to me on the other side of the street. This gentleman raised his cap to me, informed me, with icy politeness, that I was committing an offence and should appear before him the following day. When I did, he regretted that he had to fine me the sum of 6/8d (33p in today's money). Was this what I had been through five years of war for?

Such incidents did not help me settle to University life. I was in love at the time, impatient to get married and started on my career. I did not find studying any easier than before but managed to get through the necessary work so that, by doing an extra term during the summer vacation, the course was completed in two years instead of three. I missed out on all the extra-mural activities which should have made the experience much richer; that was my choice. However, I got my degree, presented with a lot of bowing and cap-raising in the Senate House. I had fulfilled the condition for getting a job. It was 1948; I was 26 and my formal education was at last finished.

### John Thorn, 1946

Cambridge immediately after the war was, not surprisingly, a strange place, its dons few, its undergraduates varying in age from 18 to 30. It was cold and grey and there was no luxury. *Brideshead Revisited* had been out a few years – its Oxford seemed another world, a far cry from the queues outside Fitzbillies, patiently waiting for a small cake. Crumpets were toasted at guttering gas fires. Brown Windsor soup, Vienna steaks, and rice pudding with a spoonful of jam were what followed the Latin grace declaimed by Pat Charvet. But we enjoyed it hugely, I think.

### Tom West, 1946

When I came up in October 1946 I was one of a small group who came straight from school. Ninety per cent of undergraduates were ex-servicemen, many of whom had served throughout the six years of the war. Looking back, I consider it was a mistake to have come straight from school. I would have benefited from doing national service at the age of eighteen and coming up when I was more mature. However, I quickly made friends with a group of fellow 'schoolboys' – not that I failed to have friends among the ex-servicemen. One disappointment was that, owing to the pressure on accommodation, I had to share a room during my first year, so that I didn't get 'a room of my own'. Jack Wild, with whom I shared (you can imagine the jokes about the Wild West corner

*May Ball, June 10th 1947.*

of the College), remained a close friend until he died in 1988. Another disappointment was that my first year was marred by various mishaps. I spent half of the first term in the Evelyn Nursing Home and recuperating at home, and my father died in the summer term. I thought I would have to leave the College because of lack of funding but the Labour Government of Clement Attlee had introduced state awards for all holders of open scholarships or exhibitions so my grant was made up to the maximum and I was able to stay on.

When I returned to College, fully recovered, in January 1947, it was the beginning of the worst winter for decades. Snow was piled up in the streets and the weather was bitter. The College had only enough coal to allow fires on one or two days a week. Jack and I had a gas fire, but, because of wartime neglect, even the gas pipes froze up so that we only had a flame about an inch high. There were only two ways to keep warm in the evenings, to go to bed or to go to the cinema. I saw more films in that term than at any other time in my life, including *Great Expectations* and *Gone with the Wind*.

In contrast, the summer term of 1947 brought the hottest summer of the century. After exams were over, a group of us went out by bus into the Cambridgeshire countryside nearly every day. I was pleased to be awarded a II.i in the Preliminary Examination. Because of my father's death and shortage of money I spent a month of the Long Vacation working at a fruit-picking camp near Cambridge. The College did not really approve of this

and I was warned to spend a good deal of the Long Vac reading in preparation for the second year when I would take the History Tripos Part I. The most remarkable event of my second year was the riot on Guy Fawkes Day when a huge mob of undergraduates assembled in the Market Place. A home-made bomb was set off near King's College Chapel where the stained-glass windows were being put back after their removal during the war and some of the windows in the Senate House were broken. Vehicles were damaged and the police did a baton charge in Petty Cury. The Vice-Chancellor, Canon Charles Raven, sent a letter to every undergraduate deploring the episode. A group of us had gone to the cinema together and found the mob outside when we emerged. We were glad to get back to College in one piece. I don't think anything like it has occurred since.

I revelled in the pleasures of English literature for a year, not least because of the distinguished cast of lecturers – Dadie Rylands himself, Hugh and Joan Bennett, the great Dr F.R. Leavis, F.L. Lucas – who entertained us in the Mill Lane Lecture Rooms. With Paul Turner's help I managed to do a two-year course in one year and gained a II.ii. in the English Tripos Part I. I had lost my College exhibition but state funding continued and I completed my degree. In June 1949 my friends and I trooped down to the Senate House, where, a month before my twenty-first birthday I knelt before the Vice-Chancellor, Canon Charles Raven, to receive my BA degree in the presence of my dear mother.

*Graduation Day, 1949. From left to right:*

*R.H. Joyce, R. Mangnall, J. Wild, T. West, H. Hughes, M. Fowler*

*Punting on the Cam.*

In September I was called up for two years of national service in the Royal Army Educational Corps. When I returned to Corpus in October 1951 to do the year's course for a teaching certificate, the College had changed. The great bulk of the wartime ex-servicemen had departed and the average age was much lower. I was more mature and found the postgraduate year very enjoyable.

### Derick Armstrong, 1947

I was one of that generation which came out of the army to go up to Corpus plus wife and very young baby. I was never really integrated in the life of the College – one foot out and one foot in – a sort of adult Tech. We were lucky enough to live in Patrice Charvet's mother's house for a year and then we lodged with Elizabeth and Desmond Lee. I never spent the midnight hours discussing Kafka over a bottle of red wine. I was a member of the Gravediggers' Society, which was very agreeable, and I played squash with Michael McCrum, who always beat me. Most of the time was spent swotting to get a piece of paper which would get me a job. I read Spanish and German – the latter was helpful as I spent 30 years in BP having much to do with Germany and Austria.

### Peter Teed, 1947

After three years in the tropics I found Cambridge excessively cold. I was on T staircase and the walk to the baths was far too long in winter. We were expected to dine in Hall, in jackets, tie and gown, which everybody accepted. Jeans had not been invented! There were, of course, no girls! Incredibly it was perfectly possible to live on one's ex-service grant, serving sherry to one's friends and buying an amazing number of books (hardbacks). There seems to still have been something left over for vacations, but perhaps I misremember.

Although I had been active in school drama, I never took any part in University theatre and the College Marlowe Society had yet to be born. I sang in the Chapel Choir and joined CUMS under Boris Ord. This was a fantastic experience. I don't know what we sounded like, but in three years we performed a remarkable range of works: Matthew Passion, B Minor Mass, Symphony of Psalms, 9th Symphony, etc!! Boris was an institution in himself.

Of course, Cambridge in spring was a total delight, especially to someone who had not seen a spring for three years. Rationing had not ended, and there was a certain amount of grumbling, but for me life in peacetime Cambridge was a delight. We old men integrated with the freshers from school surprisingly easily. The 1945 Labour landslide had passed me by in Burma, and I was at that time remarkably apolitical.

Patrick Bury supervised my Modern European History, and his gentle but profound criticism always inspired and encouraged one to 'try harder'! Gradually my knowledge and understanding of history grew and I never regretted not reading English, which was my original intention. Patrick encouraged me to apply for a Lazard scholarship, which I was fortunate to win. It enabled me to spend a lengthy and fascinating Long Vac in France, looking at French education. In my last year I was also fortunate enough to be appointed Student Librarian to the Parker Library. My duties were light, mostly to show the odd tourists some of the treasures of the Collection. Compared with today both conservation and security were virtually non-existent! The then curator of the Lewis Collection was a Mr Bicknell, a highly eccentric scholar who shuffled around the library in old shoes (no socks), with whom I was expected to take tea occasionally in his very untidy and dirty cottage.

In my last year I moved into the Marlowe rooms, and was thus a neighbour of Garth Moore. The stories of the latter's eccentricities abounded, including that he used to supervise in the bath, (but I guess this was apocryphal!). By all accounts he was a brilliant teacher. Certainly Murray Stuart-Smith made it all the way to the House of Lords. Do Law students still have to disappear to London every so often to eat at their Inn?

Living in the Old Court, one was supposed to see or hear the College Ghost. There was always a deal of wood-creaking during the night and such noises were eerie; but I was never convinced that they came from beyond!

### John Baden, 1948

Of my three years as an undergraduate I think my main memories were of the Boat Club dinners and the luck I had in being fairly slim so that I could squeeze through the Golden Gates without having to go through the Porter's Lodge if I was returning back late to College. I would add that my grandchildren still do not believe that I could do it! After coming down as an undergraduate one of my first memories is of the 600th Anniversary Lunch in Hall which was the first time ladies were allowed in Hall and my wife still has a vivid recollection of that lunch.

### D.W. Small, 1948

In March 1945, I had been offered a place at Corpus. Army service took me to London University to study a Chinese dialect, followed by a spell in Egypt as an Intelligence Officer. The College contacted me when demob came round, to confirm my place, and enclosed a formidable suggested reading list. Somehow my enthusiasm for the Classics had evaporated in the previous three years. My family had been lawyers in Scotland for several generations.

To my great relief, the College graciously consented to my switching to the Law Tripos. The months between October 1948 and June 1951 went all too quickly. First in H8 (nearest bathroom in the Old Court), then two years in 12 KP, half-way between the College and the Law Library. Reading all those law cases still left time, if properly organized, for some sport and social activities.

For some years after I went down I was Secretary of the Corpus Association, and subsequently served on the Appeal Committee. Now I look forward to my first Beldam Dinner.

### Edward Booth, 1949

I would first like to mention some memories of coming to Cambridge for the entrance examination in December 1945. It was very cold and I was accommodated in the Old Court (Q1). I was fascinated by the ancient black-painted, iron fireplace. A fire had been laid, with wood, firelighters and coal. I tried to light it, but without success. I think I spent the first day without any heating. But in the street I met my former House Captain (at Prince Henry's Grammar School, Evesham), A.T. ('Dick') Grove (then of St Catharine's College), four years older than me, who after his air service had come to finish off his Geography degree. He came to show me how to light the fire, with a fire-guard in front of the chimney, largely covered with newspaper to create a draught at the bottom. It was the real beginning of a life-long friendship. When the senior members heard that I came from a school named after Prince Henry (first son of James I), Canon Charles Smyth took me to Sir Will Spens in the Master's Lodge, to look at a portrait of Prince Henry there, supposedly by Marcus Gheeraerts the younger, a Flemish English court painter: 'Was it like the one at school?' I did not need the electric light, which the Master brought to see that it was totally unlike it. It was small, whereas the painting in the school hall was large and life-sized (it is seemingly a copy of the portrait in the National Portrait Gallery by Robert Peake the Elder.) I was told much later that Corpus was concerned about its authenticity.

When I came up in 1949 I had most to do with Patrick Bury, as Director of Studies. A deeply kind and gentle man, he had made his speciality the explosive material of post-revolution France, which was so unlike himself. I often recall with great pleasure, even connatural amusement, that not-quite-dead-pan voice (because he was also communicating the humour of irony) in which he delivered his lecture on 'The Storming of the Bastille' and how it was all a mistake.

At Corpus I was also taught by three others. John Roach had had a hard war, working as a Japanese prisoner on the Burmese railway of death. He had written a deeply researched document on an Indian civil servant. He was precise, clear, and always friendly. So was Geoffrey Woodhead, who taught me Classical History. He was an expert in Greek epigraphy. Much later I was to have a very good correspondence with him. Very different was Harry Porter, who taught me the History of Political Thought. His restrained flamboyance was an expression of life. For him Michael Oakeshott was preferred reading .

With my contemporaries and near-contemporaries, I remember many religious discussions – especially significant for me because I became a Catholic in the Lent term of my second year. Probably they verged on the distasteful for those unwillingly drawn into them. I am sorry about that. I had some good relationships with some very different groupings. Not with the Chess Club (who never played chess), who, in their woolly smoker jackets, saw their guests out of the College just before midnight with three rousing cheers. I remember the elegant discussions, of a cultural, religious, and College sort, with a group which included Peter Teed, who was sub-librarian, Alister Kneller (a lawyer, and later a judge, with whom I am now again in touch), his school friend, the late Malcolm Burgess (who taught Russian, and painted in many different forms: stage settings were a speciality, and he designed the redecoration of the Hall), Ian Barton (an excellent classicist, always so self-effacing), and Hugh Baillie (a friendly musician tutored by Boris Ord). The lighter subjects of conversation would extend from the latest *bons mots* of Garth Moore,

stories about Mr Bicknell (who worked in the library, whose rather ferocious, Edwardian appearance belied his gentleness), to the latest antique acquisitions from Gabor Cossa (opposite the Fitzwilliam). Among my own years were John Belfrage (a nephew of the BBC news-reader), and his school contemporary (I think), the late John McClure, who played the cello. ('How is the cello going?', I would ask. 'Like a bomb!' he would reply.) A quite dissimilar pair were Roger Hippisley Cox (who required encouragement to get out of bed in the morning, and who could not wait to go off to be an agricultural engineer) and Denis Whelan. The latter was a nephew of Sean O'Faolain. He had an Irish soul locked up within an anglicized ethos, which even his English studies could not release. With John Denza, who played the piano well, I could just about manage to play the subordinate part in classical duets. Besides a friendship with another Catholic, Joe Binns, whose Portuguese-Azores background fascinated me (illustrated with his latest watercolour sketches), I had a good, long-lasting relationship (we corresponded and sometimes met) with Keith Winnard, as everyone knew, a card-carrying Communist. Perhaps we were united in dissimilar earnestness. He died young. I even managed a friendly relationship with the redoubtable Donald Munro. I think also of two others who died relatively young. Nicholas Corke, who had a room near mine over the Library, who was somewhat aesthetic and remote – who died at home as the result of a gas leak, and Douglas Spankie, a really noble and agreeable character. He told me that he had taken up TA parachuting because it was a challenge. Two years below was another future priest, David Bingham (of the Mill Hill Missionaries), whom I have visited in Sarawak.

Finally I would like to say how happy I was to live at the hostel at 12 KP for my second and third years, with George and Margaret Meggison. The splendid side-view of King's College Chapel was a bonus; there was even a little excitement generated by the meetings, just under my window, of E.M. Forster (in his outmoded clothes, including a cap; with some justice someone remarked that he looked just like a London taxicab driver) and the 'beautiful and the good' of King's College.

## Graham Campbell-Smith, 1949

My year, in 1949, was among the first to have been at school throughout the war, doing national service before

*Old Court (from* Some Artistic Impressions, *Gorman).*

going up. Even those who did not do national service had to wait two years. We had experienced blackouts, which made travelling at night very difficult, few cars with tiny petrol allowances, unless you had a need e.g. a doctor, farmer, etc. and virtually no social life or parties until 1945. We were consequently more serious than might have previously been the case.

I had won a scholarship to Corpus in Maths but two and a half years maturing had altered my aims in life. Having travelled from Edinburgh overnight to London and then out to Cambridge, I found my rooms, left my luggage and proceeded to Hall for lunch. The Butler, Mr Freeman, saw me, looked up at the clock which was at 1.31 pm and said that it was closed as it was after 1.30 pm. I explained about my overnight journey from Edinburgh, to no avail. Thereafter, we had a mutual respect for each other. I made off towards the Guildhall and found a British Restaurant. These were a wartime invention, serving pretty basic meals within strict price controls. The next shock was to find that the gates shut at 10 pm, although the porter would let you in through the door until midnight. It was astonishing to find people who had commanded regiments, making life and death decisions, being treated like schoolboys!

About the second evening, there was a knock at the door and two men entered. They looked me up and down and said, 'You'll do'. 'Do what?' I asked. 'In the boat,' they said. I had captained the school shooting eight and took them to the first post-war Bisley and had hopes of a Half Blue shooting. All of these hopes went out of the window and, although I had only gillied for my father whilst fishing, I found myself in a tub at the boathouse next day. I eventually made the first boat in the Lent bumps but we took Corpus to ninth in the London head of the river race, a record which still stands.

After a few days, Sunday arrived and I found that I could not take communion in Chapel as I was a member of the Church of Scotland. I had been nurtured and confirmed in St Giles Cathedral in Edinburgh and on my first vacation, took the matter up with the Very Revd Dr Charles Warr. He took it up with the Archbishop of Canterbury and success was reached the year after I went down in 1952, too late for me to benefit but a step in ecumenism for others. I worshipped at St Columba's near Emmanuel. I was surprised on a recent visit, not a Sunday, to find it full of Chinese, probably evangelized by Eric Liddell!

I soon encountered a pre-war custom. The Dorothy Café was built in the escapist era between the two world wars. On the ground floor was an upmarket grocery and on the first floor a café/ballroom which provided coffee dances in the morning and tea dances in the afternoon. The technical college offered a certificate in English to foreigners and there were many French and Scandinavian girls au-pairing in order to learn English. Thus, although Newnham and Girton provided girl undergraduates, they tended to avoid the Dorothy Café. The foreigners and some locals evened up the numbers to some extent.

Unfortunately, Corpus had no tradition in Maths and in my year there were four of us and no tutor. We were sent to David Rees, who had been code-breaking at Bletchley Park, and later to a youngster – Michael Atiyah, both now FRSs. But the lectures I found to be very stilted and dull and, as far as I was concerned, not very helpful. I spent my first Long Vacation studying my favourite subject – astronomy – to find, on my return, that it had been removed from the syllabus. I had not read the correct notice-boards and no-one mentioned it. It was very disheartening. A fellow scholar of my year, Chris Hooley, subsequently became the College's first Research Fellow in Maths and is also now an FRS.

Getting around necessitated getting a bicycle. As many were stolen, each college had numbers, one of which was painted on the rear mudguard. I reckoned that an old ladies' bicycle would be less attractive to thieves and in fact it was never stolen. Recently, when visiting the College and knowing that a MacCurdy Dinner was not far off and that last time I got the number of my old rooms wrong, I thought I would check their location. I encountered the current impregnable security system and was shocked to think that such defences were now needed when each room has a lock and key. Why were the staircases barred? It made me realize how far civilisation has disintegrated in the last 50 years. The porter was not at the lodge but a Fellow let me in and I discovered that, by splitting some rooms, they have re-numbered my old rooms. A young lady occupant allowed me to remind myself of watering my cyclamen on the window-sill above the bank and an agitated bank employee explaining to me that a lady customer had had her hat soaked as she entered the bank.

My last year was 1952, the 600th anniversary of the founding of the College. Amazingly, the roof timbers

*An ancient Leyland.*

had lasted all that time but it was decided that they should be replaced. So, all of the roof tiles came off and new timbers went up to a plan (unlike the original) but I am sure that they will not last 600 years – they are probably not oak. Remembering that rationing of some foods had not ended, two oxen were donated by the town of Corpus Christi, Texas and were flown over, together with the men to roast them. We had an open air feast on the playing fields to commemorate the event.

Later, in 1963, again with the involvement of the Archbishop of Canterbury who had to authorize the use of the Chapel as a parish church for the day, I was married in the beautiful Chapel which my wife and I continue to enjoy revisiting, cherishing our happy memories.

**Harry Grant, 1949**
I was at Corpus for only two winter terms, while attending a second Devonshire Colonial Service Course – October 1949–March 1950. I was already married and aged 28 and lived in lodgings in Chesterton Road. I rowed in the College second boat and so met a few of the undergraduate members of the College, but I cannot recall any of their names!

**Bill Matthews, 1949**
I came up to Corpus to read History in 1949, following National Service in the RAF, in which I had had a very good time. My room was X4, where the bedder was a formidable lady called Mrs Holmes. I soon found out

who was in charge: I love cats, and finding a stray on the stairs one day, welcomed him into my room, where he spent the night. When Mrs Holmes found him asleep on the sofa the following morning, I was left in no doubt that cats were not regarded as welcome guests in undergraduate rooms.

A particular memory of my time in X4 is of the buses. These were ancient Leylands, originally petrol engined, but which had been dieselised with five-cylinder Gardners, just about the roughest engine there was. They retained the original exhaust system, and as a result were deafeningly noisy. I would hear the thing start from Guildhall and accelerate down Bene't Street, the racket reverberating off the walls. At the bottom of the street it would stop, the diesel knocking loudly, then, with a crash of gears, thunder off down Trumpington Street. As it passed my window, everything in the room rattled.

My supervisors were John Roach and Geoffrey Woodhead. I've been back to Cambridge several times recently, and have always hoped that I would meet them again, but have had no luck. I could sense their brilliance even at my age. I suspect that neither was much older than I was.

I soon made friends, and indeed there were quite a gang of us. Henry Angas is now a farmer in Australia, and we are still in regular contact. Alan Robinson has had a very distinguished career in the USA. Hugh King-Smith, who had the room above mine, joined the Franciscans and is (or was, when I last heard) in a senior position on the West Coast of America. Mike Hallett and Keith Winnard are both now sadly dead. Keith was a violent Communist, and many were the all-night arguments we had. John (Charlie) Parker has spent his working life in Norwich. John Denza played many a board game with me. None of us was sporting, and indeed we affected to despise those who rolled in mud on the football or rugger fields. At the Parker Library lunch recently, I sat next to the Very Revd Alan Warren. He came up after I went down, but his elder brother Ray was one of us. Ray was reading Music, and ended his career as Professor of Music at Bristol. He was no mean composer, and wrote a piece for the 1952 May Ball. He said we would like it, because it had tunes in it!

Henry Angas taught me to make tea Australian-style. Tea was rationed in those days, and had to be used economically, but neither of us liked weak tea. The solu-

*Botolph Lane.*

tion was to make the morning tea in the orthodox way in a metal teapot, and use half of it. Came teatime, you filled the pot up with cold water and boiled it up again. Very satisfying.

Severe rationing was still in force in 1949, and strange expedients had to be adopted to cope with a hundred or more hungry undergraduates. Pat Charvet was Steward of the College Estates at the time and these were infested with hares which, jugged, made frequent appearances on the menu. This was repulsive, and attendances in Hall were thin indeed if the word had got round that it was to be served. Occasionally they cheated by not announcing it. As you couldn't leave after grace, you had to choke it down somehow. Another revolting dish was an entrée of dried egg on toast with an anchovy on top. No doubt it was edible when first made, but by the time we got it, the toast had curled up, and the egg had a dried-up crust. The anchovy often curled in the opposite direction to the toast. Talking of meals, I've never forgotten what must be the shortest grace on record: *Benedictus Benedicat*. It reminds me of William the Conqueror selecting as his Archbishop of Canterbury the cleric who could gabble a mass the quickest.

For my last year, I moved out to lodgings in Botolph Lane run by a sweet little red-haired Yorkshire lady named Mrs Lowe. In the winter, she caught a very bad cold, and my mother sent her a roast chicken to restore her strength. Alas for good intentions – the next-door cat crept in through an open window and stole it, the chewed wreckage later being discovered in the street. My neighbour in the room below and I used to spend hours playing canasta well into the night. I wish I could remember his name.

### Robin Crawford, 1950

**The University OTC**: Most of the intake of undergraduates in the early 1950s had done two years or eighteen months of national service before coming up and most had been officers. All ex-national servicemen had an obligation to continue in the TA for a few years after their full-time service was over. For those who went up to Cambridge this obligation meant that they had to join CUOTC and do a number of afternoons of training at the military premises, which were then immediately behind the University rugger ground on Grange Road, and also some weekends of training under

CUOTC arrangements. The result of all this was that the OTC was made up of about 80% officers and barely 20% of officer cadets. This made it rather difficult for the regular army permanent staff NCOs, having to organise training periods for a large number of jovial but uninterested young officers, who thought they knew it all already!

However there was one very substantial plus, which was that there were a great number of excellent parties at the Officers Mess, which was then at Quayside beside Magdalene Bridge. These would quite often count towards training time particularly when the permanent staff were there too. Corpus provided two members of the Mess Committee at that time including the all-important Wines Member. It was a great social life in the OTC!

**The Eagle**: This was very much the Corpus local. It was quite small in those days, with only two smallish bars, although there was some seating in the courtyard when it was warm enough to sit out. It was run by a formidable but kindly couple, Ethel and Ted. Ethel ran the lounge bar where the ceiling was – and probably still is – decorated with cigar-burnt designs by wartime airmen from Mildenhall and elsewhere. Ethel was much more than the bar-lady; she got to know all her regulars and their problems. Being a motherly figure, she was a good listener and adviser. Many an undergraduate with emotional problems would come to weep on her shoulder or to seek advice. Ted handled the public bar and also made the key decisions on when to allow short-term credit and when not to. He had mastered the difficult art of turning you down for credit without causing any offence. They were a very popular and well-respected pair.

*The Eagle pub today.*

### Harry Mitchell, 1950

Most of us had to manage on modest incomes, in my case a minor scholarship from the College plus a government grant, providing a total of £300 a year or thereabouts from which to meet the cost of board and lodging in College, books, miscellaneous expenses in term time and the cost of travel between home and College at the beginning and end of term. Unlike students nowadays we were, however, spared the burden of having to meet the cost of tuition fees. I owned few clothes and wore the same pair of corduroy trousers every day of term. We all bought second-hand under-

graduate gowns, which had probably never been dry-cleaned and were often ragged. College rooms did not have the benefits of central heating or bathrooms en suite. We managed with gas fires and numerous trips in the course of the day to the communal bathrooms and lavatories in a corner of the Old Court. Taking a bath in the winter required some physical stamina, as it usually involved a walk in pyjamas and dressing gown on a cold night from one's staircase on the Old or New Court to the bathrooms in the corner of the Old Court.

The Lord Chamberlain still exercised his powers of censorship over theatrical performances at that time, powers which were eventually abolished by the Theatres Act 1968. One of the Lord Chamberlain's arbitrary rules was that nudes were permitted on stage but only if they remained in statuesque poses. Word soon got around that in a variety show at the Arts in the summer of 1952 or 1953 there were indeed nudes and certain undergraduates – not including myself, I hasten to add – decided that this was an opportunity too good to miss. They bought tickets for the front rows and boxes and went along to the theatre armed with water pistols filled with water, said to be capable of firing as many as 32 shots without needing to be refilled. When the curtain was up and the nudes were on stage these undergraduates took aim at the girls and managed a few direct hits. My recollection is that the girls were mindful of the need to comply with the Lord Chamberlain's edicts and not bring the company or the theatre into disrepute, so they stoically maintained their poses while cold water trickled down their naked bodies; one or two of them may have unavoidably shuddered a little. These antics led to a great deal of uproar in the house and there were protests from some of the townspeople in the audience who objected to having their evening's entertainment hijacked in this way. After a few disrupted scenes the curtain came down and the manager came on to the stage. His message was, 'If this behaviour continues I shall bring down the curtain and give everyone their money back – except members of the University.' The message was heeded.

Another incident which I vividly recall is the rustication of Mark Boxer, sometime editor of *Granta* and now, alas, dead. The proctors took offence at a poem which he published in *Granta* which they considered blasphemous, I think in the summer term 1953, and they made an order for his rustication a fortnight or so

*The 'Marlowe' portrait.*

before the end of term. He organized a spectacular send-off for himself. He hired a local undertaker to turn up on King's Parade on a Sunday afternoon with a horse-drawn hearse, a coffin and attendants in black with top hats and the usual regalia. In attendance also were an undergraduate dressed in the trappings of a Roman Catholic priest and numerous acolytes. One of Mark Boxer's friends stood on the hearse and delivered a mock funeral oration on the demise of the editor of the *Granta*. The 'priest' walked along King's Parade swinging an incense burner dispensing huge clouds of incense and uttering mock Latin prayers in which the word 'granta' frequently and audibly occurred. It was a great piece of entertainment. It was a hot afternoon in early summer and Cambridge was crowded with

*'The Old Court under repair' in the 1950s (from* Some Artistic Impressions, *p.96, G. Gilbert and G.A. Clarke).*

tourists who greatly relished this free unexpected spectacle. For some time King's Parade was completely blocked with crowds of undergraduates, townspeople and tourists, all greatly enjoying themselves. It would be inconceivable nowadays that the proctors would take such stern disciplinary action for what would certainly be regarded as a minor offence or more likely would not be considered now to be an offence at all. It would be even more inconceivable that any kind of disciplinary action by the proctors would be met with such a mild, amusing and good-natured reaction by the undergraduates – or have I got it all wrong and are the days of violent student protests long gone?

### Peter Hall, 1953

When I was Captain of Boats at Corpus in 1953, I was privileged to have the corner room on the first floor with a staircase which went up to a bedroom in the roofspace above. Originally, the staircase crossed with the Senior Tutor's staircase, so that his bedroom was above my room in the Old Court, and my bedroom was above his room in the New Court. The Senior Tutor at that time was Mike McCrum, so we got to know each other quite well as we had to share the same staircase to our bedrooms!

During the restoration work on the Old Court, which I think was related to the 600th anniversary, the workmen took the gas fire out of the fireplace, in what was now my bedroom above my room in the Old Court, in order to install a more modern fire. In doing so, they found two planks of oak underneath the old fire, and these were put onto the skip. When I saw this happening, I asked if I could have the oak planks, as I was building a case for a hi-fi system and thought they might be suitable. However, when I looked at the planks closely, I saw that there was a painting on them; you could vaguely see a head. So rather than build my hi-fi unit, I took them to Pat Bury, the Librarian, to ask if he thought they were of any value. He was very interested, as we could just see a date in the corner, which appeared to be the 21st birthday of Christopher Marlowe. He also found out that there were no other portraits of Marlowe and thought that it was worth getting the painting restored. The restorers did a first-class job and it was framed and hung in Hall, from memory about half-way down on the right hand side. [Nb: Michael McCrum has a different version of events].

### Peter Marshall, 1943

Toast to the College, proposed at the Corpus Association Dinner [July 20, 1991]:

I can think of no more appropriate way of meeting the honourable charge, laid so courteously upon me, of proposing the health of the College than to recall a glowing instance of its solicitude for its *alumni*: specifically the Old Members' Party on June 21, 1952, when the College was celebrating six hundred years of its existence.

Two reasons underlie this choice. The second, and more practical of the two, I leave to the end of these brief observations. The first, and more objective, reason is that I was the Captain of the Old Members' team, which played the College at cricket on that great day.... I am uniquely qualified to supply the detail of that memorable afternoon.

First, the background. The celebrations in 1952 were described as 'the Sexcentenary'. If the anniversary had fallen in this Year of Grace 1991, would we, in our current psychological and sociological obsession, have been so un-mealy mouthed? Does today's unclassical generation imagine that 39 years ago we were celebrating the centenary of Freud's birth (admittedly four years too early) rather than six hundred years of ourselves? Would there have been a prudent decision to settle for some circumlocutory evasion of the issue by talking of our 'Sesquiquadricentennial'? In those less complex days there were no such qualms. There was only nostalgia and rejoicing. No hang-ups, but quite a few hang-overs.

Secondly, the documentation. There was, I suppose, a score-book, and perhaps even a scorer, to record this epic encounter of which I speak. If so, both are lost in the mists of time. Happily the participants included the Master and Geoffrey Styler in their respective contemporary qualities of Tutor and Dean of Chapel. I therefore have to submit my account to the bar of shared reminiscence. This underlines the point that diplomacy, like the law, is perhaps less concerned with absolute truth than with the danger of effective contradiction.

When I agreed to raise the Old Members' side, it was with a lively awareness of the difficulties of the task. Some people reply to letters either late or not at all. They likewise regard the telephone as a disastrous invention. Others say 'perhaps' when they mean 'yes' or 'no'. Only the few are reliable as well as cooperative.

*Coat of Arms:*
*Old Court.*

I do not find it surprising that airlines overbook as a matter of policy. Suffice it to say that I arrived at the College on June 21, 1952, in a state of some uncertainty as to the exact strength of my forces. In fact some twelve of those on my mailing list presented themselves and indicated that, having been invited, they had every intention of playing. I therefore entered into slightly delicate negotiations with the plenipotentiaries of the College team. I proposed to them that we should play twelve a side. Twelve, I added, was an average figure. My thought was that, in order not to upset their arrangements, they would have eleven and we would have thirteen.

The College plenipotentiaries did not accord this suggestion quite the rapturous welcome for which I was hoping. They appeared not to think that I had made an offer which they could not refuse. However, the negotiations were not central to the issue. I was confident that a process of natural selection would be assured by the outstanding College hospitality about to be lavished on us: cocktails in Old Court, followed by lunch in a marquee in New Court. My confidence was not misplaced. When the time came to gather my forces for transport to Cranmer Road by the shuttle buses referred to in the *Association Letter*, their effective number had been reduced by Bacchus to the customary level.

Caesar, having collected his forces, drew up his line of battle. That is to say, I won the toss and elected to field on the eminently sound reasoning that none of the Old Members' team was in a fit condition to wield a bat with the prospect of useful results. The same argument applied, of course, *mutatis mutandis* to bowling: but the shortcomings in this sphere were not so immediately apparent. Tony Fawke managed an early straight ball, which claimed Geoffrey Styler's stumps. For the rest, the proceedings were a little one-sided. Mike Mills dropped a sitter at cover point. Perhaps a former captain of the University cricket team is entitled to try and catch a ball with his eyes shut or averted. Or perhaps he was interested in extra-sensory perception. It may be relevant that at this time the Corpus High Table was powerfully represented in the Society for Psychical Research. I recall the admirable advice given by that eminent Corpus Fellow, R.G. Thouless, in his book *Straight and Crooked Thinking*: if someone's intention is to overawe you by wearing impressive regalia, imagine what he would look like without any clothes on.

Anyway, the College score mounted rapidly until the merciful declaration by the College chronicled in the *Association Letter*. There followed one of those famous Heywood teas, for which no praise is too high. At that time there was no difficulty whatever in securing home cricket fixtures for the College. Visiting teams needed no second invitation to come again. The tea interval achieved what might have been beyond College skills or the diligence of the Match secretary.

By the time it was the turn of the Old Members to bat, a process of sobering up had set in. The batting order was arranged by the simple process of putting the Captain down as number eleven and drawing lots for the other ten slots. However any improvement in our condition was offset by an important, nay unique, distraction, which was beginning to make itself felt… the roasting of a whole ox on the midwicket/extra cover boundary.

It came about thuswise – and here again I am indebted to the 1952 *Association Letter*. A conversation the previous autumn between John Harley-Mason and some American colleagues led to the magnificent gesture by the Chamber of Commerce of Corpus Christi, Texas, of sending us a whole ox. The Lions Club added to this, no less magnificently, by sending us one of their members who was a barbecue expert, Buster Sheehy, to supervise the proceedings. A pit was dug on the edge of the ground, and half the carcass was roasted over the red-hot ashes. The publicity was considerable, as were the proportions of ox distributed to those present. As the Newsletter put it, 'what might not inaccurately' – note the dignified double negative – 'be described as a beef tea was provided on the ground'. The enthusiasm of the consumers knew no bounds. One of them felicitated Buster warmly: 'congratulations, Colonel'. Buster accepted the congratulations, but modestly disclaimed the colonelship. The Old Member in question must have been a victim of Yankee propaganda. He said: 'congratulations again. You are the first man I have met from Texas who was not a colonel'.

No batsman, whether sober or not, can be expected to give of his best in such distracting circumstances. You have to remember that there was still meat rationing in 1952. And it was not long before my team was in deep trouble. There was only one thing for it. I had to assume direct command. I went out to join Albert as an umpire. I should interject here that I take some credit for enthusing Albert with the vocation of umpiring. He showed at times

PROBLEMS OF ADJUSTMENT'/1945–52

an excessive regard for impartiality. But otherwise his services were of as high an order as those, albeit of a different kind, he rendered to the University Rugby Football team. No sooner had I joined Albert than one of my team foolishly allowed himself to be run out by several yards. As it was my end, I was able to take remedial measures. 'Not out,' I said. If challenged, my policy would have been 'never explain and never apologise'. But the College were too well mannered to protest. If J.J. Rousseau had been present, I think he would have discerned some sort of general will to achieve an outcome which avoided the distress of defeat for anyone. In any case the beef tea claimed the greater attention.

So night fell. The captains and the kings departed. The remaining half of the ox was distributed to the College staff and pensioners and to the recipients of the College Christmas Charity. And we all lived happily after. As for Corpus Christi, Texas, Buster took back with him, for presentation to the City, the College flag in exchange for the flag of the City, as well as presents for the Chamber of Commerce, the Lions Club, and himself. It was a happy circumstance that in the following year an Old Member, Alec Adams, was appointed HM Consul-General, Houston, and was able to fortify our links with the City of Corpus Christi, which was in his consular district.

# TEACHING AND LEARNING

## John Burkinshaw, 1931

Archie Clark-Kennedy was a wonderful tutor in Physiology. About four of us would go to his room in College where he would be balancing on a deep armchair with one leg missing. Our full attention was ensured firstly by awaiting the moment when he would lose his balance

and the chair would tip over, secondly by his habit of leaving the last syllables of his sentence to be supplied by his pupils. Thus: 'Expired air contains a higher level of Carbon Di …?' Chorus: 'Oxide'. Incidentally, we never referred to him as Archie, just C.K. In those days Christian names were reserved for close friends and it might be months before one got on 'Christian-name terms' with an acquaintance.

## John Press, 1938

My first supervisor was Charles Smyth, Dean of College and an eminent ecclesiastical historian. I had to leave my weekly essay in his rooms overnight and read it to him on the following day. I found reading aloud something of an ordeal, especially after he had remarked: 'That is not a bad essay, but you make it sound like Hamlet's oration over his father's grave'.

Supervisions with Charles Smyth were never dull, often yielding some unexpected bonus. He once handed me a book, saying that it was a Lutheran hymnbook that had belonged to Frederick Maurice. 'What do you know of Frederick Maurice?' When I replied that he was the founder of Christian Socialism I was corrected: 'That is not important. His real significance is that he was the man who made it possible for intelligent Victorians to remain Christians'.

My supervisor in the Lent term was Kenneth Pickthorn, Senior Burgess for the University, immortalized as Dr Gorse by Christopher Isherwood in *Lions and Shadows*, and a man famed for his outbursts of rage and flashes of arrogance. When I referred to the arbitrary government of Charles I, he exploded with disdain: 'You are supposed to be an educated man talking to an educated man, but you resemble the cook complaining to the housemaid: 'The master is an arbitrary gent'. Try to use language with some degree of precision'. One day, after I had read my essay, Pickthorn lay back as though in pain and groaned 'Why should I have to listen to that kind of rubbish?' When, with some trepidation, I answered 'Because you are paid quite well to do so,' he burst out laughing and said 'Well, I can't think of a better reason'.

Patrick Bury's supervisions in the Summer term were tranquil. While he pointed out the errors and deficiencies in one's essays he always did so gently and encouragingly, managing to find something to praise even in the least promising piece of work. I began to think that I was not wholly without merit as a historian.

## Geoffrey Woodhead, 1940

We worked all the hours we could. To aim for Part II of the Classical Tripos in eight months' time, with four years of rust thick upon our scholarship and so much of classical literature unread or forgotten, was a terrifying experience. Men who had faced the enemy in the field with comparative *sang froid* grew pale at the prospect of that confrontation with the examiners that would take place within a few short months.

John Chadwick in his biographical fragment has very little to say about that year, but makes his suggestion that, in the event, the examiners were kind and the class list lop-sided. This is a false assessment. The papers were as rigorous as any I subsequently encountered or had a hand in setting. The reason for the 'lopsided' effect was quite simply the fact that under the arrangements for demobilization, colleges could apply for the quick release from the forces of those they regarded as top-class scholars who, it was supposed, would be needed on completion of their studies for the provision of the brain-power required for national recovery. So many potential 'leaders' had perished: survivors had to be groomed with special treatment. So those who took their final examinations in 1946 were a chosen few, and it came as no surprise that a disproportionate number of classical Firsts was awarded.

Besides John and me there was a third Corpus classic, Bernard J. Sims, who subsequently became a lecturer at the University of Newcastle. He was senior to us (matr. 1937), was already married, and with his wife had lodgings in Victoria Park. Like John he read Group E, and in the event we all got Firsts with distinctions in

*Geoffrey Woodhead, Fellow 1948–present.*

our special subjects. I saw little of him except at philosophy sessions with Desmond Lee, who dealt with all three of us together. During that winter people drifted back to Cambridge one by one as they were demobilized; former Colonels and Commanders, Petty Officers and Corporals, found themselves back together on an equal footing with an equal challenge to face. Later comers had to postpone their finals to 1947, time being too short by then to attempt the Tripos of 1946. Thus the 1946 classical list was small in total as well as being overweighted at the top end. The 'happy few' were undoubtedly an elite – intentionally so, and perhaps this made their situation even more stimulating. But there was no sense of competition. We were all in it together, and we helped each other as best we could.

Of the three General Papers that then formed a major element of Part II, that on Philosophy attracted us least and therefore caused the most worry. Desmond Lee's supervisions were regular and demanding, and, as is illustrated by the dream of the bones of Anaximander which, somehow, Anna Davies learned of, they tended to prey on the mind. I noted essays not only on the Pre-Socratics (one of which, on Parmenides, had John and me discussing him one evening for two and a half hours solid); one on Plato's idea of the Good, written only six weeks after our return, even now strikes me as an excruciating challenge after so long a 'lay-off'. Indeed, on most evenings after Hall it seems that John and I knuckled down to a succession of such problems during that winter – and were consistently very late to bed in consequence. We were much helped in the Lent term by a good series of lectures put on by Arthur Peck of Christ's, which was in essence a Revision Course for Returned Warriors. Those lecture notes too I long kept by me. But at the outset, for this and the Literature paper (and in John's case the History paper also), we had to decide simply to jettison certain topics and not attempt to cover, or recover, the whole range of the subjects. Thus I decided, at the start, to do no work on Greek epic or lyric; and John, I think, gave up on the Roman emperors. We both abandoned any Philosophy after Plato, except that I was interested in Political Theory and therefore carried on with at least some Aristotle.

On one evening a week, usually a Wednesday, we foregathered after Hall with Mervyn Jones of Trinity, each providing hospitality in turn. On these occasions we read and discussed some work of literature. In the Michaelmas term we read a lot of Herodotus; in the Lent term we worked through the whole of Catullus, and followed this up with Hesiod's *Works and Days*. When at Mervyn's the evening would be concluded with a little music, often a Mozart or Haydn Quartet, he being the fortunate possessor of a gramophone and a useful supply of records.

By the Easter term pressure was so intense that my diary entries became more and more perfunctory. We continued our tea parties, and I have a note of one or two cycle expeditions. Desmond Lee gave the Corpus classical trio his final blessing at a supervision on Friday

31 May. On the following Monday we were in the Arts School for the General History paper followed in the afternoon by the first of the two special subject papers. John regarded a cup of tea after lunch on all three days as a suitable nerve-steadier. One way or another we saw it through, but by the Wednesday evening we were just about exhausted. John's parents were in Cambridge on the Thursday, on a brief visit. Full term ended on Friday 14 June, and John went down on that very day. A couple of us helped him with his kit, went to the station with him, and saw him off on a mid-morning train. And so it all ended. I went down during the following week, leaving Bernard Sims, still living in Cambridge, to send a telegram with the Tripos results when they came out.

**John Barry, 1945**
In my first year (1945–1946) one of my supervisors in History was Charles Smyth, Dean of Chapel. He set me an essay on the Elizabethan Settlement (of the Church). 'You won't understand it unless you study thoroughly the 39 Articles,' he warned, and with this advice ringing in my ears I went off looking forward to a week's pleasant study.

Not a bit of it. It was to be a week of frustration and, finally, of humiliation. I started my research, as usual, in the Butler Library. As that did not provide all the books I wanted I went on to the History Faculty Library. I consulted all the relevant books of documents but nowhere could I find the 39 Articles. Ah well, a visit to the University Library was required. I surely would track down the missing articles there.

I had a fascinating morning in the University Library, learning its ways. But nothing to my purpose was achieved. I should have to write my essay without the 39 Articles. When I came to read it to Charles I was unusually nervous but determined to make my point. 'Yes,' said Charles 'that's good. But didn't I tell you to study the 39 Articles?' Strongly resentful, I embarked on a description of all my efforts to find the wretched articles. But I had not proceeded far when Charles broke in: 'My dear John, I know that your father is a Methodist minister, but do you by any chance possess a copy of the Book of Common Prayer?' I was shattered. As a matter of fact I had two copies of the Prayer Book and knew at once how stupid I had been. But to this day I cannot understand why the 39 Articles were not included in any of the books of documents.

**Robin Crawford, 1950**

Dr Pickthorn was then a Conservative MP for Cambridge, but still supervised in History for undergraduates who were studying the Tudors and Stuarts. Many years earlier, he had written a book about that period. His supervisions were always on Friday evenings, when he returned from London. He was a fierce and forbidding character, but never dull! His supervisions were notable in two ways: first, he would often ring up the Buttery half-way through and order one glass of sherry, never two. Secondly, he would ask you to read your essay (after reminding him what it was supposed to be about) and stop you after the first two or three sentences saying 'stop, stop, that sentence is rubbish – it doesn't mean anything.' Then he would get you to read it again while he dissected it word by word to prove what rubbish it was. Sometimes the supervision never got beyond the first paragraph!

On one occasion Dick Wrathall was so depressed by this treatment that he started his essay with a paragraph taken verbatim from Dr Pickthorn's own book. The paragraph got the usual treatment, but Dick was ready for it. 'But, sir', he said, 'those were the words of your own book.' There was silence for a while, then Dr Pickthorn reached for the telephone, rang up the Buttery and ordered two glasses of sherry!

**Harry Mitchell, 1950**

The general belief was, at the time, that Oxford and Cambridge offered the finest possible education available anywhere, even though sometimes that belief did not seem compatible with daily experience. I read Modern Languages Tripos Part I and Law Tripos Part II. Lectures in the former were often of indifferent quality and my Tripos results did not suffer from missing most of them. Law was a different matter. There was a vast amount of detail to absorb and there was a need to make sure that one had some acquaintance with new decided cases and statutes which had not yet found their way into the law books, but to which the lecturers would usually draw attention. It was not a good idea to skip lectures, even though the standard of lectures varied a lot. Some of the lecturers simply regurgitated the textbook, but there were others who were famous in their field whose lectures it was a privilege and a revelation to attend. I have in mind particularly Professors Lauterpacht, Wade and Hamson, outstanding authorities in

their respective fields of International, Constitutional and Comparative Law. A great character who would certainly not count among outstanding lecturers but whose lectures on Criminal Law were nevertheless memorable was Henry Barnes, sometime Fellow of Sidney Sussex, who died more than 40 years ago. He belonged to the now extinct breed of Anglo-Irish Protestants, a graduate of Trinity College Dublin and a great patriot convinced of the supreme greatness of Great Britain and Ireland before partition. I remember one of his oft-reported sayings as 'These two islands are the centre of the world and everybody has offices in London.' It was said that in his younger days he had been something of an adventurer and had become involved in local politics, to such an extent that he briefly became President of a South American republic. However, he was warned by one of the generals that it would be in his best interests if he left the country forthwith. He took this advice, made his way back to the United Kingdom and Cambridge and some-

Granta *illustration,* – *'Work'.*

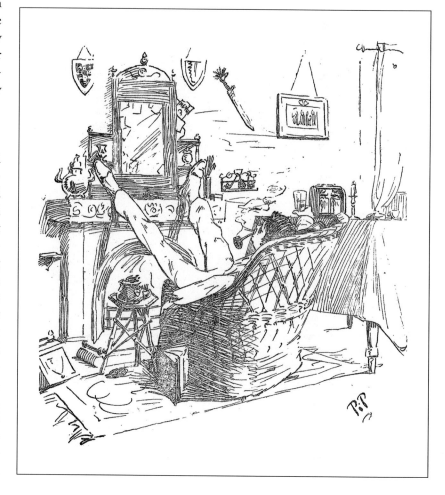

how or other became a Law lecturer. This part of his life story sounds too bizarre to be true, but it was confirmed at the time by his obituary in *The Times*. Even as undergraduates, many of us realized that the content of his lectures was not wholly reliable, though they were undoubtedly entertaining. He had a habit of quoting cases, which no one else had ever heard of and to which one could certainly not discover any references in the textbooks on Criminal Law. His summary of the facts of a particular case would often begin with the words 'Now this fellow got a girl into trouble', uttered in a pronounced Irish accent and repeated on so many occasions that we all cheered each time. His most unforgettable summary related to a man who was convicted of bestiality with an animal, to wit a duck, but according to Henry Barnes, 'The Court of Criminal Law quashed the conviction because they said that a duck was not an animal.'

### Sir Harold (Hooky) Walker, 1978

In the last term of 1978 I had the pleasure and privilege of being Fellow Commoner. For obvious reasons the College normally invites schoolteachers – indeed the Fellows are usually referred to as Schoolteacher Fellow Commoners – but when Duncan Wilson was Master the field was broadened to include at least, to my knowledge, a musicologist and me, a diplomat.

A Fellow Commoner has no duties as such: presumably he or she is seen simply as in some sense a window on to the world outside Corpus. One is, however, encouraged to live the life of the College to the full, and I had no difficulty in meeting this obligation. I even, at the age of 48, played squash for the College – in the seventh team. Squash was not in fact a game I had any skill in, but I had a reasonable eye (tennis was really my game) and I remember having a tremendous battle with the Captain of Newnham. Although she was a proper squash player and I was not, I still did not like losing to a woman.

Many of my daylight hours I spent in the Oriental Faculty reading, or rather trying to read, pre-Islamic poetry; they don't cover that when you learn Arabic in the Foreign Office. But of course the main pleasure came from colleagues, both in the Senior Combination Room and amongst the undergraduates, and through them I acquired a lasting affection for the College. I attend as many College events as I can, and I regard being asked to be Fellow Commoner as the biggest stroke of luck in my life.

### Elizabeth Smith, 1992 Fellow Commoner

The Schoolteacher Fellow Commoner at Corpus must be the recipient of one of the most generous academic foundations that are on offer at a Cambridge college, not least because of the many privileges that can be enjoyed for the rest of his or her life.

It is a unique experience that affords a schoolteacher, who may come from any walk of teaching life, the opportunity to undertake a complete term of individual study on a chosen theme, at the same time as being a member of High Table and enjoying many other rights of the Fellowship.

Halfway through the Michaelmas term I was asked by the Senior Tutor if I would help out with the general interviews for those senior school pupils hoping to come up to Corpus in the next session. It would be good for me, he said, and, just as importantly, good for College, to know what a schoolteacher's reactions would be to the whole process of interviews.

He was right, and I have always been immensely grateful for the insight it gave me into the entrance criteria, and into how other schools were preparing their pupils. Coming from Scotland, it was also good to compare notes with English colleagues and to see what similarities and contrasts there were between the A Level and Higher systems. I met a most interesting set of sixth-formers, and was extremely impressed with the manner in which Corpus colleagues handled the interviews. I never really believed that modern Cambridge was in any way guilty of the discrimination that so many commentators seem to think is perpetrated to the detriment of state school pupils, but it was heartening to have my views confirmed at first hand. The system was both fair and open, and no short cuts were taken that I could see to admit those with favoured circumstances or family connections.

# SPORT

**John King, 1931**

My scholastic achievements were of the lowest order achieving only a Third in Modern Languages Part I and an equally undistinguished Third in Law Part II.

My games record was a little better. I had a University trial for soccer, in which I managed to dislocate my shoulder and so transferred, temporarily, to rowing, where my boat, Corpus Lent second achieved the only 'oar', four bumps, of any Corpus boat while I was up – I still have the oar proudly hanging in my hall with the photograph underneath of the crew and the boat in action. The crew was: Bow E.H. Etherington, 2. J.H. King, 3. F.H. Lawton, 4. J.A. Oliver, 5. K.V. Maguire, 6. W.H.M. Clifford, 7. J.H. Burkinshaw, Stroke P.H. Nash, Cox C.F. Brooke, Coach J.B. Ansell (Jesus). Apart from that I was Captain of Tennis in my third year and played squash for the College.

**Ronnie Brown, 1935**

I spent three very happy years at Corpus from 1935 to 1938.

When the representatives of the various sporting clubs came round I decided to try rowing. I found I had a sufficient aptitude for it and greatly enjoyed it. I was fortunate in that Corpus was doing very well on the river during that period.

In March 1936 we rowed on the Tideway in the Head of the River Race (over the same three and a half mile course as the University Boat Race but in the opposite direction starting at Mortlake and finishing at Putney). We started at No. 12 in a field of 139 crews.

On the Cam the first Lent boat 1936 made two bumps and the first May boat 1936 made three bumps.

But 1937 was an outstanding year. All three Lent boats won their oars. *The Times* rowing correspondent wrote: 'The splendid record of Corpus, in each of their crews gaining their oars, is the best performance by this college on the river since 1909'.

The first May boat 1937 won their oars, with no fewer than five bumps, thanks to having to row twice in one evening as sandwich boat between the second and first Divisions.

In 1938 the first Lent boat won their oars and in the Mays the second boat won their oars. The first Boat entered the Thames Cup Eights at Marlow and won. They also entered for the Ladies Plate at Henley and reached the semi-final round, losing to Radley who were the ultimate winners of this event.

After Henley some of us joined a scratch crew organized by two Clare men to take part in a regatta at

**C. U. B. C. – THE MICHELL CUP**

An error was made in the calculation of points for the Michell Cup. The correct result is as follows:

| | Points | Position |
|---|---|---|
| Corpus | 102 | 1 |
| Magdalene | 66 | 2 |
| Christ's | 52 | 3 |
| Trinity Hall ) | 42 | = 4 |
| Third Trinity ) | | |
| Jesus | 38 | 6 |
| St Catharine's | 30 | 7 |
| Caius | 15 | 8 |
| Downing | 10 | 9 |
| Selwyn | 8 | 10 |
| King's ) | 2 | = 11 |
| First Trinity ) | | |
| Pembroke | $1^3/_5$ | 13 |
| Lady Margaret | $-22^1/_5$ | 14 |
| Sidney ) | $-24$ | = 15 |
| Clare ) | | |
| Emmanuel | $-26$ | 17 |
| Peterhouse | $-48$ | 18 |
| Queens' | $-68$ | 19 |
| Fitzwilliam House | $-72$ | 20 |

**A. Burrough,**
Hon. Sec. C.U.B.C.

Essen, Germany. That was great fun. The outstanding crews at that regatta were from the SS. After the rowing we mixed amiably with them so far as the language barrier would permit.

Corpus also won the Michell Cup in 1937 by what is possibly a record total of 102 points.

**Leslie Hill, 1936**

My arrival at Corpus coincided with the beginning of a three-year boom in Corpus rowing, due mainly to a body of keen and strong young freshmen who came up with me. One of them, Arthur Turner, got his Blue two years running and finished up as secretary of the Cambridge University Boat Club. The rest of us, though far less successful, pushed the Corpus boats quite a way up the gradings on the river during those three years.

Our first race was the Fairbairn Head of the River race, about three miles with the stream. Just before the race, we lost one of our crew, as he was rusticated for his part in a November 5th rag. Guy Fawkes Day always led to trouble in the market square at Cambridge. Undergraduates would climb street lamps and smash the glass in them, mob the police and steal their helmets, and generally go mad. Police from other districts were always drafted in, and the University authorities took a serious view of offenders.

During my last term, at the third-year table, one of the students who rowed with me decided to carry out a survey. He asked all of us whether we were virgins. All the others answered in the affirmative, but I was not going to give anything away, so I answered, 'I can think of at least three ways in which a man can be a virgin. Which one do you mean?' Everyone laughed loudly, but my colleague cried triumphantly, 'I knew he wasn't one!'

My second year at Cambridge I was in the College first eight. We won our oars in the Lents again, made three bumps in the Mays, and also won the Marlow Eights Challenge Cup at the regatta there.

My third year, I was tried for the Cambridge crew a couple of times, won the College Pairs race with a diminutive but very energetic man who was reading Theology, and had the indignity of being bumped for the first time in twenty races on my last day on the Cam. However, we got our own back on our conquerors, King's College, at Henley Regatta, where we beat them comfortably and got into the final of the Ladies Plate, only to be beaten by another Cambridge college.

### F.J. Leishman, 1937

I went up in autumn 1937 and my rooms were on the top of I staircase. Up there I became good friends with an American, Rod McNeil, a golfer, and Bill Leith, a South African and a rugby player like myself. At the beginning of the summer term of 1938, we were visited by the august figure of Arthur Turner, Captain of Boats and a Blue. He was looking for men to row in the College second May boat. After some discussion

Rod, Bill and I volunteered, on one condition: we would not have to obey any of the Boat Club's training rules and restrictions. The great man was somewhat taken aback by this, but he was so short of volunteers that he had to accept.

So we started. Our boat consisted of Bow C.C.H. Wheatley; 2. W.F. Leith; 3. C.M. Miller; 4. G.M. Stephany; 5. R.C. McNeil; 6. Myself; 7. P.G. Spens; Stroke R.M. Herbert Smith; and Cox J.McD. Broadhead.

*Rugby team of 1947. From left to right:*

*Back row: M. Graham, J. Beasley, A. Amos, J. Freeland, G. Wright; Middle row: R. Holmes, H. Thomas, C. Talbot, N. Dening, G. Smith, J. Crocker; Front row: B. Nichols, M. McCrum, S. Dawbarn, D. Sweeting, J. Higgs, M. Leslie, P. Bassier*

*Hockey team of 46–47.*

I enjoyed our training rows, as I think we all did. But having rowed over the course a few times, I decided that it was far too far, and that we should aim to make our bumps quickly. So we needed to make very fast starts. I thought I knew the solution. On each of the four nights, when we pushed out to get into position, we took with us in the boat a tin of Glucose D powder and a bottle of gin. Then from Bow to Cox we each took a handful of Glucose D and washed it down with a good swig of gin. We made our four bumps without ever rowing far past Grassy Corner. Neither of our coaches, Eric Huggins of Sidney nor our own Captain of Boats, was consulted or even informed of this unorthodox preparation, but they seemed pleased that we got our oars.

### Richard Orange-Bromehead, 1945
Although I never achieved academic distinction, during my stay on the last of the University Short Courses

(1945–46) I joined the Boat Club and rowed in the second boat. I have always been proud at having been in a boat that made seven bumps in the 1946 Lent races, four of which we achieved on one day. On that day we made an overbump, and found that we were at the top of the division and would have to row again at the bottom of the next. Our coach comforted us with the fact that the bottom boat of the next division were a lot of old Blues who would set off in style but had had no training so provided we kept going we would catch them! And so it proved.

### Malcolm H. Thorndike, 1953
The Senior Tutor (Michael McCrum) invited me to comment on the architect's first draft of plans for a proposed new boathouse to be shared with Sidney Sussex College. The Boat Club's Officers, together with our senior coaches, John Shaw (Fellow) and Bernard Lucas

*May breakfast.*

ing and trying out his own rules. Sir Frank Lee was a great encouragement to the College and to me personally, and not just through his patronage of croquet. I remember his announcing at Hall dinner the assassination of President Kennedy and before that the Cuban missile crisis. He was quite open about things but nevertheless appeared to be in control, in so far as he could be. This made an important contribution to the maintenance of morale in difficult times.

For 1963–6 I was able to put seven Cs after my name. CCCCCCC = Captain of Corpus Christi College Cambridge Croquet Club.

### M. Lea Rudee, Visiting Scholar 1971–72

I was a Visiting Scholar (now called Visiting Fellow, I believe) at Corpus for the 1971–72 academic year. We lived in a flat in Selwyn Gardens adjacent to Leckhampton. In the spring of 1972 I played tennis regularly at Leckhampton sports field, in a foursome that included the then Master, Sir Duncan Wilson, the current Master, Haroon Ahmed, and the current President, Chris Andrew. My wife and I attended the May Ball, 13 June 1972, and were included in a group organized by Haroon and Chris for a breakfast picnic at Wandlebury Ring the following morning.

### *Corpus in Cuppers Final Shock* – Harry Mount, 1982

More than anything at Corpus, more than the laidback supervisions of John Hatcher or the inspirational words of Michael Tanner, I remember the cricket, and particularly the year when, in defiance of the proud Corpus tradition of sporting mediocrity, we reached the Cuppers final.

With its tiara of trees and hint of the Cambridgeshire fields beginning just behind the pavilion, Leckhampton always seemed to me the prettiest ground in Cambridge. Perhaps the excellent teas put on by Mike Hayward and his successors did no harm in attracting visitors either. Home games suited me fine; the grassy, somewhat characteristic wicket and the swing-inducing foliage were just the thing for my style of bowling, and that style, which would have been horribly exposed at a higher level, turned out to be just the thing for college cricket.

Thanks to that, and to being an eternal student, I contrived to play for the Corpus team for ten years from '82 to '91, and in that time saw several generations of cricketers pass through. First up was Chris Grindal's

(Assistant Bursar), got together with people from Sidney Sussex and we duly submitted our report on 21 November 1955. The recommendations included the installation of 'sliding racks' and a plea for larger changing facilities. The boathouse now in place incorporates many of the features we suggested. However, the designers did not envisage its use by four boat clubs and no-one foresaw that within 30 years or so some members of the College would be women!

The [Boat Club's] estimated annual expenditure was £1,193.11.2d which included the proposed purchase of a new shell eight for £300 and a new clinker eight for £185. A set of oars cost £66. An item of £3 covered maintenance of guns and ammunition! This was not for shooting the opposition nor any tutors, but covered revolvers and blank ammunition fired by coaches cycling on the towpath to signal 'Go for your bump now!'

### Peter Hallett, 1962

My contemporaries at Corpus seem to remember me as a mean croquet player. I was very fortunate in being able to take advantage of the croquet facilities at Leckhampton. Sir Frank Lee provided the croquet set and the lawns and facilities at Leckhampton were about the best available in the Cambridge colleges at the time. Sir Frank Lee enjoyed a game of croquet and had a small lawn set up in the Master's garden. Somehow he generally managed to win by a small margin. Garth Moore also played but he was particularly interested in invent-

1982 team, featuring a remarkable (especially for Corpus) intake of natural athletes like the fast bowler Chris Davis, the football Blue Aubrey Swift and (when he could be persuaded) the future head of Radio Five Bob Shennan. That lot were even better at football than at cricket, but they carried us to a thrillingly close Cuppers victory against a very powerful Jesus team and might have done the same in the ensuing quarter-final against Trinity had rain not intervened to shorten the match. In the following years the team, on paper, seemed at times even stronger, with the arrival of quality players like the rugby Blues Mark Bailey and John Ellison, the Corinthian all-rounder Mark Burgess, and the prolific batsman Rupert Levy. But despite much good cricket, the focus somehow wasn't quite the same as it had been in that first year.

In the late 1980s the cricket was still fun but successes were rare, and the heights we had touched at the beginning of the decade seemed a distant memory. When I returned from the States for a final year at Corpus in 1991, playing cricket was the last thing on my mind. And so it would have remained had Alan Lewis and Chris Baddeley, two players I remembered as talented freshers, who were now graduates and the senior pros of the team, not come to drag me away from the computer and off to the nets.

As the season began I soon realized that this was an excellent team, perhaps not quite as strong man-for-man as some of those of the early 1980s but with a remarkable spirit, and superbly led by the affable Yorkshireman Mark Reid. There were no stars, but quality throughout the team, and, like the England one-day team of the time, we batted (after a fashion) down to number eleven and could put forward six or seven front-line bowlers. This made us especially dangerous in the limited-over format followed by Cuppers. Opponents would wait in vain for the beginning of our vulnerable tail or the arrival of our weak fifth bowler. If someone had an off day someone else would be there to step into the breach. Our particular secret weapon was a skinny middle-order batsman called Andy Powell. Andy would slouch to the wicket in a sweater several sizes too big for him, looking barely strong enough to carry his bat, let alone wield it in anger. Opposition captains sized him up, scented blood and brought the field in. This was the cue for the rest of us to stop what we were doing and watch, for we knew that, despite his unpromising physique, Andy had a tremendous eye and a beautiful golfer's swing with which he could hit the

ball to the furthest corners of Leckhampton. By the time other teams woke up to what was happening Andy would have raced to forty or fifty and changed the course of the game. In the first two rounds of Cuppers both Churchill and Fitzwilliam collapsed before us, their morale broken by his unlikely onslaughts.

That took us into the quarter-final against Girton and another easy victory hastened by some excellent bowling from Mark, who was still taking wickets even though captaincy was having a Nasser Hussain-like effect on his batting. Even the team mascot, my baby son, got in on the act, with an imaginative if happily averted attempt to decapitate the spectating Mistress of Girton, Baroness Warnock, with a cricket ball.

Come the semi-final and little Corpus were drawn against the big boys of Trinity, future England centurion John Crawley and all. Happily the mighty Crawley was away on Cambridge duty, but the Trinity team was still packed with Crusaders and bad attitude. The latter began to surface as Alan and Chris built a solid opening stand, and may not have been entirely unconnected with the inscrutable behaviour and unconventionally bare feet of our twelfth man and umpire, Phil Johnson. Whatever Trinity felt about us, however, was nothing to the vitriol they were turning on each other, much of it either issuing from or directed at their own captain. After my own stint as umpire I gleefully returned to the

*C.C.C. Boat Town Bumps, July 1979. Professor Rod Thompson (stroke) and some of the crew receiving last minute towpath advice from the college bursar, Alec Clark-Kennedy.*

pavilion to announce, echoing Bob Taylor at Headingly in '81, that the wheels were coming off.

Trinity were, however, still formidable opponents, and made it clear that they didn't think our total would pose them too many problems. Exhausted by his magnificent 78 in the draining heat, Alan switched places in the bowling order with me in order to open with our paceman, Alex Large. They did a great job, and by half way through the Trinity innings we were ahead on points. Word came from the pavilion that Trinity were waiting for our fifth bowler, but due to our reshuffle our fifth bowler was our usual opener, and before the Trinity captain had realized his error I had him caught behind by keeper Adrian Smith. For the first time, doubts

began to gnaw at Trinity's confidence. In a last throw of the dice the Trinity captain brought himself on as umpire, but even a string of bizarre decisions were not enough to stop his team falling increasingly behind the run rate. Mark bowled the last over to the proverbial breathless hush, and then Leckhampton exploded, the home crowd invading the pitch and chairing the team off. The celebrations lasted long into the night and the hangover (I have a dim and nasty memory of home-made cider) long into the following week.

'You've got to come over, we're in the Cuppers final,' I croaked down a transatlantic line to a disbelieving Simon Boughey, one of my old Corpus friends from the early 1980s. Simon gallantly dropped everything and

*Mens Hockey 1st XI 1992–93. From left to right:*

*Back row: Ian Campbell, Paul Munro, Richard Wade-Martins, James Mackenzie, Edward Barratt;*
*Front row: Phil Johnson, Milo Carver, Nick Kenefick, John MacCormick, Andy Lawrence; Inset: Elizabeth Smith*

came, but sadly the final was a bit of an anticlimax. Bad weather meant that it was postponed until after the exams, and by then we'd lost a bit of focus and the incessant rain had turned our usually sprightly pitch into a soggy strip of plasticine, thus neutralising our strong seam attack. We were, moreover, up against Pembroke, another little college who equalled us in team spirit and were even more canny: for the first time that season we found ourselves being out-thought. A big home crowd eager to cheer Corpus on in our first ever Cuppers final saw our batting reined in by tight bowling and clever fields. Mark at last got a start, only to hit a ball into the trees at midwicket and, in the delay while it was found, lose his concentration and then his wicket. Our total never looked like being quite enough, especially once Pembroke's Blue Mikey Morris got going. To add injury to insult I pulled a muscle and had to limp off, to watch from the boundary as we capitulated lamely. For the first time, we'd all had an off day together. A desolate evening followed, but spirits were revived on an end-of-season tour to Somerset, spent mainly in the pubs of Wellington as the rain teemed down outside…

### Elizabeth Smith, 1992 Fellow Commoner

Never did I dream that I would end up playing in a Cuppers hockey final, and certainly not for the College men's XI. By some quirk of the ancient rules governing College hockey, any member of College, either student or staff, male or female, could participate in the cup competition, even if the same rules did not apply for normal league fixtures. I had never played in a more 'gentlemanly' team, nor have I since, even if it caused some concerns as to which changing rooms I might use! These boys were terrific, and I know many of them will not only have gone on to greater things in the world of hockey, but also on to greater things in the academic and professional world.

Nor indeed did I dream that I would ever be part of a coxless four on the Cam that comprised a motley crew of Corpus Watsonians, (the former pupils of my school in Edinburgh), although the less said about our rowing prowess the better.

*1977–78: One of the most successful College teams.*
*Division III, Winners – P.9, W.9, F.39, A.16. From left to right:*

Back row: M. Scholfield, D. Hartley, S. Peacock, P. Chaplin, B. Hawthorne, S. Fraser, J. Hatcher, F. Small, P. Rossiter; Front row: A. Shennan, R. Bromage, J. Devitt (Vice-Captain), D. Grant (Captain), D. Fodin (Secretary), I. Dillon, I. Churchill

# CHAPEL

*The inside of the Chapel.*

### Harold Last, 1935

Attendance at Chapel was of course voluntary, and had been for some years. Congregations at services were small. The 8.30 am sung Communion on Sundays was the best attended. This was a service of simple dignity, celebrated by Sir Edwyn Hoskyns very beautifully. He had a good voice and a good ear. All the Chapel services were strictly according to the Book of Common Prayer (1662). There were no special biddings or additional Collects and no recourse to the 1928 Prayer Book. The music was led by a small undergraduate choir consisting of six choral scholars or Bible clerks (two from each year) and a few suitable volunteers. Within their limitations as a male voice ensemble this group of singers was quite expert. The old Flight organ was adequate in accompaniments, if for little else. It was originally blown by a very unsatisfactory hydraulic motor, difficult to manage and prone to leakage. Certain 'interested parties' encouraged the leakage until water threatened to flood not only the small Chapel but the adjacent Spencer room as well. Within a week or so an electric motor was installed! At Sunday services and on red-letter days, old-fashioned open-fronted surplices were worn, otherwise it was the inevitable College gown.

### John Press, 1938

Early in the Michaelmas term I took part in a ceremony that would nowadays be regarded as distinctly odd. All first-year scholars and exhibitioners, except non-Christians, assembled in the Chapel, where the Master sat enthroned in front of the chancel. One by one we knelt before him, put our hands between his and swore an oath of fealty in the name of the Father and of the Son and of the Holy Ghost. We were told that this was an Anglo-Saxon ritual, but I have always wondered how much it owed to the Anglo-Saxon Chronicle and how much to the Master's theological inventiveness.

### John Roach, 1938

Charles Smyth kept a fairly close eye on the ordinands, and he expected us to keep a certain number of Chapels in the week as a discipline. He was himself a fine preacher, and he never got into the College pulpit without saying something worth hearing. He had a quizzical streak too and used to preach commemoration sermons on worthies of the College's past. It must have been at the end of my first term that he preached on Richard Love, the Master who had been appointed by Charles I, had survived every regime in the Civil War and Commonwealth, and lived to be made Dean of Ely by Charles II. His text (Proverbs 30, 26) was 'The conies are but a feeble folk, yet make they their houses in the rocks'. The meat of the sermon has long since gone, but that text is unforgettable! Smyth shared to the full in the rather high and dry Toryism of the place. For example, we regularly celebrated the feast of King Charles the Martyr on 30 January in Chapel.

## John Fitch, 1941

In my second year, my supervisor was the Dean of Chapel, Canon Charles Smyth, whose polished lectures on the history of political thought I well remember. One evening Charles intimated that he wanted to come and see me and Hetley Price. When we met together, he told us he had had a great disappointment. He had put in for the Dixie Chair of Ecclesiastical History, which had fallen vacant. It was something on which he had set his heart. But the electors had set aside his claims in favour of Norman Sykes, of Emmanuel. Charles's keen disappointment led to his subsequent decision to turn his back on his University, although he later returned after ten years as a Canon of Westminster and Rector of St Margaret's.

Charles was at one time editor of the *Cambridge Review*, which at that time seemed largely in clerical hands. I recall a lively correspondence between the two brilliant 'Caroline' ecclesiastics – Smyth's adversary being none other than the then Regius Professor of Divinity and Master of Christ's, Charles Raven, and the subject: the duty/advisability (supposed by Smyth) of clergymen always to wear their 'dog collars' in public. Smyth was never afraid of controversy, and very much the professional priest and, to do him justice, pastor.

On rare occasions the Senior Fellow, the Revd C.A.E. Pollock was invited to read the First Lesson at Evensong. It was the famous passage from Joshua 6 describing the Fall of Jericho, Authorized (King James) Version of course. Pollock, very old and frail, read in a quavering voice and using a large magnifying glass, which was highly visible as it slowly travelled along each line. It seemed to go on and on, very slowly and deliberately until he came to the words 'the walls of Jericho' (long pause) 'fell down' (very long pause, the reader saying audibly 'I can't read it… I can't read it'. Further pause followed by loud, triumphant 'FLAT'.

## Brian Macdonald Milne, *Rector of Landbeach and Vicar of Waterbeach*, 1983–88

When new colleges were established in the Middle Ages, benefactors often endowed them with land, manors, or advowsons, which were the right to appoint parish priests. This meant that ordained members of the colleges might also be priests of neighbouring parishes. On marrying, the college was often able to provide Fellows with a parochial appointment, which entitled

*A stained glass window in the Chapel.*

> LETTER OF CORPUS ASSOCIATION, 1964
> *SPENS MEMORIAL*
> *All who contributed will be glad to know that the clock given by them in memory of Will Spens is now in position above the west window of the Chapel.*
>
> *In the past, Corpus men have had to rely on the sun and a strange hieroglyphic on the north wall of the Old Court to keep their time pieces regulated. Now, even though the sun may be late, there will be no excuse if they are.*
>
> *The clock, which has a terracotta centre, rim, figures and hands in bronze with a green patina, may in one sense be described as a striking feature in the adornment and interest of the New Court, but in another sense the description is misleading, for it does its work with silent efficiency, telling the time to those who want to know it, refraining with wisdom and kindness from reminding the others of the inexorable march through the hours, the quarters, and the halves.*
>
> *What more fitting memorial for a man who was wise and kind beyond measure, punctual and efficient in all he undertook and who worked without thought of time for the College and its members.*

*Corpus Chapel by*
*Derek Abel.*

Left: *The Chapel in the early nineteenth century.*

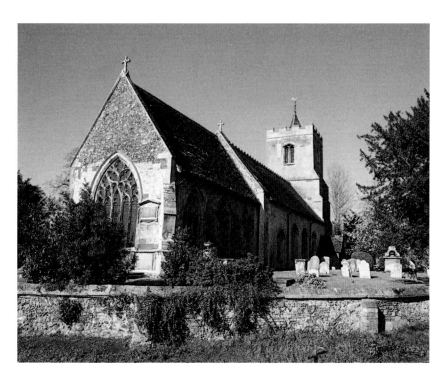

Above: *Saint Andrew and Saint Mary, Granchester.*

Far right: *The tower of St Bene'ts Church, with the Old and new Courts beyond. Herbert Kailton, 1903.*

Below: *The Spens clock in New Court.*

somewhat taken aback when Garth Moore challenged them, saying that he had not seen them in chapel, but he had seen them in St Bene't's! One of the events continuing to link the church with the College is that the vicar is still nominated by the College and the parish has long agreed with the idea that he should be a member of the Anglican Franciscan Order, the Society of St Francis. Friars were already ministering there when I was an undergraduate in the 1950s. They then occupied the Oratory House in the Madingley Road (taken over from the Oratory of the Good Shepherd, another Anglican Order). Some of us from Corpus and other colleges would go there for gatherings on Sunday afternoons with Brother Michael (later Minister-General of the Society, after being Bishop of St Germans in Truro Diocese), Brother Barnabas (who later had a professorship in Manchester), Brother Lothian (the vicar) and other members of the Society. In more recent years, the Brothers have occupied College property at numbers 14 and 15 Botolph Lane.

them to the use of a parsonage house. Thus they had a 'living'. Many of the early colleges were situated near parish churches, which they used as their chapels until they were able to build suitable chapels of their own. Thus St Bene't's (St Benedict's), the oldest church in Cambridge, was adopted by the new College of Corpus Christi in 1352 as its chapel and used until 1579. When I was an undergraduate, we were told that the front pews were reserved for members of the College wearing their gowns. There was a little rope barrier across the end of the front pew on each side. Sometimes members of the College who did not rise early enough of a Sunday to attend the sung communion service in Chapel would make their way to the slightly later service in St Bene't's. The gallery joining the College to the chancel of the church originally had a window looking down onto the altar, so members of College could actually observe the mass from above without leaving the College building! A winding staircase leads down from the first floor of the gallery to the lower one, and it has two tiny windows which look into the church. Mr Evelyn Garth Moore used to occupy the rooms there in my time and, after the service in Chapel, would sometimes look through those 'spy-holes' on his way down the staircase to his bathroom on the lower floor. Undergraduates who were unaware of this were

Saxon Tower
of Benedict's Church

# Music

## Harold Last, 1935

Mention should perhaps be made of a special concert, which took place early in my final year (1939). It took the form of a recital of J.S. Bach's Four and Three Klavier Concertos, and was given by four players who had all at sometime been organ scholars of the College during the inter-war years. Four Steinway grand pianos were hired from London for this performance and the pianists were Boris Ord, John Dykes Bower, Wilfrid Dykes Bower, and Harold Last. There was a capacity audience in the Hall, many musical visitors from other Colleges coming to hear quite a unique recital, which was duplicated during an ensuing vacation in the Governors' Hall of St Thomas' Hospital.

## John Roach, 1938

One amusing product of that time was a comic opera, written by Geoffrey Woodhead and put on at the College May Week Concert in June 1958. *The Royal Commission, or the Bursar's Bantling* was a take-off of events in 'one of the older and rather more obscure Cambridge colleges in the early summer of 1881', at the time when Fellows of colleges were given permission to marry while retaining their Fellowships. I was cast as Dr Theophilus Perch, the villainous Domestic Bursar. It transpired, not unnaturally, that the Fellows had been married all the time; they simply kept their wives at Hitchin! I can't sing for toffee, but I managed somehow, and the evening was an uproarious success. I fear that we crowded so many people into the Hall that we must certainly have breached all fire regulations. I still have a tape of the opera, given me long afterwards by Geoffrey Styler, when he visited me in Sheffield. To play it brings back very happy memories.

## John Assheton, 1938

A group of us freshmen soon became friends. We played a lot of innocent poker in our rooms for modest stakes. We shared and developed a love for classical music which has supported me ever since. We went regularly to wonderful concerts on Sunday afternoons in Covent Garden opera house, mostly given by the LPO under Sir Thomas Beecham. The day return rail ticket from Cambridge to London was 4s 2d. Another memorable musical occasion was a recital by Fritz Kreisler somewhere in Cambridge. He was then in his sixties but still one of the greatest violinists of his day. I can see him now, with his great shock of white hair. As an encore he played Beethoven's *Rondino* – trifle, but never was trifle more deliciously served.

## Raymond Warren, 1949

Corpus had no resident music don at this time but Boris Ord was originally a Corpus man and was a good friend to generations of Corpus men, so we went over to King's for our musical instruction. I shall never forget my first arranged supervision, shared with Andrew Pusey. As we expectantly headed up the stairs of the Gibb building, there seemed to be rather a lot of noise coming from behind the door, and on knocking and entering we found a sherry party in full swing! Of course, Boris invited us in and introduced us to a number of the leading musicians of the day – I remember meeting David Willcocks (then at Worcester) and Anthony Lewis (then professor at Birmingham and later to be Principal of the Royal Academy). Such forgetfulness on Boris's part was by no means exceptional, but his exceptional musicianship made it on the whole worth staying with him as supervisor. In those days the Music Faculty was divided (to put it rather crudely) between the musicologists and the musicians and Boris was firmly in the latter camp. But the Faculty was changing fast, largely as a result of the brilliance of the young Thurston Dart, who bridged the gap by being eminent as both scholar and performer.

One of my earliest recollections is of sitting in my room in New Court on weekday afternoons and hearing someone *very* competently playing systematically through all the preludes and fugues of the second book of the '48'. I soon discovered that the sounds were wafting from the rooms of the Dean of Chapel, Geoffrey Styler. I couldn't have done it half as well myself, and I was supposed to be a professional! The Chapel choir under the organ scholar John Bell consisted only of tenors and basses (no women, of course, in those days) but they sang their somewhat limited repertoire extremely well. Their singing of the *Lauda Sion* sequence on Corpus Christi day has remained one of the high spots of my musical life. I was intrigued by the way they used the English Hymnal (SATB) to harmonize the hymns in, generally, three parts. The baritones sang the tune an octave lower and the basses the bass part at pitch. The tenors pencilled in a wavy line in their books which wandered from alto to tenor part, whichever made for the better harmony but of course skilfully avoiding consecutives. It was a triumph of musical ingenuity in those pre-photocopier days! Another memory is of playing the cello in very cramped conditions in one of the ground floor rooms of the Old Court with the windows open, to provide incidental music (mostly Morley and Dowland) for a very lively May Week production of *The Knight of the Burning Pestle* in the court outside – a magical setting for such a performance.

My greatest feelings of gratitude to the College aren't primarily about things musical at all. I think of the opportunities of meeting eminent people of other disciplines, from whom there is always so much to learn, and above all for its creating an environment where friendships could be cultivated across the subjects. This was a big bonus for someone like me who had only narrowly decided to go to university rather than the Royal College of Music.

**Alan Vening, 1952**
The system at Corpus was to have an overlap of organ scholars. My senior was Keith Bond, already an FRCO and a graduate of Manchester University. Keith lived in I3 along the corridor and between us in I2 was a first-year choral scholar, Robin Pardoe. He had a wonderful tenor voice and we quickly got together to sing many things, most memorably the Britten folk song settings.

The Master of Corpus in my time was Sir George Thomson. Sir George was always kind to music and musicians, entertaining the choir with an annual feast in the Lodge. He attended every Sunday service as was expected, though he denied belief and avowed knowledge of only two pieces of music; one was the National Anthem and the other wasn't.

For my first two years I had piano lessons with Boris Ord every Tuesday afternoon from 2.00–3.00pm. He proved an excellent teacher and revealed to me not only how to play Mozart in the classical fashion but also Schumann. Boris once said that a big regret of his was never to have played a big romantic piano concerto. A surprise, this, for he was famous for the meticulous, pure and refined style of the King's choir.

We used purely College talent in the Chapel, unlike some colleges which invited professional artists, but were never short of worthwhile items even though we were the second smallest college after Peterhouse, with fewer than 200 undergraduates.

The Chapel organ of these days was in a sorry state. It was rumoured that it used to be powered by water and that the air supply dropped when the Master took a bath! The organ was greatly improved in 1961 by Hill, Norman and Beard, but seven years later the Chapel at last had an instrument worthy of a Cambridge college, built by Mander.

October 1953 brought a new wave of choral exhibitioners. John Pardoe and Peter Nicholson (tenors), Alan Warren (baritone), Peter Stroud and Peter Vincent joined the College. John fancied himself as a big operatic tenor in the style of Caruso, or at least Mario Lanza, and was most upset when one press reporter described his voice as a light, lyric tenor. Peter Nicholson was meant to be a tenor but had smoked so much during his national service that his highest note was E at a struggle and had to be treated as a baritone. One venture was *The Lord is a Man of War*, a duet for two basses from *Israel in Egypt* by Handel. We did this for massed male voices, one side versus the other. We must have made a splendid sound but did not impress the new Chaplain, Roland Walls, who described it as the worst text in the Bible.

*The day after the May Ball, 1956. From left to right and back to front: John Robson, Peter Vincent, John Pardoe, Robin Jargoe, Alan Vening and Jill Alderton (later Vening)*

One of my duties as organ scholar was to meet with Roland and Geoffrey Styler each Monday evening to choose the music for the following Sunday and have a post-mortem on the previous day's offerings. I confess I did not find these meetings the most exhilarating part of the week, but suppose that they had to keep some sort of curb on their enthusiastic and wayward charge. Every Tuesday lunchtime I had to walk to the Cambridge University Press with a fair copy of Sunday's music for the printers.

Vaughan Williams' *Pilgrim's Progress* had been staged at Covent Garden in 1951 but with limited success. Boris Ord was determined to give it the production that the work deserved. I was given two small roles and engaged as a rehearsal pianist. Boris made it clear that once we accepted this commitment it must take priority over everything else. This landed me in a quandary. An invitation arrived for me to dine with the Master in the Lodge. This clashed with a rehearsal. One does not refuse an invitation from the Master. I went to Boris with the problem. He was unbending. So I wrote an apologetic letter declining the invitation, giving the reason. A few days after the rehearsal Boris asked me to evening drinks in his rooms. When I arrived he introduced me to Susie Jeans, the famous organist and wife of Sir James Jeans, the astronomer royal, and to his other guest – the Master of Corpus. Thus did Boris thank me, in the nicest way possible, for putting him first.

The summer term of 1954 was a momentous one. Peter Tranchell, another OC, had written a satirical cantata with Harry Porter called *Daisy Simpkins*. He had offered it to King's who weren't interested so, luckily for Corpus, we were offered it instead. *Daisy Simpkins* was a very witty and sophisticated work for two pianos, solo roles and chorus. It contained some delicious tunes but was far from easy. The leads chose themselves – the dashing young undergraduate was John Pardoe and the beautiful female lead just had to be Janet Edmonds, whom I had met through the Madrigal Society and who had sung a small soprano part in *Pilgrim's Progress*. Before the days of photocopying I spent much time writing out parts for the singers to learn. Admission was by invitation alone. Previous Corpus May Week concerts had been fairly staid affairs – but now over 350 guests came and it was a great success, the first of a line in this ilk.

On Ascension Day in Cambridge there were no examinations. There was, of course, an 8.30 am communion service in Corpus Chapel. At 8.30 I had failed to ascend. Apparently at the start of the service everyone looked up at the organ loft for the first hymn but there was no sign of life. Keith Pemberton decided to rescue the situation, but walked slowly down the Chapel with loud footsteps. Geoffrey Styler couldn't wait. I woke two minutes later, realised the situation, jumped out of my bedroom window and ran across the lawn still in pyjamas. I played the rest of the service but, naturally enough, did not receive communion. At the end I waited a very long time and then crept down the organ staircase. Waiting at the bottom was Geoffrey Styler. I expected a rocket, but he burst out laughing and I fled. Apparently he dined out on that story for weeks!

The Corpus May Week Concert of 1955 was *The Literary Delinquent* written by Harry Porter and Neil Sutherland. The leading roles were again taken by John Pardoe and Janet Edmonds. This proved amazingly popular in rehearsal and was a worthy successor to *Daisy Simpkins*.

By now I was well in with the Cambridge theatre crowd and mingled with them at the Arts Bar for lunch everyday. During the summer vacation of 1955, I received a letter from Peter Tranchell to say that I had been elected President of the Musical Comedy Club. This would ease the path, he suggested, for me to compose the next musical comedy.

While this was in the cooking pot I had two splendid commissions. The first was to write incidental music for John Webster's play *The White Devil,* which was put on at the ADC for a week and starred Dan Massey. I wrote this for the newly formed College orchestra but they couldn't manage it, so I recorded it on Queens' College organ. This proved very atmospheric and did my reputation no harm.

The other invitation was to give an organ recital in King's. It was short notice but a great privilege as current organ scholars from other colleges were rarely, if ever, invited to play at King's. I chose to play, among other things, the Bach *Fantasia and Fugue in G minor* and Mulet's *Tu es Petra.* Both, I was told, were played very fast. John Pardoe page-turned in the organ loft, an interesting juxtaposition for a former chorister.

Returning one day for lunch I was amazed to see a crowd in the Old Court being given an impromptu entertainment by none other than Danny Kaye. How I would have loved to produce a piano to enable him to sing. He was absolutely amazing and was on a flying visit to Cambridge on behalf of UNICEF.

We were already into November when we found we had only three weeks to produce an acceptable script for the musical comedy planned for February at the Arts Theatre. Peter Vincent and John Pardoe produced in remarkably quick time the opening scene and they had a title – *The Girl Next Door.* We asked Bruce Cleave of Queens' to produce. He had little experience but was well known as a set designer. Pardoe's talent for publicity ensured a front page spread in *Varsity* and the Arts Theatre accepted us. The opening night was Monday 6 February 1956 and it was already the end of November. During the week before we opened I worked right through the nights, kept awake by Peter Nicholson brewing endless cups of coffee. It was actually finished at 4.51 am on the morning of the opening night.

Monday 6 February arrived and found me utterly exhausted and depressed. At the performance, when the audience didn't laugh where I thought they ought to, I got more and more upset and almost walked out at the interval. At the end I dashed out, shouting at poor Malcolm Burgess, who had designed the sets, not to be so *'fey'* and went immediately to bed, so missing the first-night party. The next day I was woken at 4.15 in the afternoon by John and Peter with the press reports which they read to me. Even in my exhausted state I realised that they were not damning – far from it. My spirits soared and I thoroughly enjoyed the second

night's performance. Attending that night in a box was the Professor of Music, Paddy Hadley. Imagine my surprise and delight when, next day, a package arrived containing a letter which said that he had been a devotee of musical comedy since the days of Lionel Monkton, but rarely had he enjoyed a musical more. Moreover, he included a page of manuscript of Hadley in the style of Vening as sung by Miss Greenwood. It is one of my most treasured possessions.

On the Friday there was a midnight matinee. To this had been invited three VIPs – Margot Fonteyn and her husband Tito Arrias and the comedian Jimmy Edwards. Tito Arrias was the Panamanian Ambassador so during the day I dashed to the Music School library to find the Panama National Anthem – Charles Cudworth produced it. I hurriedly arranged it for our forces and we proudly played it after our own National Anthem.

I went over afterwards and asked him whether it was all right. 'It's the first time I've heard it all through,' he replied.

The performance went splendidly, partly because a drunk Dan Massey at the front of the Circle kept laughing and applauding!

[From *Pitch Imperfect* by Alan Vening.]

## John Bertalot, 1955

The Corpus May Week concerts were, in those days, devoted to musical comedy. Dr Harry Porter, then a junior Fellow, and my predecessor, Alan Vening, were both heavily involved in Footlights. I was to write the music for the 1957 and 1958 productions: *Cinderella and the Wicked Dean*, scripted by Peter Vincent, who was later to write scripts for *The Two Ronnies* on TV, and *The Bursar's Bantling*, written by Geoffrey Woodhead. We couldn't think who could take the central part of the college Bursar, which was affectionately based on our actual Bursar, Dr John Roach. Finally someone suggested that John should play himself, which he did, brilliantly.

Three outstanding events took place in my first term in 1955. There was a state visit by the Queen and Duke of Edinburgh. I was standing in Trinity Great Court when their car drove down the ramp towards the Master's Lodgings. The young Queen was radiant in emerald green and the Duke next to her was in his scarlet doctoral robes. Six trumpeters stood on the tower to play a fanfare, and the sun shone from a clear blue sky.

A few weeks later, Boris Ord, my supervisor, sent me a note saying he couldn't see me that day as he ought to see Dr Schweitzer receive an honorary doctorate. I felt I ought to see this historic event too. The Chancellor, Lord Tedder, was magnificently dignified in his Chancellor's robes; Dr Schweitzer, his hair awry, looked like a sack of potatoes. The public orator told us in Latin why the doctorate was being awarded, the Chancellor held out his hand to Dr Schweitzer and everyone in the Senate House cheered.

Lastly, the young Billy Graham led his first Mission to the University and I played the organ for most of the services held in the University church that week. His visit has affected many lives since.

The Chapel organ was the worst in Cambridge: Three manuals – by Flight and Son, who had gone out

Organ Scholars, 1968 (top):
*Back row: G.T.B. Wright, J.G. Price, Wilfrid Dykes-Bower, Harold Dexter, Alan Vening, John Bertalot, Sir John Dykes-Bower, R. Parker.*
*Front Row: Graham Mayo, Canon Charles Smyth, A.S.M. Dickens, Keith Bond, Revd. Geoffrey Styler, Edward Higginbottom, J. Price-Jones, Michael Davey, D.C.H. Borgnis.*

Chapel Choir, 1957 (above):
*Back row (archway): ?, Roger Clarke, Michael Morton, Peter Stroud, Fergus Harris, Peter Scott, Brian Macdonald-Milne, Richard Warren, Oliver Haywood, ?, John Clark. Front row: Norman Warren (standing), John Bertalot, George Atherton, Graham Miles, Bill Roberts, Revd. Roland Wells, Gilbert Travis, Anthony Gable.*

of business in 1876. It had two sets of 8ft and 4ft flutes on every manual and not much else besides. At one Choral Evensong I was accompanying the choir in Stanford's *B flat Magnificat*. I turned over a page and found that the middle four pages were missing. Immediately I had a violent headache, and played the next few pages from memory whilst my assistant ransacked the organ loft for the missing pages. He found them just as we came to the end. Ever since I've always checked my music before playing for a service.

There was a rumour that someone had left £40,000 (an enormous sum) to buy a new organ, but we weren't told when this munificence would be put to use. The new organ was built in 1968, when Edward Higginbottom was organ scholar. There was a gathering of past organ scholars to celebrate the event, headed by Sir John Dykes Bower of St Paul's Cathedral, who had been Corpus's second organ scholar after Boris Ord. At the inaugural recital that night, Catherine Crozier from the USA played Charles Ives' *Variations on America* (i.e. God Save the Queen). The Senior Tutor had a fit of the giggles and so did most of the rest of us.

Roland Walls, our Dean of Chapel, and Geoffrey Styler, College Precentor, were wonderful people. Roland was such a gentle soul with a lovely smile, who never forgot his humble beginnings and was ever conscious of the high privilege of being numbered with so many gifted colleagues. Geoffrey is still with us and has hardly changed a hair. He and his lovely wife, Audrey, used to play sonatas for violin and piano at our monthly Bene't Club concerts. Audrey's translucent personality and gracious smile blessed all whom she met.

I counted it the greatest privilege to have been organ scholar at Corpus. There was a time when we boasted more cathedral organists than King's or John's: Boris Ord at King's, John Dykes Bower at Truro, Durham and St Paul's, Harold Dexter at Southwark, Robert Joyce at Llandaff, myself at Blackburn, Edward Higginbottom at New College and Mark Lee at Bristol. And Geoffrey Styler knows us all.

### Michael Harverson, 1957

When I was President of the Fletcher Players, the main items in our programme were a play in the Old Court every second summer and a musical comedy, performed in the Hall, as part of the annual Bene't Club May Week Concert. Members of the Society also devised the

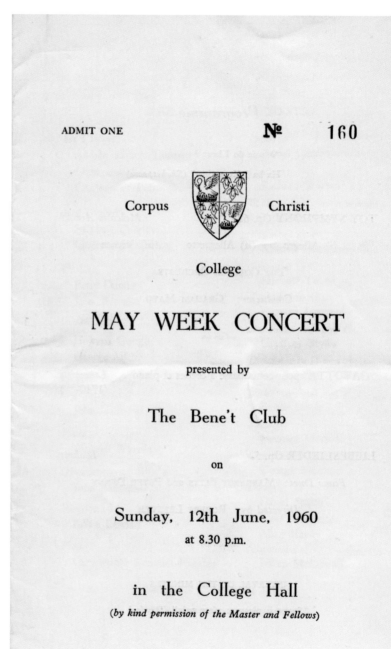

ADMIT ONE     № 160

Corpus    Christi

College

## MAY WEEK CONCERT

presented by

### The Bene't Club

on

**Sunday, 12th June, 1960**
at 8.30 p.m.

### in the College Hall

*(by kind permission of the Master and Fellows)*

script for a *son et lumière* production about the history of Corpus in the Old Court, also in 1959. The Sequins, a band of variety artistes – to give us a very flattering name – earned a few old shillings by providing entertainment after club or society dinners in non-university Cambridge and on Poppy Day, at least in 1959, with a review entitled *Opium for Half-a-Crown*. In March 1960 the Fletcher Players, directed by Anthony Everitt (1959), performed Marlowe's *The Jew of Malta* in the Hall and Professor Christopher Andrew (1959) had a role as one of the three Jewish businessmen! Proceeds went to the World Refugee Year Appeal.

By tradition the musical comedy was produced or written by the current president of the Fletcher Players, with music composed by the organ scholar; it made light-hearted fun of some of the features and perceived foibles of senior members of the College, very thinly disguised. In 1958 Brian Macdonald Milne (1955) produced *The Royal Commission*, or *The Bursar's Bantling* written by Geoffrey Woodhead (1940) and composed by John Bertalot (1955), in which John Roach (1938) played his putative predecessor as Domestic Bursar at the Porterhouse of 1881. This was followed in 1959 by *Bears and Squirrels*, or *Dons et Lumières* by Bill Ritson (1956), composed by Alan Vening (1952) and directed by Alun Jones (1956), in which Corpus alias Porterhouse had become Albert Hall.

So, it fell to my lot to think up a topic, devise a plot and write a libretto for May Week 1960. This was the time of the struggle for supremacy in space between the USA and the Soviet Union so I elected to give the action a pre-Star Wars setting. By the end of the Lent term the libretto was ready and despatched to the composer: not the current organ scholar, who felt no calling to follow the example of Arthur Sullivan, but Alan Vening, who came to the rescue again. Somehow an agreed version became available for rehearsal, directed by Anthony Everitt in the weeks before, around and after the Tripos examinations.

A makeshift stage, constructed of tables, dominated the end of the Hall, and the Senior Common Room of that era functioned as our green room. Friends were recruited to play the female parts. Those who could genuinely sing were assigned the roles that were intended to hold the action together and that were at all musically exacting. Bill Roberts (1956), for example, played the young male lead, and Michael Morton (1957) his father, the Monarch of the Moon.

Graham Mayo (1958) had his hands full, holding together a band of definitely amateur singers on the stage, and this on an evening when he was also concerned with conducting madrigals and part-songs in the Old Court and directing part of the serious side of the evening's entertainment, provided by the College orchestra.

It tickled our fancies in those days to insert into the programme minor notes or quotations, concocted or genuine, intended to divert the audience. *Red Moon* had no serious or satirical mission. TW3 lay a few years ahead. In the salad days of Cambridge in 1960 light-hearted fun was the arguably rather tame aim of productions such as this 'Lunar Lampoon'. The senior members of the College not only put up with our feeble jibes, they supported the performances and showed their appreciation of such determined attempts to contribute to the social life of the College.

## Peter Ryde, 1957

On Rag Day 1958, a small group from Corpus staged what was claimed at the time – accurately, I think – to be the first ever *son et lumière* presentation to be put on in Cambridge. It took place in the Old Court, which was illuminated by specially installed banks of fluorescent tubes arranged on the ground in groups along the north, east, and south sides. The control system allowed all or part of the walls to be appropriately lit in a variety of colours, and for certain scenes, such as Marlowe at work, lights would come on within one or two of the upstairs rooms. The audio (with which I assisted) was played through a PA system from a specially prepared tape, with narration, dialogue, music and sound effects. The performance, repeated every half hour throughout the evening, lasted about twenty minutes and provided a dramatized history of the College, based on selected incidents from Patrick Bury's booklet.

Though, technically speaking, it was undoubtedly crude, and the vast array of cables which disfigured the Old Court for a couple of days provoked a good deal of unfavourable comment, we felt it was a notable 'first' for Corpus. Unfortunately, it turned out to be useless as a fundraiser, for although it was well attended the takings barely exceeded the very considerable costs. But it was fun to do – the town riots, staged for the microphone one autumn afternoon, produced a satisfying degree of consternation amongst our elders – and as art for art's sake, I remember it with defiant affection and only a modicum of embarrassment.

*'War on Want' lunch
by the river.*

### Leonard Pearcey, 1959

The two most immediate memories come from opposite ends of my three memorable years at Corpus.

The first in the autumn of 1959 was of a war-on-want lunch by the river. The immediate friendships of the first frantic days of that first term had settled into a different and more permanent grouping for those lunches. That in turn gelled into another group that spent our middle year in the happy hostel run at 8A King's Parade by Mr and Mrs Collins.

The second, in my final term in 1962, revolves around the departing tutor Michael McCrum. As Vice-President of the Amalgamation Club (that year we held the Vice-Presidency of all college amalgamation clubs and launched an inter-college postal system – I wonder if it still exists – warmly welcomed by *Varsity*), I'd already had the privilege of getting to know him through our regular meetings and officially looking after him at parties (actually it was the other way round). We staged a musical sub-

titled with great subtlety *Dial M For Michael* and then a smoking concert when I sang, with Peter Denny at the piano, to the tune of *Der Vogelfänger bin ich ja* from Mozart's *Magic Flute*, his 'The Tutor is available to see undergraduates' notice, ending, with more subtlety, after the days of the week, with 'but never Never on a Sunday, a Sunday, a Sunday cos that's his day of rest', as made popular by Melina Mercouri in the film of that name. We presented him with a Georgian Silver Coffee Pot inscribed 'Michael McCrum, Tutor, Corpus Christi College Cambridge, 1951 to 1962'. He told me the other day that it's still used regularly.

### Richard Shephard, 1967

There were, of course, the big formal events such as the installation of the new Mander organ. But Corpus music-making in the 1960s seemed to revolve round two poles, the Bene't Club and the choir. Both organizations were the cause of much merriment and laughter.

*Rostropovich, who in 1974 stayed in the College as the guest of the master.*

The choir was an all-male institution and I, for one, found it all rather odd. The soprano part was sung by baritones an octave below pitch. This led to some very odd chord spacing and the general sound was muddy. This may, of course, have had something to do with the large number of wrong notes which characterized most performances. Sung Eucharists at a very early hour on Sunday mornings did not, perhaps, show off our vocal prowess to the full. The incumbent organ scholars used to provide a warm drink, allegedly tea, before the warm-up practice. I wish I could claim that either the drink or the practice improved the shining hour.

The Bene't Club met fortnightly in the Master's Lodge. Lady Lee presided over the occasions with benign good humour despite the feeble behaviour of many of us. I vividly recall a male-voice part-song breaking down in hysteria: Kathleen Lee stood up and said in a Joyce Grenfellesque way, 'Now don't be so silly: start again!' On another occasion, an oboe sonata of mine was given its premiere. The soloist had to face the corner in order to avoid being put off by members of the audience. One of the listeners developed a nose-bleed during the first movement, and the whole thing was punctuated by the sound of stifled mirth. I came across the manuscript the other day, and can quite understand the reception the piece received.

The other, rather larger-scale piece which I essayed during my time as an undergraduate was a re-working of *The Beggar's Opera*, which we performed as the May Week play, and then took on tour to the Minack Theatre in Cornwall. I learned much from this exercise, in particular that it is unwise to score for cellos if the per-

EXTRACT FROM *THE TIMES*, 29 MARCH, 2002
*Dirty tricks and the KGB*
by Christopher Andrew (Fellow)
*Mstislav Rostropovich's 75th birthday on Wednesday brought back vivid memories of the beginning, in 1974, of the great musician's lengthy exile from his native Russia. His exile started in Corpus Christi College, Cambridge, whose Master, Sir Duncan Wilson, was both a former Ambassador in Moscow and a close friend of Rostropovich and his wife, the soprano Galina Vishnevskaya. The Wilsons' younger daughter – herself a distinguished cellist as well being fluent in Russian – had been a pupil of Rostropovich and one of the very few Westerners to be housed during her studies in the Russian section of the Moscow Conservatoire.*

*With Rostropovich to Corpus (where I was, and remain, a Fellow) came his beloved cello. As the College Butler, Ron Storey (then, as now, one of the most popular members of the College), began unloading the luggage from the car that had brought Rostropovich to Cambridge, he picked up the cello case. 'Nyet, nyet!', shouted Rostropovich, waving his arms.*

*'My cello I will carry myself!'*

*That evening, as Rostropovich came in to dinner in a packed Corpus Hall, the students gave him a spontaneous standing ovation. Afterwards, he chatted with some of them in an animated, engaging mixture of Russian, English and German. The warmth of the College's welcome reflected not merely respect for Rostropovich's musical genius, but also deep admiration for his defence of human rights in the Soviet Union. During the past few years he had dared to give refuge in his dacha to the persecuted writer Aleksandr Solzhenitsyn, and to defend publicly Russia's leading dissident, Andrei Sakharov, denounced by the KGB chairman and future Soviet leader Yuri Andropov as 'Public Enemy No 1'. Rostropovich was – still is – one of the heroes of our time.*

formance is likely to be plagued by mists rolling in from the sea off Penzance. By the end of the week's run, the glue in the cello had disintegrated, and the cellist was left with what appeared to be a pile of matchwood.

In the late sixties there was no music don in the College. Our academic work was directed by David Willcocks who was a friendly, if somewhat remote figure over the road. There were undoubted benefits in not having a senior member of the University presiding over music-making in the College. We had the freedom to do roughly what we liked.

One hitherto unchronicled musical activity was a tour by a group calling itself the Bene't Ensemble. About eight of us drove off to the west country and performed in Bryanston School, Gloucester and Bristol Cathedrals, Tewkesbury Abbey and Cheltenham Ladies College. I can recall a spirited rendition of *The Lambeth Walk* in this last venue, the piece ending with an athletic leap by the present Precentor of Salisbury and a breathtaking catch of the flying singer by two others of us. What the Cheltenham Ladies thought remains cloaked in a merciful obscurity.

### Don Neville, 1974

It all began in 1974 when John and Polly Bird, John Bintliff, Mark Goldie, Tony and Maureen Ottridge, and others who can be seen in the photograph (below), gathered informally around the piano at Leckhampton to sing madrigals in the manner in which they were designed to be sung – for the fun of it. The following year, the group decided to brave a more public display of their talents, and Don Neville was asked to add a few extras to the group and prepare the slightly augmented team for a performance. This request lead to the inaugural concert that was held at the old Music School in Downing Place on 13 March 1975. The main work was the Brahms *Liebeslieder Walzer* accompanied by duo pianists Edward Higginbottom and Stephen Harrison – and just to prove that there was no favouritism, the two pianists exchanged ends of the piano part-way through. Of course, the choir had to have a name, one that simply meant 'a choir of graduate students.' Unfortunately, antiquity did not leave us a convenient title, so to Galen Graham fell the task of inventing an approximation. Thus, if 'Collegium Laureatum' sounds a little grandiose for a bunch of amateurs, all that was intended was a clear distinction between this group and the prestigious undergraduate choir.

Thereafter we extended the hospitality of Leckhampton to all graduates of the University. As a result, our numbers exceeded the 100 mark, Doug Mills became the official accompanist, and the second concert at the Guildhall on 19 February 1976 featured the Rossini *Petite Messe Solennelle*, with soloists Elaine Blyth, Beatrix Bown, Trevor Brown and Peter Harrison

and with Edward Higginbottom providing the organ backup to Doug's piano accompaniment. The Rossini Mass, the Dvojak *Mass in D*, along with a Bach motet, brought Don Neville's time with the choir to an end, and the baton passed to Theodore Boorman.

### Nicholas Marston, 1977

I went up to Corpus as a choral exhibitioner in 1977. The College did not have its own Director of Studies in Music at that time, and men – we were all men in 1977! – reading for the Tripos were 'managed' from King's, where the organist and Director of Studies was Philip Ledger.

I managed to remain in Cambridge until 1989, and for much of that time I was involved with Corpus music, mostly in the Chapel, as I'm not an instrumentalist. The organization of musical activities fell very largely on the shoulders of the organ scholars, and my relatively extended presence about the place gave me ample opportunity to compare and contrast. The pattern of things remained (and remains) pretty constant: Evensong on Sunday and Wednesday (not the least advantage of the advent of women in the College was the death-blow it struck to the traditional men's voices service on Wednesdays: Wood's *View me, Lord* is one anthem I never want to sing again), Eucharist on Sunday mornings and feast days. Lunchtime recital series, usually on Fridays, came and went – I recall Quentin Poole playing the Mozart *oboe quartet*, and a string quartet playing Beethoven's *C minor quartet, op. 18 no. 4*. I occasionally contributed an organ recital, and remember pondering the unpopularity of such events on one occasion when, at the starting time of 1.15 pm, I was the only person in the Chapel: not even my pageturner had come.

*The Collegium Laureatum Choir.*

There were usually around four undergraduates reading Music in my time, which made a decent core for practical activities. Despite there being no internal DoS, support from the Fellowship was strong, and music was regarded as an important component of College life. Richard Bainbridge, then Senior Tutor, was unfailingly helpful and enthusiastic (my Chapel position at the westernmost end on decani gave me a clear view of him during services, and one could always read enjoyment, or otherwise, clearly on his face); but Geoffrey Styler, then as now, was the presiding genius, whether as Precentor, pianist (often accompanying his beloved wife Audrey's violin playing), host of Middleton Cottage concerts, or simply as the College's living musical memory since the immediate post-war years.

The arrival of Geoffrey Lloyd as organ scholar in 1980, along with a fine crop of instrumentalists such as Nick Benda, heralded a period of ambitious and successful music-making both in and out of Chapel. In an effort to prevent the congregation feeling excluded from the choral music, there was a tradition of congregational parts being issued for the canticles; and where these did not already exist, it was the organ scholar's rather tiresome duty to provide them. Thus it was that Geoff and I, sitting one Sunday afternoon in I9, dreamed up what probably remains the only congregational part for Rubbra in A flat. The approach was simple: an isolated word or two here and there in the main body of the text (echoes of that bass drum part), and then the whole of the Gloria doubling the organ manual part. Those familiar with Rubbra's setting will get the message, as, it seemed, did the College: the congregation seemed strangely reticent about joining in thereafter.

*Camelia in Old Court.*

# DRAMA

**Harry Porter, 1945**

As an undergraduate Malcolm Burgess designed sets for the ADC, including *Boris Godunov* in Russian. As a research student from 1948 his topic was the Russian theatre in the age of Catherine the Great. He designed the 1950 Greek play at the Arts, and at the end of 1949 he joined the Footlights committee as 'décor master'. (The Footlights President at the time was Adrian Vale of Corpus). The minute book noted 'the enthusiasm, nay frenzy of the décor master, longing to design romantic sets with red and white spotted mushrooms'.

The May Week revues of 1954, the fifth for which Malcolm designed the sets, and 1955 were the peak of Corpus's association with the Footlights. In 1954 Neil Sutherland 'was elected musical director, and everyone was very pleased'. The cast included John Pardoe, who also appeared in 1955, when the music director was Alan Vening, and three Corpus men were in the band – Alan Warren, Andrew Mortimer and Christopher Bennett. Both revues transferred to London. Vening composed *The Girl Next Door*, book by Pardoe and Peter Vincent (also Corpus), which was presented at the Arts early in 1956 by the University Musical Comedy Club (of which Vening was President). The cast included, from Corpus, Timothy Todhunter and Peter Nicholson, with John Pardoe as an Elvis-style pop singer. *Granta* enjoyed his 'gyrating his Charing Cross Road shoulders – everything from the whiteness of the teeth to the puddle blue zoot was perfectly observed.' A Research Fellow of Corpus at that time, I contributed four lyrics.

Also in 1954 Malcolm designed the musical comedy *Zuleika* at the Arts, music by Peter Tranchell of King's,

*Harry Porter.*

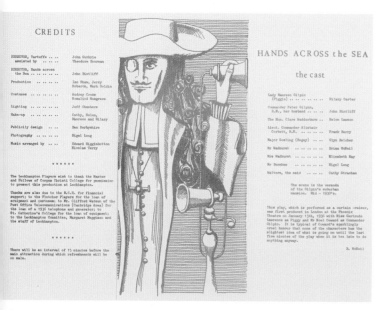

based on Beerbohm's *Zuleika Dobson*. From Corpus, John Pardoe was the Duke of Dorset, and Alan Vening assistant conductor. When the work was produced in London in 1957, sets were by Osbert Lancaster, a 'big name'. Kenneth Tynan thought them 'drab' – and Malcolm, 'absolutely horrible!!!' Malcolm was always torn between theatrical design and academic life, but academia prevailed. In 1962 he returned to Cambridge as lecturer in Slavonic Studies, having in 1960 transformed the Hall at Corpus. And in the mid-1970s he refurbished the Chapel (the Chapel committee accepted chandeliers, but vetoed too much gilt). He was eventually elected to a Corpus Fellowship in 1974, but died of cancer in 1978. In the tribute paid at the memorial service in the Chapel, it was suggested that the Deity had surely arranged for 'the heavenly halls to need that extra little bit of gold leaf'. The Burgess Footlights, which survive, are now in the Club archives.

A familiar rubric in the mid-1950s was: 'At the Pianos, Alan Vening and Peter Stroud'. (Stroud was to be Footlights President in 1957). The rubric was prominent in the programmes for three Corpus May Week concerts, 1954–1956. The music was for operetta style pieces, each lasting about one hour, for which I wrote the books. The first and most elaborate was *Daisy Simpkins*, or *the Spinning House*, a 'Concert Entertainment', 'through-composed' by Peter Tranchell of King's. Concerning Cambridge in the early 1890s, the libretto was based on two cases (telescoped into one) involving the

traditional powers of the Vice-Chancellor and proctors over local 'loose women', who, found in the company of a member of the University, could be imprisoned in the 'Spinning House' in Regent Street. There was a chorus of undergraduates and another of 'light ladies', and a cast of twelve, including the Senior Proctor (Neil Sutherland), with John Pardoe as the undergraduate hero. This work has been revived at Homerton, Selwyn, Christ's and Caius. Neil Sutherland wrote the music for the 1955 *The Literary Delinquent: A May Week Frivolity*, a simpler affair, a comedy with a dozen musical numbers. John Pardoe was 'Harry: a Delinquent', and Alan Warren, as the vicar, led a memorable sextet, *Clay in the Hands of the Potter*. The piece was directed by Michael Mayne, later vicar of Great St Mary's and Dean of Westminster.

The music in 1956, for *The Dutch Uncle: A Swan Song*, was by Alan Vening. Tim Todhunter was the Bishop of Wells and Winches, John Pardoe a Senior Chorister, and Peter Nicholson 'an Ecclesiastical Chancellor' – was Garth Moore amused? *The Times* reported, in part, 'Although set in a crumbling bishop's palace where only faith holds the death-watch beetles from massing for a final assault, *The Dutch Uncle* was performed recently in the hall of Corpus Christi College, Cambridge. This bizarre contradiction between squalor and elegance was thoroughly in keeping with the deliberate artificiality of Mr H.C. Porter's text... [the] thread of plot was the excuse for 13 well-made lyrics which were set with sophisticated variety by Mr Alan Vening. Mr Vening can produce agreeable melody and aggressive syncopation; but he is at his most inventive as a mimic, excelling in the unexpected use of full-blooded recitative, or four-part chorale harmonisation set in ludicrous contrast to the text.'

Corpus, because of the initiative of the Master, Michael McCrum, was the only college to do anything about the Footlights Centenary in 1983. Former Corpus 'Footlighters' were invited to a Footlights Reunion Dinner on Saturday 10 December. The senior guest was Geoffrey Wright (1931), who in his second year designed the 1933 May Week revue, and wrote music for two lyrics by Robert Hamer (1930), who later wrote and directed *Kind Hearts and Coronets*. Wright wrote most of the music in 1934. After going down, he contributed music and costume designs for the 1936 and 1938 revues.

## Brian Macdonald Milne, 1955

I soon attached myself to the Corpus Christi College Dramatic Society. I felt that an annual play in the Old Court was certainly not enough, and when I was elected President, with James Groves (later ordained) as my Vice-President, I felt we should be rather more adventurous. We continued with the Old Court Play in the Easter term, preferring Tudor or Restoration plays, not least because of our Elizabethan alumnus, Christopher Marlowe, and also the dramatist of the early Jacobean period, John Fletcher, both of whom are prominently commemorated on a wall plaque in the Old Court. We attempted to show our respect for the drama of their periods by presenting the plays in the costume of the time they were written, and using the Old Court itself as the stage – having people entering by the staircases, or appearing when appropriate either leaning or looking out of the windows. There was no extra staging, as we felt what was there was quite adequate. I myself directed a play by Philip Massinger, *A New Way To Pay Old Debts*. James Groves was a gifted costume designer as well as a forceful performer. As the College was single sex, we had to audition undergraduates from women's colleges for the parts requiring female gifts. Unlike the Elizabethan dramatists, we did not have young men or boys playing the women's parts!

Our emphasis on the drama of these periods, and our consciousness of the College's heritage of drama, led me to wonder why we used the rather long title, 'Corpus Christi College Dramatic Society'. Other Colleges often had rather snappier titles for their dramatic societies. The University itself had already claimed Marlowe for a leading body so why not use Fletcher? Thus it was that the name 'The Fletcher Players' was adopted. But alongside that, the society decided to do more about revue and cabaret, and a small group of six was formed to perform the Rag Week Revue in I6 and to do cabaret at social events. As we decided to wear evening dress for these performances, we felt that a slightly over-the-top name would be appropriate, so we called ourselves The Sequins! We were six: Alun Glyn-Jones (who succeeded me as President), Bill Ritson (a natural comic!), Bill Roberts (a fine singer, also in the choir), Michael Tubbs (our pianist, who later became music director at the RSC, Stratford-upon-Avon), David Soulsby (double bass), and myself (writer, singer, comic, director, etc). Alun and Bill Ritson were later

ordained – largely because of the influence of the Dean of Chapel, Roland Walls – and Bill became one of the leading authorities on the theatre among the clergy of the Church of England. Among the more senior members of the College showing a similar enthusiasm for the theatre was Harry Porter.

As a result of these activities, I was invited to join the Footlights, whose musical director at the time was Alan Vening, another Corpus man. Their main activities in those days – other than the well-known annual revue – were the Smoking Concerts held in Dorothy's Café, then situated upstairs in Sidney Street.

*Alan Glyn-Jones in doublet and hose for the production of* A New Way to Pay Old Debts, *June 1957.*

Members of the Bene't Club, the Fletcher Players, and others came together for a concert one year which included a dramatic element – a production of *The Bursar's Bantling*, directed by Geoffrey Woodhead and starring John Roach as Dr Perch, with music by Beethoven and John Bertalot! The lyrics had many topical references, including mention of 'Bucks' and 'Beds'. A number of Fellows participated or were impersonated. I wore my kilt and was intended to represent Dr Henderson. A good time was had by all!

Another production, this time by the Fletcher Players, also combined music and drama and even included poetry. I contacted Clive Sansom, who had written a collection of poems about Biblical characters and events entitled *The Witnesses*, and he gave permission for some of these to be incorporated in the text of the play, which I wrote. It was an attempt to combine theology and music and drama. The aim of the play was not only to try and present the outline of the 'Bible Story' in a nutshell, but to use music as an integral part of the drama. No attempt, therefore, was made to present the Creation in word or action, but only in music and light. The play was also designed for performance in church buildings of any shape, Corpus Christi Chapel being difficult to use if you do not want all the action to take place in one spot at the east end. It ended with a reference to the Eucharist. I called it *The New Creation*, taking the title from Paul's Second Epistle to the Corinthians, and

described it as a 'Modern Miracle Play'. The music was specially composed by our organ scholar, John Bertalot. We needed women to play various parts, and I was fortunate to have a woman undergraduate recommended to me to play the part of the Virgin Mary, some of whose lines were from one of Clive Sansom's poems. This person was Bernardine Wall, who later became known more widely because of her part as a witness in the court case involving the publication by Penguin Books of *Lady Chatterley's Lover*. (She was the undergraduate who was presented by the defence to state that she had not been 'corrupted' by reading the novel). We took this play on tour to College livings around Cambridge, namely Landbeach, Little Wilbraham and Grantchester, none of which were ideal for drama. Our 'business manager' was Keith Hinde, later resident at Denny House in Waterbeach.

*A dress rehearsal at Leckhampton for* The Massacre at Paris, *by Marlowe, 1966.*

### Tom Faber, 1953
#### *The Gravediggers*

According to Patrick Bury's *History* of Corpus, the Gravediggers Society was founded by the Revd Arnold Joseph Wallis, 'to help bridge the gulf between dons and undergraduates'. The date of the first meeting is not recorded, but Wallis became a Fellow at the age of 22 in 1879, and the Society celebrated its centenary at a memorable dinner held in April 1980. It is not quite as old as the Chess Club, therefore, and it has never enjoyed the same social prestige within the College. But whereas members of the Chess Club degenerated into a society devoted to the less taxing pastimes of eating, drinking and dancing, the Gravediggers still meet to read plays.

Wallis, who came to Corpus from Trinity to be a college lecturer in Mathematics, was 'a high-minded earnest man of small stature and unassuming appearance'; and Pollock, another mathematician from Trinity who was appointed a college lecturer three years after Wallis and who subsequently presided over the Gravediggers for many years, was undoubtedly high-minded too, despite 'his tendency to yawn in Chapel'. In their day, Shakespeare provided the Gravediggers' principal fare, but during my own time as an active member the Society restricted itself to one Shakespeare play per year, the other meetings being devoted to the whole spectrum of the British theatre, from Marlowe to Tom Stoppard in chronological terms, or from Marlowe to Edgar Wallace on a scale of earnestness.

The first meeting which I attended was probably in the Michaelmas term of 1953: I was yet another small and unassuming import from Trinity, though a physicist rather than a mathematician and with no claim whatever to high-mindedness. I attended meetings, though at rare intervals towards the end, for the next 40 years or so, and I always enjoyed them, though there are some Restoration comedies and some plays by Shaw that I no longer wish to read through yet again. Meetings used to start, and no doubt still do, at 8.30 pm, which gave just enough time to Fellows who had dined in Hall for one fortifying glass of port. Coffee and biscuits (sometimes paid for out of the undergraduate Secretary's own pocket and sometimes charged to a fund at the Senior Tutor's disposal) would be served, and the host or hosts for the evening – Fellows were expected to host one meeting each year, and other meetings were hosted by non-Fellows in pairs – dispensed wine at half time. Sometimes there was a crate of beer behind a sofa for consumption after the reading was over, but to the best of my knowledge gravediggers remained sober at play-reading meetings and were in bed before midnight. The Secretary's job was (and still is) a burdensome one: he had to secure copies; he was primarily responsible for the casting; he distributed reminder cards; and above all he was expected to write extensive and witty minutes after each meeting, and to read them out at the start of the next. Compared with his, the duties of the undergraduate President – to preserve traditions, maintain order, make a speech at the annual dinner, and supervise the process

*The Gravediggers.*

whereby new members are selected – are undemanding.

The minute books of the Society are preserved; I understand them to be complete for the years between 1885 and 1913, when the Society was allowed to lapse, and between its revival in 1922 or 1923 and the present day. They provide a permanent record of numerous special occasions, such as the meeting to read *Under Milk Wood* which was held in my rooms (Y2) during the 1950s: E.M. Forster attended as a guest, and no-one who heard him read the line 'I will put my pyjamas in the drawer marked pyjamas' can have forgotten it. They also provide a permanent memorial to the industry and inventiveness of generations of Secretaries, and to the dignity of generations of Presidents. I shall name none of these, but a few Fellows who were particularly stalwart supporters deserve mention: Patrick Bury, who in 1953 was nearing the end of what must have been a long stint; Patrice Charvet, renowned for suggesting at the end of each meeting that next time we should read *Mrs Dane's Defence*, a melodrama which one enterprising Secretary contrived to unearth and which proved extremely feeble; John Roach, regularly cast as (in his own words) a 'wise old counsellor'; Michael McCrum (as Tutor, and later as Master); Frank Lee (as Master); Theodore Boorman, who left the residue of his cellar to the Society when he died in 1981; Richard Bainbridge (as Senior Tutor); Chris Andrew (another Senior Tutor); and latterly Alison Smith and Chris Howe.

During the summer of 1959 I married a girl who came from a 'rich stage background'. At her suggestion I invited the then President and Secretary to arrange a meeting at our small house in Drosier Road, and to ask members to bring girlfriends with them. The invitation was accepted, but no girls apart from Penny turned up, and we spent the evening reading *The Apple Cart* in which there is one female part and one only. The food which she provided for the occasion was of such a standard, however, that there was strong demand for a repeat, and in no time at all one or more extramural 'Ladies Nights' were regular features of the Gravediggers' calendar. I find in the College archive a scribbled note which probably dates from 1965, written by one Secretary for the information of his successor. One of the first tips in it is to visit Penny Faber at the Old Vicarage, and Kathleen Lee at the Master's Lodge, to inquire about Ladies Nights in the Lent and Easter terms respectively: '[They] will say yes [and] will provide all booze and eats'. Jenny Andrew was being equally hospitable a few years later. Since Corpus went mixed, the Society has of course had members of both sexes and, according to the Society's written constitution, as revised in 1996, every host is now required to 'provide good food and wine according to the standard that has come to be expected'.

The new constitution also lays down that 'a skull is to be present at each meeting, if not in being then in spirit'. When skulls first appeared at meetings I am uncertain, but it was perhaps at about the time (1974?) when the Society first adopted a tie in the Corpus colours with a white skull on it. Rightly or wrongly, I associate them with Richard Bainbridge, and I blame him also for the tradition that every meeting should start with a reading of the gravedigger's scene in *Hamlet*, a tradition which has now, I trust, been abandoned.

I have left until last an account of the annual dinners which are the highlight of the Gravediggers' year. They have not always been as sober as the play-reading meetings described above. In the 1950s, under the auspices of Michael McCrum, those attending were required to sit in a close circle after dinner, holding a sheet stretched taut between them. A feather would be placed in the centre, whereupon every one blew very hard until the feather was forced out of the circle; the person underneath it as it crossed the line would then remove an article of clothing, and the process would be repeated. In the late 1960s, under the auspices of Richard Bainbridge, dinners were regularly enlivened by pyrotechnics. The cigars which were provided as a matter of course in those degenerate days came in metal tubes, closed at one end, which could be made to nestle into one another; a very satisfying explosion could be achieved by placing a charge of match heads in tube A, blocking it with tube B, and heating the match heads over a candle. The object of firing tube B into the New Court, and breaking the windows of Richard's dining room in the process, was never quite achieved, but those present were sufficiently sobered by the noise to retire to his study for a relatively quiet round of 'Adverbs', otherwise known as 'In the Manner of the Word'. During Michael's Mastership, when the annual dinner took place in the Lodge, the inexhaustible resources of the McCrum dressing-up box were placed at our disposal. Fireworks and 'Adverbs' then gave way to charades and 'Murder in the Dark'.

*Room 00: Perhaps the most prestigious undergraduate room in College.*

CHRISTOPHER
MARLOWE
1581·1587

JOHN
FLETCHER
1591·1594

ANTIQVAE DOMVS
GEMINVM DECVS

## Mark McCrum, 1977

*The Playroom*

It was autumn 1979. I was in my second year at Corpus reading English, an eager would-be playwright. My only problem being: there was nowhere in Cambridge dedicated to new writing. If you wanted to stage an original play, you had to produce it yourself. This meant raising funds to hire a venue, which might be as much as – whisper it – £50 and then persuading the relevant Powers-That-Be that an original work, rather than a punk rock version of *Hamlet* or a searing new presentation of *Danton's Death*, was the thing to do.

I was living in a tiny back room in the undergraduate hostel at 8 King's Parade. My view was of the scruffy back yard of the Eagle, the dons' car park and, beyond that, the empty space at 11 St Edward's Passage. Once this had been the Girton Ladies Waiting Room, in the days when Girtonians needed somewhere to re-apply their powder and lipstick after a long bicycle ride and before facing the critical stares of their male peers. Now, with Wolfson Court up and running, the place had become defunct.

I managed to get a front door key from the porters and check the building out. The walls were peeling and battered, there was plaster dust and litter all over the bare boards of the floor, and the main room was an odd L-shape, not ideal for a theatre, even the fashionable and groundbreaking 'studio' I had in mind.

But it was empty, and central, and a substantial space. I got talking to another apprentice playwright, Caroline Oulton, herself a Girtonian. She was equally enthused. Over numerous cups of thin Nescafe in front of the glowing gas fire at 8 King's Parade we hatched a plan. She would gee up the University and creative-writing side of things and I would tackle the Corpus authorities.

Fortunately our Senior Tutor at the time, the twinkly Dr Richard Bainbridge, was a keen dramaturge. Famed for his performance as Rattie in a May Week production of *Toad of Toad Hall*, he ruled the roost in both Fletcher Players and Gravediggers. The other key figure to be talked round was the splendid Bursar of the day, Alec Clark-Kennedy, a handsome ex-naval man with a sharp line in blue blazers and a complexion that spoke eloquently of his keenness for sport, rowing in particular.

After much discussion, the idea of an experiment was born. We would be allowed one season of plays at St Edward's Passage and see how it went.

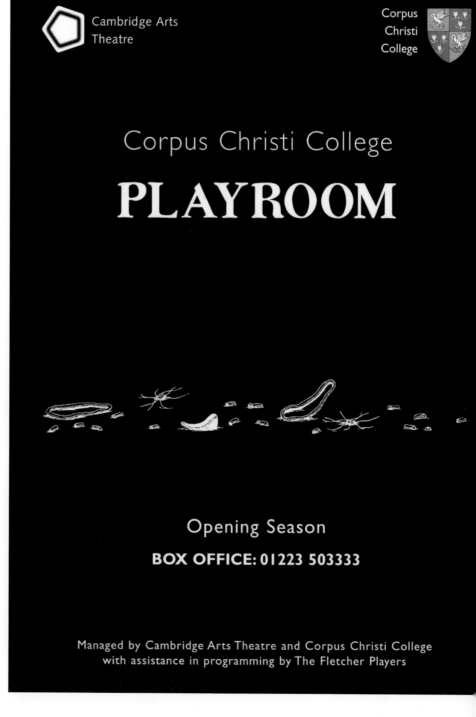

Cambridge Arts Theatre

Corpus Christi College

## Corpus Christi College

# PLAYROOM

## Opening Season

### BOX OFFICE: 01223 503333

Managed by Cambridge Arts Theatre and Corpus Christi College with assistance in programming by The Fletcher Players

*Playroom programme, re-opening season 2002.*

A team of friends moved in with stepladders and rollers. In a single weekend the horrid green of the walls was repainted with a theatrical black. The Fletcher Players' ever-competent technical team swung into action and had soon erected a raked stage and lights on scaffolding. A programme was printed. The opening night would feature Simon McBurney in a play by Caroline together with a parody of Pinter's plays I had written entitled *No Man's Land Betrayed*. The following week there would be a play called *Latin* by a tall, rather donnish chess-player from Queens' called Stephen Fry; and so on ….

Our debut was a success. Both arms of the L-shape were packed. The fact that the laughter of the two sec-tions wasn't entirely in sync didn't seem to matter. Oliver Letwin (his ambitions then set on being a don at Trinity rather than Shadow Home Secretary) gave us a rave notice in the *Cambridge Review. Stop Press* were equally kind, though keen to point out that there had been nobody on the door to collect the ticket money.

We were on our way. At the end of the term Dr Bainbridge judged his experiment a success. The Playroom was something the Fletcher Players could be proud of. I made very sure I cast him as the lead role in the May Week show. As a result, the following year I got the room I wanted and the Playroom became a fixture.

---

**Welcome…**

…to the opening season in an exciting new phase of development for Corpus Christi College Playroom, as Cambridge Arts Theatre and Corpus Christi College (through its own student drama society, the Fletcher Players) join together to inspire a broader range of dramatic productions for the venue, and to give it a greater lease of life outside of term.

As you'll see from the events on offer in January and beyond, this uniquely intimate and atmospheric studio theatre in St. Edward's Passage, which boasts former student performers such as Stephen Fry and Emma Thompson, will continue to be dedicated to student drama production for much of the year. The weeks in between will see professional and community-based events run by the Arts Theatre, with an emphasis on youth drama, new writing and non-mainstream performance which complements the Theatre's existing special needs strand.

We hope that this new partnership will encourage more people to get involved in the life of an important venue – whether it be by staging a production or by coming to see the vast range of work on offer – and we look forward to joining with you in an exciting future.

Ian Ross
Executive Director, Cambridge Arts Theatre

Christopher Kelly
Senior Tutor, Corpus Christi College

### Wednesday 30 January – Saturday 2 February

**7.15pm**

The Fletcher Players present

**Making Space**
A Quartet of New Adaptations

To mark the re-opening of Corpus Christi College Playroom, the Fletcher Players are performing a suite of four short adaptations and devised pieces. Taken from the writings of Edward Gorey, Raymond Carver, Federico Garcia Lorca and Wyndham Lewis, all four pieces explore the frustrations of physical and emotional disorientation and the possibilities of escape.

**9.45pm**          Saturday matinee, 2pm

The Fletcher Players and Activated Image present

**Latin!** by Stephen Fry

Back in 1979, when men spoke Latin and girls hadn't been invented yet, a young chap with a floppy fringe was asked to write for a new theatre called The Playroom. LATIN! was Stephen Fry's hilarious, outrageous response. Mark Farrelly and Tom Noad shine in the tale of how a prep school master's intimacy with his star pupil lands him in amo, amas, a mess.

### Tuesday 5 – Saturday 9 February

**7.15pm**

Clare Actors present

**My Mother Said I Never Should**
by Charlotte Keatley

What are little girls made of? Sugar and spice and all things nice.

The role of woman in twentieth century life is explored through four generations. Each female is presented with different opportunities to break away from her dependence on men and gain freedom by having a career, the struggle becoming easier with each generation.

**9.45pm**

Cambridge University Theatre Company present

**The Cenci** by Artaud

THE CENCI is Artaud's masterpiece. His dramatisation of the tyranny of Count Cenci remains the landmark in the development of twentieth century theatre and is the earliest example of the Theatre of Cruelty.

Poignant, dark and powerful, the story of Count Cenci and his daughter reveals man in his lowest incarnation and asks us 'can murder ever be justified?'

**Tickets for all performances £5.50 (£4 concessions)**
**BOX OFFICE: 01223 503333**

### Tuesday 12 – Saturday 16 February

**7pm**

The ADC presents

**Coming in to Land** by Stephen Poliakoff

In a tale that could be lifted from today's headlines the ADC explores the struggles of refugees in a dislocated world. Illegal immigrant Halina's best chance of asylum rests with marrying a city lawyer. While beginning to cohabit, Halina starts to plan a more independent, potentially perilous, stay. This impassioned psychological thriller pits the individual against the state, using the gripping story of one woman to illustrate the plight of many.

**10pm**

The ADC presents

**The Dumb Waiter** by Harold Pinter

In the basement room of a deserted house, two men wait impatiently for instructions on a job they must do. But their predicament takes a suprising turn as bizarre messages are sent from the supposedly abandoned floor above…

One of Pinter's earliest plays, THE DUMB WAITER is both a dark farce and a suspense thriller. Combining humour with tension, Pinter forces the audience into the role of detective in a play where the questions are left unanswered.

### Tuesday 19 – Saturday 23 February

**7.15pm**

Wicked Theatre and
Big Jacket Productions present

Sex, drugs, rock 'n' roll.
Funk, junk and birth control.
Life's a bitch and then you die.
So f*** the world and let's get high.

This dark comedy will plunge you into a world of disposability, disconnection and dysfunction. Relationships are reduced to transactions and love isn't the only four-letter word when things get messy between friends. A gritty urban tale of people with nothing better to do than Shopping and F***ing.

**9.45pm**

K-C Productions present

**Spoonface Steinberg**          by Lee Hall

SPOONFACE STEINBERG is a beautiful monologue delivered by a 7-year old autistic child who is dying of cancer. The narration is laced with extracts of various arias sung by Maria Callas, which reflect Spoonface's love of opera, and lend the play a melancholic beauty.

This is a unique opportunity to see a poignant play about love, hope and death, through the eyes of an autistic child with a rare and inspiring outlook on the world.

*All proceeds will be donated to Cambridge University Support for the Homeless (CUSH).*

### Tuesday 26 February – Saturday 2 March

**7.15pm**

The Fletcher Players present

**The Freshers' Play**

Written, directed, performed and produced by Corpus Christi College first years, the show will be newly conceived and will offer something a little different for its audience. It is so fresh in fact that, at time of print, we don't know what the play will be! However, from the precedent set by past Freshers' Plays (PERRIN'S FAULT, OBLIVIOUS, BED AND GOD) we can guarantee you an entertaining and enjoyable evening…

**9.30pm**

The Fletcher Players present

**Nuts** by Fausto Paravidino

A group of friends raid a house which one of them is supposed to house-sit, leading to conflict and accusations of misplaced loyalty; ten years on, they meet again, this as adults in a grotesque totalitarian state, oblivious to their past relationships and facing each other as torturers and victims.

Written in the aftermath of the Genoa protests, this politically charged play by an award-winning Italian playwright is part of the interNational Connections Festival.

**Tickets for all performances £5.50 (£4 concessions)**
**BOX OFFICE: 01223 503333**

# DINING

*Graduation Dinner, 2001.*

**Frederick Lawton, 1930**

Budgeting so as to be able to pay my College account at the end of each term was not difficult. The College provided one meal a day. This was dinner, which had come to be served at 7.30 pm in Hall. All members of the College, Fellows as well as undergraduates, dined together, the Fellows on a raised dais at one end of the Hall. This was known as 'High Table'. There were three rows of tables down the length of the Hall, seating separately the undergraduates of each year of intake. There was a table for BAs at the end of the middle row. Dining together in Hall was regarded as an important aspect of College life. Undergraduates were expected to dine at least five nights a week. If they habitually did not do so the Tutor would require them to explain their frequent absences. The College charged a small sum for each dinner. My recollection is that it was 3s 6d. The food was ample and good. I enjoyed dining in Hall. I got to know those other members of my year with whom I had neither academic nor sporting contact.

For other meals the College provided a Buttery from which undergraduates could draw 'battles', that is provisions such as milk, bread, tea and the like. It was also possible through the Buttery to order meals from the kitchen. Meals so ordered were brought to undergraduates' rooms by the 'Buttery boy' and charged to College accounts. I kept my College account under control by never using this Buttery meal service. I always had a light breakfast and luncheon in my room, using 'battles' or other provisions which I had brought from the shops. Making tea or coffee was easy as there were gas rings in the 'gyp' rooms on each staircase.

**Leslie Hill, 1936**

Lunch was a magnificent affair at Corpus. Our fees were relatively high, and the College food was the best in the University, with the possible exception of Peterhouse. Lunch was not compulsory, one could eat *table d'hote* or *à la carte* at that meal. I myself seldom had lunch in Hall, as my allowance of £300 a year from my parents and £40 from my exhibition did not go far. There was always a large array of cold meats and pies, and an imposing selection of hot dishes on the menu. I particularly liked the camembert.

**Richard Winterbotham, 1946**

An abiding memory is whalemeat. Food was in shorter supply after the war than during it and whalemeat came onto the menu to prevent undergraduate starvation. Whether the cooking was at fault or the main ingredient beyond redemption, all my complaints resulted only in my being appointed to the Kitchen Committee.

Another serious shortage was cake, an essential for undergraduate tea. Long queues could be seen in the market place on Saturday mornings waiting for Mr Grodzinski and his weekly supply of cakes, made largely, we thought, of sawdust.

**Robin Crawford, 1950**

Corpus was a great place to learn about wine, although not at all in an academic way. There were none of today's earnest wine-tastings – just a lot of very nice wine and a great deal of expert knowledge available, if one took the trouble to make use of it. This knowledge centred on the brilliant combination of Pat Charvet from High Table and Bert Lawrence in the Buttery. Pat Charvet was half

French and a man of enormous charm, kindness and patience (with rather stupid undergraduates). He used, for many years, to travel annually in France for the purpose of tasting and buying wine for the College that was both good wine and excellent value. Of course, this was mostly for the Fellows since the enormous cellars under two sides of New Court are (as far as I know) mostly reserved for the Fellows. But he also bought equally for the much more limited pockets of the undergraduates. This was where Bert Lawrence came in!

Bert was a quiet, shrewd character whose great hobby was racing. If he knew you were a racing fan he always had a tip or two whenever you entered the Buttery. His success rate at finding winners was not wonderful, but his knowledge of form and breeding was! He would usually give his tips in the form of a pun or a rhyming couplet. But when it came to wine, you were onto a winner every time if you asked him nicely for advice. He knew what each of us could afford (very little in my case) and tailored his suggestions to match it, without being in the least bit condescending. But there were a number of undergraduates who thought they knew a good deal about wine – perhaps they did – and they were not offered advice or help from Bert. In his quiet way, he simply showed them the list of wines and fetched their choices without a comment of any kind. I do believe I knew more about good claret when I left Corpus than at any other time in my life – even now when I can almost afford it!

### P.G.B. Wills, 1952

It was not until the last College party after we had taken our final exams that Michael McCrum revealed that, as Senior Tutor, he had taken over Admissions from the Dean on 1 January 1952, to find to his horror that there were some gaps in admissions for the following September. He spent, he told us, a somewhat hectic few months telling schools that Corpus was, of course, a very exclusive College, with particularly high standards, but if they had an exceptional case, he might just find a place for him that year. People like me, turning up out of the blue, with College connections – not only through Uncle Dick, who was a good friend of Pat Charvet, but W.J.A. Wills (1946) who is my cousin – were something of a godsend.

None of the 1952 entry was able to achieve First Class Honours in any subject, though the College cricket team was almost of County standard.

Many years later, in the 1980s, I was sitting next to the Permanent Secretary of the Foreign Office at lunch, and was able to inform him how some of the tension between India and Pakistan had been ameliorated over the previous decade. When things got a bit tense, 'Sammy' (S.M. Khan (1953)), a Minister in the Pakistan Government would ring 'Natwar' (K. Natwar-Singh (1952)), a Minister in the Indian Government, and between them they would quietly work out a way to calm things down. They would then go to their respective Cabinets and persuade them of the solution they had reached. The thing that surprised me most, I suppose, was that the Foreign Office didn't realise that they had both been at Corpus at the same time.

### David Harkness, 1958

The embellishment of the Coat of Arms above the Fellows dining table in Hall remains less than clear. It must have been in late 1960 or in 1961. It followed generous hospitality in the Lodge… or maybe just after a successful Chess Club evening. The Hall was reached, I think I remember, through the service lift. Tables were built into a pyramid, and chairs were added. Where the paint came from I do not recall. My job was precarious but unskilled: holding a candle aloft so that the artist could pick out in red the lion and unicorn genitals. The work completed, the tables and chairs were restored, more or less to their normal configuration. Nobody had been killed. At breakfast the next morning there was much satisfaction in the illuminated masculinity of the animals in question. Had it really been us who had managed to complete this artistic feat in a less-than-steady state the evening before? An examination of my dinner jacket seemed to bear out the probability. It was covered in candle grease.

### Tom Faber (Fellow), 1953
*Redecoration of the Hall in 1960*

By the late 1950s the Corpus Hall, refloored and redecorated by T.H. Lyon in 1913/14, was more than a little dingy, and, after an attempt to improve it by installing strip lights above the panelling had proved unsuccessful, a committee was set up with complete redecoration as its brief. The committee sought advice from two experts, as well as two other local architects whose names are not mentioned in the committee's minutes. They both recommended that the second row of portraits which hung

Left: *The 'embelish-ment' of the Coat of Arms.*

DIEU ET MON DROIT

above the panelling should go, and that the old electric lights suspended from the ceiling should be replaced by chandeliers. In most other respects, however, their opinions were markedly different.

'The problem is made extremely difficult' wrote David Roberts on 20 November 1959 'due to the lack of authenticity in the materials used for the roof and that the whole room is a version of a Medieval Hall, with the result that the roof has neither the structural force of the Medieval originals nor the elegance of the early nineteenth Century… The most that can be sought is a scheme which resolves the Hall clearly into a roof, walls with panelling and windows. In order to achieve this clarity I suggest:

1 That the entire roof structure… be painted so as to look like wood, with the exception of certain pendants and pieces of carving, which can be picked out in gold. I should like to emphasise that the only colours should be brown and gold.

2 The stone work to the windows should be cleaned with water.

3 All plaster work in the walls should be painted white.' And so on. A small sketch of a carved pendant was attached to show the discreet gilding recommended, and the report concluded as follows:-

'I should like to emphasise that I have considered much richer and more splended schemes, but quite apart from the problem of expense, I am convinced that the architectural form of the roof if emphasised by colour would merely appear flaccid and weak. I feel that my proposal would, if carried out, result in a calm, dignified room.'

The contrasting three-page report by Malcolm Burgess, written in the same month, starts with an extensive 'Historical Note' and ends with a lyrical 'Note on the Drawing', i.e. on the elegant full-sized watercolour of the whole room which he provided. Here are excerpts from the last section.

'It must necessarily be realised that no artist's sketch can ever give an adequate and complete idea of a finished scheme. The play of light and shade, the variation between daylight and artificial illumination, the effect of shadows, the very view-point of the beholder will be ever altering and changing the decorative effect. I have made the sketch flat and undramatic for this very reason. When considering my suggestions, therefore, imagine the grey-blue-green and dull gold patterned wall surfaces in some places glowing lighter, in other

spots appearing quite dark and sometimes fading into the shadows altogether. Imagine the pictures coming into prominence at night with the strip-lighting focused on them and the more brilliant pools of light cast by the chandeliers. By night the walls, the play of light on the gilding and the vermilion colour of the roof should all combine together and produce an impression of richness without vulgarity, sumptuousness without pretensiousness [sic] and interest without profusion.'

The two schemes were not compared by the committee but were presented directly to the Governing Body on 27 November 1959. Needless to say, the Burgess scheme was preferred. I voted against it as did Michael McCrum.

*A private dining society at Corpus.*

A few of the details in Malcolm's 'project [to] recapture the élan and spirit of the Tudor-Gothick era' were subsequently varied. The wallpaper (which was printed specially for the College using original William Morris blocks) became primarily blue and red, rather than grey-blue-green and gold. The 'Crest' or royal arms from Landbeach church, which was to have been left 'in its present state of decoration', was repainted – in part by undergraduates who thought that the heraldic beasts would look even livelier with some vermilion on their private parts. And a picturesque but decayed wooden pelican which had previously been in the Old Court (where now there is a modern replacement for it) was brought indoors, cleaned of old paint and bitumen and re-filled where it had rotted, provided with one new chick, transformed by silver paint, and fixed above the entrance to the Hall in a curious gilded picture frame. But otherwise the Hall as it now is reflects the

designer's original intentions, and whether or not it lacks vulgarity, pretension and profusion remains a matter of opinion.

It should perhaps be recorded, for those who do not remember him, that Malcolm was an ex-foundation scholar of the College of great liveliness and charm, who was elected a Fellow in 1974, only four years before his premature death at the age of 51. In 1959 he was attached to the University of London and studying the Russian theatre, I believe, while devoting a good deal of his energy and enthusiasm to theatrical design. Later, he supervised the redecoration of the New Combination Room and, during his time as a Fellow, of the Chapel. T.H. Lyon and David Roberts were both architects. Roberts was generally respected in 1959 for his restrained treatment of Mallory and Benson Courts in Magdalene, and for other buildings of his in Cambridge, including the shared Corpus/Sidney boathouse.

*1952 pencil drawing of the Hall, by Brian de Grineau.*

Lyon was responsible for the black and white paint which is used to good effect in the Old Court, though some of the subtleties of his original design have been lost in subsequent repainting. He was also responsible for giving the Old Combination Room its present appearance (cf. Plate 20 in Patrick Bury's *History*); here too some subtleties have been lost.

### Tom Faber (Fellow), 1953
#### The Dining of Women

The first woman to have dined in the Corpus Hall is said to have been Lady Bragg, who was invited to a Queenborough Feast when she was Mayor, not long after the 1939-45 war ended, and was deemed for that one evening to be a man. Then (as now) Fellows' wives attended the Dorothy Spens dinner on Corpus Christi day in a different room while their husbands caroused in Hall. Like all Mayors, Lady Bragg must have been asked to nominate councillors to be invited to the same feast, and no doubt she knew enough to nominate male colleagues only. A later (male) Mayor, less well-informed, nominated several female councillors. When he was asked to produce a second list of invitees, several worthy women were deeply offended, and guests attending the feast were faced by a picket of angry feminists as they arrived at the main gate

In 1956 the Governing Body (GB) agreed to a forward-looking proposal that, in addition to the Dorothy Spens dinner, an evening reception should be held in the Master's Lodge to acknowledge the efforts of the wives of married Fellows on behalf of the College. Full evening dress was worn in pre-war style, champagne was offered, and there was dancing to Ken Stevens and his band on floors newly polished with french chalk, a brazier in the garden, and bridge in the Master's study. That event started at 8.30 and finished at 1.00 am and was not preceded by dinner in Hall. It proved so successful, however, that it was repeated two years later and this time there was dinner. (Legend has it that one of the gyps said to Garth Moore beforehand: 'I take it, Sir, that the ladies will be dining at separate tables'.) That too was successful and, the thin end of a wedge having been inserted, Ladies' Receptions at Leckhampton and Ladies' Dinners in Hall (never again followed by dancing) became regular features of the Corpus calendar.

We then moved cautiously to the idea that Fellows might sometimes invite female guests to partake of the normal High Table dinner. That idea was referred to the Hospitality Committee in February 1964, and proposals which would have allowed female guests to dine on up to two specified nights each week were put to the GB; the committee recommended that 'no attempt [should be] made to confine lady guests to any special category but that Fellows should be asked to consider some self denying ordinance with regard to their "nearest and dearest"'. The committee's proposals proved too radical to secure general acceptance, but motions to the effect that female guests who were academic colleagues of their hosts and *not* their wives or fiancées should be permitted on two specified nights per term were passed. The pattern thus established remained essentially unchanged for the rest of Sir Frank's Mastership, despite a difference of opinion as to whether or not the Matron of Addenbrooke's was an academic colleague of the Quick Professor in Immunology.

The arrival in the Lodge of Sir Duncan and his wife Betty, who not unreasonably expected to accompany her husband in Hall from time to time, stimulated fresh thoughts. A motion favouring 'the general principle of non-discrimination in the entertainment of guests in Hall' was passed by a 2 to 1 majority at a GB meeting in April 1972, and after further discussion at the July meeting it was agreed that female guests could in future dine on Mondays, Wednesdays, Thursdays and most Saturdays. Furthermore, it was agreed that such guests could include wives, though Fellows were to 'exercise their good sense about how often'; the relevant minute implies that wives would be welcome on Saturdays (except when there were graduands to be entertained) and not turned away if they appeared from time to time on other nights. Unsurprisingly perhaps, wives were only rarely sighted thereafter, even on Saturdays, but another innovation which we owe to the Wilsons was well supported from the start: I mean the so-called Designated Nights at which Fellows and their wives may entertain married couples. The plan for Designated Nights was approved in November 1973, and there were several female guests at the Queenborough Feast in 1974.

## Michael Weston, 1963

On the day JFK was shot in 1963, I was in my first term at Corpus. Hall was at 7.30 pm and I was running late. I had the radio on in my room and for the previous 30 minutes it was all about President Kennedy, who lay critically ill after being shot. Just as I was racing out of the door, I heard the news that he had died.

I raced into hall, just ahead of the Master and Fellows. The Master, Sir Frank Lee, took the unusual step – either before or after grace, I don't remember – of announcing to us all that JFK had been shot and was gravely ill. I realised at that moment that I was the only person in Hall who knew that JFK had died. In the moment of silence that followed the Master's announcement, I stood up and said: 'Master, just before I left my room to come to Hall, I heard on the radio that John Kennedy has died.' I sat down, and there was complete silence. All that could be heard during Hall was the click click of knives and forks.

Everyone seems to remember where they were when John Kennedy was killed. To us undergraduates, at that time, he was the new hope for a brighter future for the world, and at that moment it seemed as if that hope had been extinguished.

## M.J. Kelly, 1964

I was demonstrating anatomy at Cambridge and supervising in Corpus in 1970. Some twenty of us had finished dinner and gone into the New Combination Room. Dr Harley-Mason had on his right an American guest, who expressed his appreciation for the excellent port. Harley-Mason then declaimed in doom-laden tones that the news from Portugal was pretty bleak for all of us in Cambridge. Met with somewhat blank stares, he elaborated:

'Dr Salazar died today and left-wing iconoclasm may well triumph. *The Times* says that they intend to nationalize their vineyards. Gentlemen, this may be the end of vintage port.'

The American guest enquired anxiously how much port the College had left.

'About two or three pipes,' Harley-Mason said mournfully. He then explained: 'Port is sold in pipes. Corpus buys it in pipes. A pipe contains about 760 bottles.'

'Oh well, then that's alright, isn't it,' his guest ventured. 'No, it isn't. Our stores will only last till the turn of the century, and after 2000 everyone is going to have a pretty thin time of it at Corpus.'

# POSTGRADUATE LIFE

### David Arnold Keys, 1920

A fascinating insight into College life during the years after the First World War can be gleaned from memories recorded by David Arnold Keys. He was the first member of Corpus to gain a Cambridge PhD, which he received in 1922. He was a Canadian physicist who first came to Britain during the War as a naval officer working on explosives. He took that opportunity to work for a short while with Professor Sir J.J. Thomson in the Cavendish and returned in 1920 to work with him on the physics of discharge tubes. His son, now in retirement, is in the process of editing his father's autobiography, the first volume of which has recently been published. He has kindly donated to the College a copy of this volume, which deals with the years to 1924. Life was clearly very relaxed and contact between senior and junior members far greater than it is today. In December 1924, David Arnold Keys married. The first extract deals with his time in College, the second from after his marriage when he lived on Huntingdon Road.

*I wrote to Sir J.J. Thomson telling him I would like to come to Cambridge and received a reply that he had arranged for me to have rooms at Corpus Christi College where his son George was a Fellow.*

*I got an easy chair for my room and a small three-legged stool with a Corpus College monogram carved on the seat, a wooden affair, also a proper electric lamp. I soon found that every day I had a small new loaf of bread, and the bedmaker took away what I did not eat, telling me that it was part of her wages. I was on the same staircase as Sir Geoffrey Butler, my rooms being on the floor above P3. I had a study and bedroom and a gas burner… I made my own breakfast and lunch and had dinner in Hall with the undergraduates.*

*On Friday we had dinner at Pickthorn's rooms at Corpus. He is Dean of College. We met his sister and Mrs Spens and Goodhart, a Fellow of Corpus and an American…. That afternoon a message came for me to attend a banquet at Corpus in Hall. It was a 'Name Day Feast.' I went and met some distinguished people there, including Lord Balfour, the Vice Chancellor of Cambridge, several admirals and a few earls. It was the occasion of the great 'Feast'. Sir Geoffrey told May (Keys' wife) that when I take my degree, Tuesday next, I will be invited to sit at the Fellows table in the dining hall.*

### Bruce McAdam, 1955

As far as I know, the role of Corpus in establishing 'Cavendish Mansions' has not been reported. This links

Fanshawe House, Corpus and Caius with the Cavendish Laboratory in a tale of collegiate Cambridge.

In September 1955 new research students were given rooms in Fanshawe House, which comprised No. 7 (12 rooms) and No. 12 (6 rooms plus housekeeper's flat) Selwyn Gardens. Meals were taken in No.12, although dining in Hall at Corpus at least once a week was encouraged. Close friendships developed; the fourth May boat for 1956 included seven of us. (We were the BA boat, and not very successful.) After the first year most students were expected to find their own lodgings, so in July 1956 we went searching. Three from Fanshawe – Harry Atkinson, John Valleau and I – joined with Ken Davey (Caius) to rent a large house at 7 St Barnabas Road. Harry was the advocate who persuaded the agent that two New Zealanders and two Canadians would look after the house.

Our own corporate life soon developed: dinner was promptly at 7.15 pm, usually with several guests; the rattle of mugs near midnight enticed us from our study/bedrooms for a late gossip; we had a spare attic room for visitors – Jock Hoe was one for many months.

From mid 1957 as each of us finished his thesis or married, our original four moved out and each found a colleague to take his room. John McKellar, Archie Howie, John Silcox were among the second generation to inherit 7 St Barnabas. I left in May 1958, completed my PhD and moved back to New Zealand and thence Australia. Visits in 1970 and 1977 showed that St Barnabas continued as a haven for Cavendish students.

I am not sure when the elderly owner died and the agent moved to sell the house. Archie Howie sought help in finding alternative accommodation from Mr Dibden(?), the Cavendish Secretary. The outcome was surprising; Cavendish bought the house, renovated it, opened two attic rooms formerly used for storage and continued its use as a home for research students. Some years later, when No. 5 St Barnabas Road came on the

*Cavendish House.*

market, they bought that and merged it with No. 7 to provide more rooms.

Renamed Cavendish Mansions, it is smaller than Leckhampton House but, as a development from Fanshawe House in the McCrum years, it began with the same collegiate values that Corpus instilled in its overseas students. The Cavendish Laboratory is no longer just across Free School Lane, but their histories remain linked.

### Peter Lewis (Fellow), 1960
#### Leckhampton, from *A History of Leckhampton*

When, in February 1961, Michael McCrum proposed to the Governing Body that the College should set up a Graduate Research Centre based on Leckhampton House, no similar institution existed anywhere in Britain. Even today, over forty years later, no undergrad-

uate college in Oxbridge has a campus for postgraduates that remotely compares with Leckhampton as it is now. In other words, we are unique – and it is important to know how Leckhampton arose and how it has evolved since its creation. A full *History of Leckhampton*, which will contain many illustrations, is in preparation, but will not be published until well after our 650th anniversary celebrations are over. It seemed appropriate, however, to include here a short history of Leckhampton, with some personal memories of the 1960s when so much was happening so fast.

First, it is important to realise that Leckhampton exists as we know it today only because of the fortuitous coming together of the ideas of two Cambridge academics who never knew each other because they were born nearly a century apart. The first was Frederic William

Peter Lewis.

Michael Noakes
1979-80

Henry Myers, who was born in 1843, and the second is Michael William McCrum, who was born in 1924. Frederic Myers was brought up in Gloucestershire, was a Fellow of Trinity for a number of years, and then became HM Inspector of Schools in 1872. He conceived the idea of building himself a home not unlike many a Cotswold manor house in a rural setting about a mile west of the centre of Cambridge: this home was completed in 1881 on land leased from Corpus. Michael McCrum, who became our Master in 1980, was Tutor at Corpus from 1951 until 1962, during which period he became much involved in University affairs. He served on the Council of the Senate from 1955 until 1958 and on the General Board of the Faculties from 1957 until he left Cambridge in 1962 to become Headmaster of Tonbridge School. During the late 1950s and early 1960s the University was much exercised by two not unrelated problems: the plight of the many University teachers and research workers without College Fellowships and the need to cater satisfactorily for the increasing numbers of research students. In 1960 the University appointed a committee under the chairmanship of Lord Bridges to advise on possible solutions. Michael McCrum was a member of that committee and was particularly interested in ideas for new collegiate structures to help solve both problems. With the death in December 1960, of Louis Clarke, who was the last tenant, the lease of Leckhampton House reverted by prior arrangement to the College in 1961. That gave Michael McCrum the opportunity to put his ideas into practice, and he proposed that we should use the property to create an entirely new type of graduate campus, which would still be part of the undergraduate College. By September 1961 the house had been converted in time to receive its first complement of two Fellows and seven research students before the beginning of the new academical year. By that same autumn the College had agreed to build, in the grounds of the house, accommodation for many more research students and a few more Fellows. This, the George Thomson Building, was opened three years later. The College also began to buy the adjacent houses in Cranmer Road, first No. 17, followed soon after by No. 23, until we owned all the last five properties on the south side.

Another important component in Michael McCrum's proposals was that the College should elect a large number of new Fellows whose primary allegiance would be to the new graduate campus at Leckhampton but would still be full Fellows of the Old House. Changes of statutes were therefore immediately initiated to introduce a sixth category of Fellowship, category F. After the customary long gestation period with the Privy Council, the new statutes came into force, and, on 23 April 1962, eleven new Fellows were admitted. More Fellows were admitted during the next few years and by 1969 the total Fellowship was approximately double what it had been in 1961. Thus it was, during the decade of the 1960s that Leckhampton was born and grew up into something we would recognize today, and that is the period on which this brief history will concentrate. Before that, however, it is interesting to mention a little of the earlier history of Leckhampton House.

In September 1878 F.W.H. Myers took a 99-year lease of one and a half acres of the land that Corpus owned to the west of Cambridge. Frederic Myers, who was brought up in Gloucestershire and went as a dayboy to Cheltenham College, came of a distinguished family. As an undergraduate at Trinity he carried off most of the College and University classical scholarships and prizes. He was elected to a Fellowship in 1864 but resigned five years later. In 1872 he was appointed HM Inspector of Schools, a post he held until shortly before his death in 1901. I think we can safely picture Frederic Myers by the mid-1870s as a member of a wide but select intellectual circle in Cambridge, where he was seriously considering making a permanent home for himself. He chose a plot of land in what was then a rural setting yet within easy reach of the older Colleges. His formative years in Gloucestershire had obviously made a deep impression on him. He appears to have modelled his new home on a type of manor house common in the Cotswolds. Probably because stone was so expensive in East Anglia, the house is built mainly of brick, but stone was used for the important architectural features such as the mullions and the balcony. Even the name he chose for his home when it was built was a reminder of his schooldays: from the playing fields of Cheltenham College, Leckhampton Hill forms a dramatic feature on the skyline, and it seems likely that this memory stimulated him to choose the name he did. He asked his maternal cousin, William Cecil Marshall (1849–1923) to design the house for him. Later Marshall was to design a number of other buildings in Cambridge, both for private individuals and for the University.

It should be emphasized that Frederic Myers had chosen to live out in the country while still remaining within easy reach of the centre of Cambridge. When he bought the lease on the land in 1878, what is now Grange Road contained only three private dwellings and a farmhouse, plus the University Rifle Butts and Armoury, which were sited there specifically to be well away from any habitation. Cranmer Road and Selwyn Gardens did not exist and Selwyn College would not be built for another four years. Nevertheless, Myers would have been within easy reach of the College, for it is approximately three quarters of a mile from the Porter's Lodge at Corpus to the front door of Leckhampton House. Trinity would have been under a mile away – no distance to walk or ride in those days. Leckhampton House was the forerunner of a major development that took place to the west of Queens Road during the next two decades. The House was an important building in its own right: even in 1960 it was still marked by name on the standard one-inch Ordnance Survey map, the

only private dwelling in the whole of Cambridge to be so honoured.

Until his death in 1901 Frederic Myers lived in his new home with his wife, his son Leo Myers, born there in 1881, and two younger daughters. During this period Leckhampton was one of the centres of Cambridge intellectual life, for Frederic knew many of the literary and political figures of the day. Frederic is best known as one of the founder members of the Society for Psychical Research, and many psychical experiments were conducted in the house and in the garden. His wife, born Eveleen Tennant, became a most gifted amateur photographer, and she took photographs of many of the well-known visitors to Leckhampton House. After the death of Frederick Myers, the house had a very chequered occupancy until 1937 when it was let to Louis Clarke, who had been Director of the Museum of Archaeology and Ethnology from 1922 but had just been appointed Director of the Fitzwilliam Museum. In this final phase, Leckhampton House became like an

*1975 ball invitation.*

annex to the Fitzwilliam, which received the bulk of Louis Clarke's splendid collection under his will. Both the first and last of these phases of occupation are fascinating reflections of life in Cambridge and are dealt with at length in the full *History*, but here we must now move on to the events of 1961.

*Felling after a storm at Leckhampton.*

Louis Clarke died in December 1960. The College had bought the remainder of the lease from the executors of Leo Myers in 1949 and had arranged with Louis Clarke that, when he died, the College should gain possession, but only after a specified interval to allow for the disposal of the many treasures stored in his house. In January 1961 his executors intimated to the College that they would be willing to surrender the lease six months early on 25 June 1961. The Executive Body promptly accepted the offer and thus began what proved to be one of the most hectic nine months in the history of the College.

The question of building on our central site was due to be discussed at a meeting of the Governing Body scheduled for 17 February 1961, but shortly after the Executive Body had agreed that we would gain possession of Leckhampton House in June, Michael McCrum circulated a paper proposing that Corpus should establish a 'research centre' at Leckhampton. He envisaged it as an organization 'parallel' to the College but an integral part of it with possibly as many as fifty Fellows (including perhaps a Sub-Master) and fifty research students. There was a preliminary discussion of this paper by the Governing Body on 17 February when a small committee was set up to consider his scheme in more detail. During the next two months there was intense discussion among the Fellowship about the idea of some form of research centre at Leckhampton. The College was then very small with an active Fellowship of only seventeen plus the Master and six Resident Life Fellows. Fellows dined and combined frequently. Furthermore, Tuesday was always a 'Fellows-only' night at which College business was routinely discussed; in fact, College business was usually the major topic at combination on a Tuesday with the Master presiding and most College Officers present, but no guests. As a result of these informal discussions, and of the more formal ones by the committee set up in February, attitudes gradually changed and early in May Michael McCrum circulated a second paper proposing a revised version scaled down to meet fears that the whole project might become too expensive for the College to afford. Thus the number of Fellows was reduced to 25, including a Warden who would be an existing Fellow of the College, but the target number of graduate students was kept at 50. Christopher Longuet-Higgins was elected the first Warden of Leckhampton for a period of five years to run from 1 August 1961. He had been a Fellow since 1954 and was Professor of Theoretical Chemistry. His election as Warden contributed enormously to the success of Leckhampton in its early years.

At a specially convened meeting of the Governing Body held on 13 May 1961 we discussed at great length the second paper by Michael McCrum and a document drawn up by the small committee appointed in February. There was general agreement to use Leckhampton House as a research centre and a much larger committee was appointed to produce a definitive scheme, and their final recommendations were ratified, without dissent, at a special meeting of the Governing Body on Friday, 23 June. Thus, in less than six months, the College had reached a momentous decision, but we had just twelve weeks to prepare Leckhampton House for its first occupants.

Even in 1961 twelve weeks was an extremely ambitious target. Now, 40 years on, it would be impossible. The greatly increased bureaucracy at national, local and College levels would now make twelve months a more realistic target. But we did reach our target—just! That we were able to do so was due largely to the sheer enthusiasm for the whole project shown by everyone involved. The executors' solicitors were very co-operative in that they readily gave us permission to enter the house at any time convenient to us. Thus we were able to survey the house, draw up tender documents, admit building contractors and make all the necessary arrangements to start work on Monday, 26 June, the day that the property became legally ours. Earlier, I had agreed to succeed Henry Chilver, now Lord Chilver and an Honorary Fellow, as Bursar for College Buildings and I therefore took over responsibility for all the work of conversion from its inception: hence my involvement with Leckhampton from the very beginning. The conversion was made more difficult by two unusual innovations of Louis Clarke. He had had an enormous safe constructed to house the most valuable items of his collection, and later, when he became very infirm, he installed a lift to take him up to his bedroom. The safe was a 'walk-in room' with a ceiling and walls of reinforced concrete a foot thick, and the lift, situated roughly where the bar is now, was large enough to take his wheelchair plus his manservant! To demolish the safe took a gang of men with pneumatic drills over a fortnight, and removal of the lift left much remedial work to be done. In spite of all the alterations and renovation required, however, the house was ready for occupation by the third week of September.

The first member of College to move into Leckhampton House was John Roach, who was Domestic Bursar. He describes the circumstances of his move on Wednesday 20 September 1961 in an excellent article entitled *Leckhampton: the early years (1961–1965)* published in the 1984 *Association Letter*. On the day after, several research students moved over from No. 7 Selwyn Gardens. Then Christopher Longuet-Higgins moved in from College and the last of the seven research students arrived, from Canada, on the Sunday afternoon. Incidentally, four of those original seven, and their wives, arranged to meet for a fortieth reunion and spent a very enjoyable and nostalgic weekend at Leckhampton in September 2001. Three of them were from Canada and the fourth from USA. Their reunion confirms both the comradeship engendered by the atmosphere created in Leckhampton House and the high proportion of stu-

*The George Thomson building.*

dents from overseas living there. In those early days the house had something of the air of a pre-war 'country house' about it. Breakfast was served for all nine residents seven days a week, and a good breakfast it was too. It gave ample opportunities for the exchange of ideas between the research students and the Fellows, which resulted in several initiatives that still survive to this day. Thus the 'Sunday teas', which are still a popular institution, started right at the beginning, and about a year later the Stephen Hales Society was formed, originally to provide a forum for research students to talk about their research, but now the speakers are more often Visiting Fellows. Dinner was served two or three times a week, but initially only during term time, and was often followed on Sundays by a musical entertainment.

The provision of extra accommodation for both Fellows and students by building near the House was a key element in the scheme proposed by Michael McCrum. In November 1961 the Governing Body chose Philip Dowson of Ove Arup Associates as the architect for just such a project. A small Building Committee was formed which included two of the resident research students as permanent members with full voting rights: John Earnshaw, a first-year Canadian engineer, and Jim Dodson, a second-year biologist. With the average age of the Fellows on the Building Committee around 40, the advice of the research students was instrumental in making sure that the facilities provided were the best possible for the age group that were going to be the main users. The story of the designing and construction of the new building will be covered more fully in the full *History*. Here it is sufficient to mention that the contract was awarded to William Sindall Ltd, a well-known Cambridge firm responsible for many College and University buildings both before and since. The work was never more than three weeks behind schedule and, with the help of a young architect from Ove Arup who camped out in the building for the last few critical weeks, the building was completed on time – a rare event indeed in the history of College and University buildings in Cambridge. The building was fully occupied by the end of the September and was very appropriately named after Sir George Thomson, who declared it open in October 1964, in the middle of a thunderstorm. By the spring of 1965, six months after the GTB had opened, it became obvious that the Leckhampton complex had reached a 'critical mass' which gave it a corporate identity with a distinctive

life of its own whilst still retaining its links with the Old House. The Games Room on the ground floor of the south block of the GTB, now the Library, became the main focus of social life for the graduate students and was used for a wide variety of activities. An important factor in generating a strong sense of community was having so many Fellows concentrated with the research students together on the one site – a total of thirteen Fellows with 38 graduate students, but for various reasons, mostly financial, the number of Fellows with rooms at Leckhampton was drastically reduced from 1967 onwards.

Many changes have occurred since those early days. Thus total postgraduate numbers have been gradually doubled over the years (from 88 in 1968 to 165 in 2000) as extra accommodation became available from the conversion of adjacent properties in Cranmer Road. In 1968 the new Dining Room came into use and dinners were served there five nights most weeks and a cooked breakfast provided nearly every morning. In 1971 the College began the practice of setting aside each year four units of accommodation, mostly at or near Leckhampton, for the use of academics, who were called Visiting Scholars, now called Visiting Fellows, and many of them played a significant role in life at Leckhampton. In 1977 the University introduced the MPhil degree, which has resulted over the years in more and more graduates taking one-year courses, subtly altering the interests of a significant proportion of Leckhampton residents. In the late 1980s the College took the innovative step of creating the category of Research Associate, aimed at providing a College attachment for Postdoctoral Research Workers. During the 1990s two new societies were started. The first, called the Leckhampton Society, was started by the present Master when he was Warden. It has very informal meetings organized by the MCR at which postgraduates talk about their work. The second is called the Cross Talk Society and is organized by a committee drawn from the Research Fellows and Research Associates. It meets about once a month at Leckhampton and aims to bridge the gaps that have developed between the various academic disciplines. It has a number of members from outside Corpus. Dining habits have also changed, with bar meals served on Monday, Wednesday and Friday instead of a formal set dinner. The bar meals are very informal and have become popular with the postgraduates: the more senior members prefer the traditional format on the Tuesdays and Thursdays.

*Drinking from the horn at the Commemoration Feast.*

## Neil Dunlop, 1960

In the 1960s, Engineering students who passed a qualifying exam in the winter before they came up, could take a full BA at the Engineering Department, in two years. That gave them a third year to do a Part II, or any other subject that would accept them.

They sat the same exams at the end of the second year as all other Engineering students did after three years, so the only way to pack all that learning into the time was to omit Soil Mechanics and take a Long Vac term at the end of the first year.

Having been admitted by Michael McCrum, such was the fate of me, Jock Baines, Tony Bristow, Peter Holliday, and Richard Hall, under the watchful eyes of Dr (later Lord) Chilver, and the late, and much missed, David Maull.

In the months leading up to that Long Vac term, Leckhampton House came back to College management. The garden had been maintained only for a few yards behind the house, and the rest of the garden had been left as jungle for nearly 30 years.

Michael McCrum asked for volunteers, and his sons and a mixed bunch of about eight intrepid explorers, armed with machetes, bow-saws and axes, set out one Saturday morning to hack their way through the forest and see if we could find the remains of the pool. I must emphasize that I am not exaggerating here and all traces of paths had long since vanished under a canopy of bushes, tree trunks and branches. The only way forward was to hack and saw through the growth, taking turns to pioneer, with the others cleaning up and widening the path behind.

Being quite small at the time, the junior McCrums were very useful surveying for short distances ahead by scrambling under the canopy, as the darkness meant we could not see far ahead, or be sure of what was underfoot.

Experts in logistics and planning will have spotted that the first evidence of a lost pool may be that the leading pioneer steps over the hidden edge, and moves rapidly downwards for most of the depth of the pool, into eight inches of black slimy stuff. We had anticipated this, but it was still a shock when it happened, luckily at the shallow end, and not to me.

We pulled the poor chap out, and cleared enough of the edge to see that it was a large pool, with tree trunks up to six inches diameter growing through it. We retraced our steps, with a small excursion to try to find the Rose Garden also mentioned on the plans, and left it to the contractors who arrived shortly after.

I attended various events at Leckampton after that, and marvelled at how quickly the garden had been turned into the haven that it is.

## John Earnshaw, 1961
### *The Canadian Engineers*

We were among the first student residents of Leckhampton House in 1961 when it was first used by the College. In those days we were called 'the Canadian Engineers': Peter Barnard, PhD (1960), Brian Gregory, PhD (1960), and John Earnshaw PhD (1961).

Michael McCrum, as Senior Tutor, had convinced the College to create a new class of Research Fellows and to use Leckhampton as the centre for a new graduate centre. Two Fellows, Christopher Longuet-Higgins and John Roach, prepared to occupy rooms at Leckhampton, and the first graduate students moved in. We three, 'the Canadian Engineers', were among those, and I think we created a rather unexpected lobby group of foreigners who set out to establish instant traditions by our rather brash 'student power'. In a strange un-Canadian way, we initiated a common Sunday Tea to which we invited all residents, Fellows and their families. We suggested that some modern paintings be purchased to update the environment, and the College obliged, even letting Peter make the selection and invite the artists to tea. We found a way to share with each other what our community of Research Students and Fellows was researching by starting monthly meetings of the Stephen Hales Society (a name given by Archie Clark-Kennedy, then the College's most senior Fellow). Brian suggested that a weed-infested lily pond at the foot of the garden be converted to a swimming pool, and we were happy when an interested Fellow, Ronald Henderson, wrote out a cheque to pay for the conversion (before leaving for an appointment in Australia). John was invited to serve on a Building Committee chaired by Sir George Thomson, Master, to locate and design a new Graduate residence, the George Thomson Building, where he was later its first occupant. He remembers the day that Henry Moore knocked on his door to ask for help lifting *Seated Man* (a gift to Leckhampton from Sir Frank Lee, Master and a friend of Moore) from a lorry that he had driven himself from his studio.

### Nigel Long, 1974

If I am remembered, it will be for the time my car ran away and ended up embedded in some new gates at Leckhampton. I was worried about what sort of rebuke I would receive for this. In fact, I received in my pigeonhole a postcard from the Dean which simply said – 'Psalm 24 – Verse 9'. I looked it up and found that this reads – Lift up your heads, O ye gates; even lift them up, ye everlasting doors; and the King of Glory shall come in.

### Eric H. Schallen, 1987

The Master undoubtedly understood the richness that diverse cultures brought to the College, for of four students selected to share breakfast in the Master's Lodge with HRH Prince Philip, three were not from the United Kingdom. Prince Philip was in Cambridge on 7 July 1987 to present honorary degrees to the King and Queen of Spain. I was coached briefly but succinctly on decorum ('Don't speak until you are addressed first', etc.) before the appointed morning. Eight of us – the Chancellor, Vice-Chancellor, Mrs McCrum, an assistant to the Chancellor, three students and myself – sat around a small table. The Chancellor took most interest in the research of Amanda Vincent, a Canadian, sitting across from me, whose study of seahorse behavior would grace the cover of *National Geographic* only a couple of years later. He apparently found pulsed lasers and nonlinear optical fibers less fascinating, so we didn't talk long.

*Henry Moore* –
Seated Man.

### Linne Mooney, 1992

At dinners I met many of the members of college, talking enthusiastically about my research in medieval manuscripts and listening, fascinated, as they told me of their research in economic history, Neanderthal man, Cold War spies, historical botany, twin stars, and other subjects about which I knew even less: electronic engineering, architecture, physics, biochemistry, computer science, and maths. I approved and happily embraced this opportunity for cross-fertilization among fields of research and it has enriched my research since then.

Meanwhile, at Leckhampton, I had been invited to give one of the Stephen Hales lectures, and I attended

*Ball invitation, 1980.*

others given by Fellows of the College, including Chris Andrew and Oliver Rackham. In Leckhampton gardens I learned to play croquet by English rules; and my sons, New England bred and therefore accustomed to the cold water of our recently ice-bound lake, were the first ones into the pool in the spring. I became a regular at the Sunday afternoon teas at Leckhampton, and learned the routine well enough to volunteer to take my turn in setting up and serving them, bringing along chocolate chip cookies for the North American postgraduates to have a taste of home. I also signed up to help with Leckhampton Garden open day, delighted to feel so much a part of the College as it opened its gates to garden-lovers from Cambridge and environs.

### Tarik O'Regan, 2000

Although I was among the last inhabitants of ailing 17 Cranmer Road before the 'Great Refurbishment' of 2000-1, I felt at home immediately in what I soon came to realize as being a mini Oxbridge College. The beautiful grounds, architecture and multi-faceted community together with such domestic niceties as a bar, dining hall, and common room (complete with television), made for an exact, postgraduate (I daren't say elite) microcosm of the main College. The tranquil nature of Leckhampton House and its accompanying buildings also meant a perfect place in which to compose. It was ultimately this environment, coupled with immense support from the College that led to a life-changing decision to go wholeheartedly into music as a career.

# ADMISSION OF WOMEN

**Tom Faber (Fellow), 1953**

*Turbulence over Gate and Guest Hours*

In his sequel to Patrick Bury's *History* of Corpus, Geoffrey Woodhead writes of Sir Frank Lee that his Mastership (1962-71) 'came at a time of great change in both College and University, and, latterly, of considerable turbulence in the academic community as a whole'. A Joint Consultative Committee (JCC) was established by Frank Lee as early as January 1969; he chaired it himself initially but seems to have handed the job to me after my return from sabbatical in America. It was to act as a safety valve, and to reduce the perceived risk that

Corpus students might start to indulge in 'direct action', by providing a forum for discussion between senior and junior members. Several domestic issues were dealt with at its early meetings, but dissent focused on two in particular: those of 'Gate and Guest Hours'. Before long, in the face of persistent pressure by representatives of the JCR, the GB (Governing Body) began to grant concessions – by a substantial majority of votes on each occasion but with noticeable reluctance nevertheless. In May 1969 it was agreed that, while the main gate of the college should continue to be locked at midnight, undergraduate members and guests of either sex in their company could in future pass in and out through that gate until 2.00 a.m. A year later, in May 1970, it was agreed that undergraduates living in college who wished to accommodate male guests overnight could do so in their own rooms provided that all guest rooms were already booked, but that female guests could only be accommodated overnight in the guest rooms in No 8 Trumpington Street.

Under Duncan Wilson, the JCC was replaced by an *ad hoc* committee with the Dean of College as chairman, which was to concentrate entirely on Gate and Guest Hours. Yet, in March 1974 Albert Jaggard, the Head Porter, found a 'Gate and Guest Hours' banner on the roof of the Chapel and risked his life and limb to remove it before any students woke up.

In June 1975 the *ad hoc* committee was in its turn replaced by a 'Guest Hours Committee', with me as chairman, and following much further dialogue a motion was presented to the GB in January 1978, that 'This College would like to see the Guest Hours regulations amended to remove the distinction between

*Graduation Day.*

men and women guests'. By that date, allegedly, guests of either sex were allowed to stay overnight in 16 of the other colleges in Cambridge. The motion was debated at a subsequent GB meeting, in March 1978, and was defeated by the narrowest of margins. The Senior Tutor felt able to include one further concession in his revised regulations dated May 1978. His notice, which makes clear that camp beds were available on request, specifies that female guests may stay overnight in rooms other than guest rooms (and presumably in college rather than in No 8 Trumpington Street) provided that their hosts have previously secured permission from the Senior Tutor or Dean of Chapel; *however*, permission will not be granted unless the officer concerned is satisfied that arrangements have been made for guest and host to sleep in separate rooms. (Limits on the number of nights for which a guest might stay are defined in

the same notice, but such limits applied equally to males or females and were meant to inhibit undesirable squatters, suspected of taking drugs, rather than co-habitation.)

The last rounds in the battle are represented by an unsuccessful plea from the JCR, dated February 1980, for the introduction of a 'late key system as in several other Colleges', and by a motion passed by a large majority at a JCR meeting in December 1980. The latter protested once again about 'discrimination against women' in the regulations for guests; it pointed out that female guests might well be mothers or sisters rather than girlfriends; and it rehearsed an old argument, that the rules were regularly broken with impunity. But it concluded with what reads like a wail of despair: if only the College were to go co-educational the issue would be resolved.

The statutes of the University were revised to make mixed colleges possible in 1965, and King's College was admitting female Fellows, and presumably female students, by 1970. I have no doubt that the idea that Corpus might in due course follow suit was regularly discussed between individual Fellows from then on, but it took several years to surface at a GB meeting. Those who had served under Sir Will Spens were apt to quote his view that if Corpus was not in the van of progress it had better be in the rearguard; and I doubt if the idea of a mixed Corpus appealed to Frank Lee, though he worked hard to bring the college's statutes up to date in other ways.

A letter from a Life Fellow concerning Guest Hours which was circulated to members of the Governing Body (GB) during the Lent Term of 1978 contained the following remark: 'I think the time has probably come when the College should start admitting women on a par with men, or at least planning to do so'. It was with that remark in mind that five active Fellows wrote to the Master in April 1978 to propose that the statutes of Corpus should be changed to enable the college to admit not only female students but also female Fellows. Their letter was discussed by the GB in July 1978. 'The view was [then] expressed that the admission of women was a subject which had been left on one side for many years without bad effect for the College [and that] to consider it at this point would only revive dissensions caused by the debate on Guest Hours'. Nevertheless a working party was set up to examine the implications of going mixed. Its report was discussed in March 1979 and more thoroughly, with Life Fellows present, in the following May. By then the JCR and MCR had been informed and had both voted strongly in favour of the proposed change. Similar proposals were said to have been discussed in all the other colleges in Cambridge, of which two had decided to remain all-female and four to remain all-male.

To change the statutes of the College requires a two-thirds majority, and a straw vote taken after the discussion in May suggested that this might not be forthcoming. The proposal was shelved in consequence, though on the understanding that it would be kept under review. In the event it was not brought forward again until the next Master (Michael McCrum) had been in office for a year: it was presented, together with numerous supplementary papers, to a meeting of the GB attended by Life Fellows in October 1981. Curiously enough, opinion in the JCR seems to have swung against co-residence during the two-year delay, but the number of Fellows who abstained from voting for the relevant motion was much smaller than had seemed likely in 1979. The first two female Fellows were admitted in October 1982, and the first female students in October 1983.

The chief thing I remember about the first lot of girls whose studies I directed is that most of them were mad keen on rowing and came to supervisions with their hands in bandages because of blisters.

### From *Association Letter* 51, 1972

At the annual Queenborough Feast in February, ladies were admitted as guests for the first time in honour of Mayor Jean Barker. As a sign of gratitude for the dangerous excellence of the hospitality on this occasion, she presented the College afterwards with a small silver box to hold saccharine tablets (thus enabling Fellows to refrain from excessive consumption of sugar).

### Diane Dawson, 1982

Over drinks, soon after Charlotte Erickson and I had been admitted as Fellows of Corpus, Bernard Williams, then Provost of Kings, was speculating on why Colleges late to elect women as Fellows regularly elected American women as their first female Fellows. I boringly suggested supply and demand: in the late 1970s and early 80s there were relatively more American than English women academics. He had a better explanation. To the male College Fellows who had opposed admission of women for so long, American females were not really women – having to sit next to one at High Table would not be like sitting next to a real woman like your daughter, wife or mother. Corpus fits the Williams pattern!

After the trauma of, for the first time, having to write a female name (in Latin) on a voting slip, they discovered they had elected a card-carrying member of CAMRA. At the request of the new Fellow, beer appeared on the drinks tray in the Master's Lodge. Perhaps my finest hour (in the service of the College) was the defence of the Eagle Public House. The defence was necessary because some of the senior Fellows of the College wanted to close the pub (get rid of uncouth beer drinkers) and turn that historic building into a music practice room or boutique. For a year the battle was fought in the Investment Committee, the

Executive Body, the Governing Body, on the streets and in the pubs. With Chris Howe and Raymond Page we founded the 'Interested Users Committee' and we succeeded. Corpus Christi was founded by the City to serve the City. Their first woman Fellow followed in this tradition, fighting for the preservation of an historic City institution.

### Davina Anderson, 1983

My first memory of Corpus was coming up for an interview in the Autumn of 1982. My first interview was with Peter Lewis, and another Fellow who was a biochemist. I was completely unprepared for the first question which was 'so how does it feel to be the first woman interviewed in this college for 650 years?' The next interview with Hew Strachan was also a bit bewildering; I was all ready for some questions about my extracurricular interests and plans for my 'Gap year', but instead we discussed the ways in which women might be made to feel welcome in the College, and various aspects of adapting facilities to women's needs. It was true that I had always been in co-educational schools, but I had never given a thought to the possibility that the process of transition might be rather daunting for anyone else running an institution.

Coming up to Corpus the following October seemed a bit unreal. We all joined in with whatever was going and I never really noticed that in fact we comprised a very small proportion of the college members. There always seemed to be visitors, the Porters were delightful (Taff immediately – and embarrassingly – coined the nickname 'Fairy Princess' for me, which he delighted in passing on to my future husband, 15 years later!) and no-one seemed to mind that I misplaced my keys at regular intervals.

The College authorities were eager to please and when we asked why there wasn't a fridge on every floor, they just appeared overnight.

*Students studying in the Butler library.*

As my surname was Anderson, I was the first to be interviewed, the first to graduate in 1986 and the first woman to be congratulated at the door by Mr Miller, head porter at the time. I suddenly realised – belatedly, in that rush of my heady undergraduate days – that I had participated in the history of the College, and it had almost passed me by. It was with some determination that when I returned to do my PhD at Cambridge, I made sure that I registered with Corpus again, and eventually joined that solemn procession from Old Court down King's Parade to the Senate House for the last time.

### Kate Langford, 1983

The chance to be among the first intake of female undergraduates was what sealed Corpus as my first choice, and the reality did not disappoint. Most of the older, male undergraduates were delighted to see women in college, and the 'uncle' system worked particularly well in providing us all with an entry into the necessarily male-dominated college life. Of course, there were a few men who were known to have opposed the admission of women, but the majority of them soon appeared to be won over and we were treated with much affection. I remember gloomily taking my place for a Commemoration Dinner, where I had been seated next to a Fellow known to be one of the women's fiercest opponents. I thought I would be ignored all evening and dreaded the prospect. In fact he was utterly charming and entertained me with stories of the Mitford sisters.

I took to rowing, and the success (or otherwise) of that first women's four became something of a point of pride to the male members of the Boat Club. On the eve of the Fairbairns Race several of them sneaked off up the river and, under cover of darkness, painted a pel-

ican and the slogan 'Go IV it Corpus' on the railway bridge adjacent to the Pike and Eel. I remember the cox shouting this out to us and the tremendous boost it gave us as we rowed by.

When asked what the admission of women had meant to them, to a man the older male members of college would lament that the partitioning of the Crystal Palace (the communal Old Court bathroom) had meant the end of the Edwardian dinner plate showers. To all those thus deprived I apologize, and I hope that with the passing of the years you now feel it was a reasonable price to pay.

### Crispin Rapinet, 1983

I think that there were certain Corpus institutions such as some of the older or gayer Fellows or the Chess Club who had some difficulty with the concept of admitting women, but ultimately the reality proved less frightening in the flesh than it might have appeared to some on paper.

We were lucky that the first Corpus women were a great bunch. Intellectually far superior, socially adept and generally perfectly capable of showing the blokes how to enjoy life at university to the full. The admission of women was a very constructive and positive experience for Corpus. Because we were, for whatever reason, a year that got on very well together, irrespective of our different interests, it just kind of happened without any great hullaballoo. The bar was a relatively civilized place to go for a drink towards the latter part of the evening, and the formal dinners in Hall were much improved by a spot of feminine company, which went some way – though not all the way I am pleased to record – towards restraining the laddish behaviour of the more diehard breadroll throwers.

# ACROSS THE DECADES

*Michael McCrum.*

**Michael McCrum, 1946**
**Master 1980–94**

Amid the multitude of personal memories over fifty years as a member of the College, rowing and the river come first to mind since rowing continues to be the most popular sport with both men and women undergraduates. I had had enough of being shouted at in boats as an ordinary seaman in the RNVR during naval war-service. However, I thought, when I was appointed Second Tutor in 1950, that perhaps after all I should learn the art of rowing so as to share the agony and the ecstasy of the many College oarsmen. When no one from the College was looking, I launched myself in a sculling boat twice from the boathouse, but on both occasions rowed only a few feet before tipping over and capsizing, to the evident delight of some old men sitting on the bank opposite. I concluded that I was not cut out for rowing. On another occasion, following the first womens' boat on my bicycle, I rode at full speed into the river at Grassy Corner in my effort to avoid collision with a mother pushing her baby towards me in a buggy. Members of the College who witnessed this debacle told me later that I surfaced smiling, which surprised me. Being much involved as Senior Treasurer of the Amalgamated Clubs, I was of course closely involved with the building of the new Corpus–Sidney boathouse, an innovation in architectural style at the time.

The most memorable College event of my early years as Tutor was, of course, the celebration of the College's sexcentenary in 1952. Though this is fully recorded in the 1951 Letter, it is perhaps worth drawing special attention to the ox-roasting on the College playing fields during the afternoon, simply because it so nearly did not happen. The ox, presented to the College by the city of Corpus Christi, Texas, was prevented by the then Ministry of Food from being delivered to the College because it contravened the food rationing legislation. To circumvent this the ox was flown to Eire, cut up into four large pieces and thus allowed entry and given an appropriate welcome by the many members of the College who had come together for the occasion.

Two other much less important, but significant, events during my Tutorship were the discovery of the so-called Marlowe portrait in 1954 and the visit of two Russian research students in 1956. I was sitting in my room on A staircase one afternoon when an undergraduate brought me a rather dusty picture, painted on wood, of a young man in sixteenth century dress, which he had found in the Bursar's garden on a pile of builders' rubbish thrown out from the Master's Lodge after the departure of the retiring Master, and which he thought might be of interest. Through the thick dust it was possible to make out an inscription: *Aetatis suae 21 Anno Domini 1585, Quod me nutrit me destruit*. Since Marlowe was born in 1564 and the Latin inscription seemed appropriate, it was at least possible that this was a por-

trait of the playwright. So we took the portrait to Professor Bruce Dickins and he insisted that the picture should be cleaned and restored. Since then, although there has been no further evidence of its identity, the picture has hung for many years without title in the hall and has become the accepted portrait of the playwright and improperly reproduced in several books as such. [Nb Peter Hall has a slightly different version of events.]

The event that concerned two Russian research students has a certain historical interest. N.K. Kochetkov and E.A. Mistrukov came into residence in the Lent term of 1956 to work with Dr John Harley Mason. They were among the first, if not the first, Russian students to come to Cambridge after the war, and it was regarded as a feather in John's cap that they had come with the express intention of learning about his work in organic chemistry.

On arrival they proved difficult, insisting they should share only one of the two rooms that they had been allocated in Fanshawe House. In order to persuade them that it was normal for each student to have a separate room I finally had to dress formally in my cap and

*Snow in New Court.*

gown and order them to accept. At the time I thought that Kochetkov simply wanted to keep a close eye on Mistrukov's activities. However, despite his suspicions of the College intentions and dislike of such luxury, they gave in.

Mistrukov, the younger of the two, soon made friends and settled into College life. Meanwhile on the international scene Russia invaded Hungary in the autumn of 1956, and Cambridge was invited by the government to admit some fifty Hungarian students who with many others had fled their homeland. We were asked to admit one such and were glad to welcome Peter Nagy. Some time later, in the following Lent term, walking through King's to the Backs one afternoon I observed Elektron Mistrukov punting Peter Nagy along the river and wondered how this had come about. Mistrukov later explained that he had arranged the trip so as to give himself the opportunity to apologize privately for Russia's appalling behaviour. Subsequently, when the time came for the Russians to return to Moscow, Mistrukov wanted (but was not allowed) to stay in England.

Mention of Leckhampton reminds me of many aspects of my activities on or around the College playing fields, both as an undergraduate and later as Senior Treasurer of the Amalgamated Clubs. I arranged the planting of the trees on the south and west side of the fields, persuaded the College to build a second and more modern squash court, incidentally giving Sandy Wilson, member of the College and later distinguished architect of the British Library, his first commission. It was also through trespassing as a student into the adjoining garden at Leckhampton to recover mislaid rugger or tennis balls (while it was let to Louis Clarke, the Director of the Fitzwilliam Museum) that I first discovered the wonders of the garden, including the disused swimming pool submerged by weeds and shrubs. So that when the property reverted to the College sooner than expected when Dr Clarke died in 1961, my idea of developing a postgraduate campus there and keeping that splendid garden for College use was seized and implemented by the Master and Fellows. A further memory of that redevelopment was the great luncheon picnic we had one summer's day for all those undergraduates and others who helped me and my family to clear the swimming pool of all those decaying trees and bushes that had masked its existence in recent years.

So much for tutorial memories, with one last occasion: my first visit to Canterbury Cathedral in attendance with the Master, Sir George Thomson, and the Librarian, Mr Patrick Bury, as guardians of the College's Canterbury gospels at the enthronement of Michael Ramsey as Archbishop in 1961. On that, the first of three similar and subsequent visits, we became involved, while we were waiting at the west end for the long procession of priests and choir to take their places, in a discussion with the Dean and Chapter, represented by the redoubtable Canon Shirley, of the morality of the College's retention of the Gospels given us by Archbishop Parker. This ended suddenly with the arrival of the new Archbishop at the west door and Canon Shirley's final loud remark: 'Morality be damned!'

Another memorable visitor to Cambridge was the former President of the USA, Ronald Reagan. Invited by the President of the Union to address them, he spoke with unexpected fluency and expertise, thus giving the lie to the view promoted by the British media, particularly the television series 'Spitting Image', which normally pictured him as completely brainless. Since the President of the Union that year was Martin Harris, an undergraduate at Corpus, I was well placed at lunch to converse with Reagan, and he gave me a detailed account of his famous argument in Iceland with the Russian President, Mikhail Gorbachev.

### Geoffrey Styler (Fellow), 1948

I was admitted to a Fellowship in Chapel after evensong early in March 1948. The Master, Sir Will Spens, gave the address himself; Michael McCrum was an undergraduate chapel-warden at the time, and Peter (now Sir Peter) Marshall was the pillar of the choir. It was a great satisfaction to me that exactly fifty years later, both of them were again able to be present at the party to celebrate my 50th anniversary as a Fellow. By then they were both of them honorary Fellows, and at the service each read a lesson. The only thing in Spens's address that we could remember was a reference to 'the commonly held opinion that one cannot serve God and Mammon.' Himself widely involved in public affairs, he was at the same time a totally committed Christian, utterly realistic and also highly principled: and to the problems of combining effective action and Christian loyalty he gave a lot of thought and could give much useful advice. One biblical text that I am sure he never challenged was 'Be ye cunning as serpents.'

My wife Audrey and I received a warm welcome from the Master and his wife Dorothy, as well as from the Fellows and their wives, in particular: Patrick and Betty Bury, who were the first to invite me to a meal in their house, Archie and Phyllis Clark-Kennedy, our predecessors as tenants of Middleton Cottage and Pat and Eleanor Charvet, and Professor and Ivy Vincent; he was invariably 'Vinca' even to his family. To me they were all Olympian figures, no less so as we got to know and love them. The College can never have had so fluent and entertaining a conversationalist as Archie, and so courteous and impressive a President as Pat Charvet, nor a Fellow with such a sharp wit as Vinca.

In the sexcentenary celebrations of 1952, the highlight was the barbecue of an ox, at a time when the meat ration was still only 2/6d a week. It was given by the members of a club in Corpus Christi, Texas and one of their number (Mr Buster Sheehy) came to supervise the sauce. After his departure, Mr Garth Moore observed one evening that he thought we ought to return the visit. 'Would the college pay for me to go to Corpus Christi, Texas?' he asked. 'Certainly,' replied Vinca; 'One way.'

Two other laconically colourful characters were Dr George Carter, the long resident bachelor guru of the college, and Professor Bruce Dickins. George once observed cheerfully, on about 10 June: 'Another fortnight, and the nights will be closing in;' and Bruce Dickins, when asked who might know the answer to a question that defeated him, replied, 'Shouldn't think anyone does if I don't.'

Have things changed much? A certain stiffness was characteristic of the College when I first knew it, and there has been a great relaxation. Spens, though essentially a very kind man, was precise and correct. He talked freely, interestingly and authoritatively on many subjects, but outside those he became silent. He liked to move as soon as possible into the NCR. When the time drew near to elect his successor, almost the only criterion we identified was that he should be someone who ate more slowly. But since everybody did, that didn't help. The Fellowship was much smaller; I think there were just eighteen of us. Inevitably with the growth of numbers we became more diffuse. But there has been no real drop in the number of colourful characters and of friendships.

Many members of staff over the years in all departments have given warm friendship and I can mention only a few. Reg Hayward, the groundsman, who com-

bined the highest standard of conscientious efficiency with a gentle and playful kindness; Bert Lawrence the Buttery manager, who also took immaculate care of the Chapel linen; Curtis, the prima donna kitchen manager, who attacked with a knife and fork any food that the undergraduates returned uneaten to check that there was nothing wrong with it; Collins in the college office, who also waited at High Table, and Bernard Lucas, already Bursar *de facto*, who later on became a Fellow and Bursar by name; and there have been numerous secretaries, some of great distinction.

The first Head Porter that I knew was Harry Cator, an impressive figure with the smoothest of manners and always the best of explanations for being unable to do what you wanted. He was tall and athletic and had been a proctor's 'bulldog'. It was said that he was once on the

*Flowers in Hostel Yard.*

heels of a gownless Corpus undergraduate and called out 'You must run faster, sir, or I shall have to catch you.' The story sounds apocryphal but it was vouched for in my hearing by his actual proctor, the Revd Percy ('Perks') Gardner-Smith, for many years Dean of Jesus. Cator was succeeded by Chapman, less colourful and in the admiring words of Spens himself 'damned efficient.' The confidence was obviously shared by a timid colleague who was on duty one breakfast-time when a small fire was reported from a gyp-room. 'Did you have to deal with it?' I asked him sympathetically. 'No, sir' he replied, 'I knew Mr Chapman would be arriving at 9 o'clock so there was no need.'

For many years Fellows still had the services of gyps. About the last to survive was Ormond Jones, who died recently and is remembered with unusual affection. He had been butler to our benefactor, Aubrey Bateman, and when Bateman died, Dr John Roach, who was Domestic Bursar, promptly realized that such a rich man must have had an excellent butler; so he went to Exeter, without

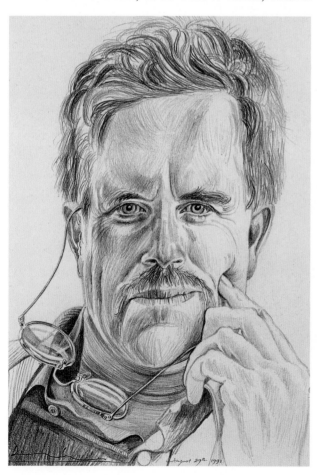

delay, and engaged him as a gyp. Ormond stepped easily into the rôle and its legends. *Inter alia* he reproved the Dean, Roland Walls, telling him that he ought to spend more on his shoes. My gyp was George Lewis, the last of those with a long history behind them. He would arrive in the morning to waken me; in cold weather he would light the gas fire and put my clothes in front of it to warm, quite unworried by the many patches my shirts had collected from my mother in those days of post-war shortage. He came again in the evening to return my shiningly cleaned shoes, draw the curtains and turn down the bed. He was not usually at a loss for words. I showed him once some new cushions of a bright green that I had bought, and asked if he liked them. 'Very nice, sir' he replied, adding 'and they'll tone down in time, sir!' One evening as we came out from dinner in Hall, Garth Moore who was wearing a rather garish pullover asked me if he needed to change before going to coffee with Sir John and Lady Lennard-Jones. 'Let's get the expert opinion,' I said and referred the question to George Lewis. His reply was masterly: 'Coffee with a Fellow? Yes, sir; coffee with a Fellow and his wife? No, sir!'

The College has had some great butlers: Matthews was close to retirement when I first knew the College, but I met him enough to recognize his stature. Sir Desmond Lee told me that when he became a Fellow, Matthews said he needed to know how many glasses of port the new Fellow was expected to drink in combination, and left no doubt that the expected answer was 'one'. The best story I heard about him was from an old member. An undergraduate found a caterpillar in his salad and showed it to Matthews. 'You can't eat that, sir,' said Matthews, taking the plate away. He came back with it saying, 'You can eat it now, sir; the chef has cut it up for you.'

But the age of great men is not past. Ron Storey, our present butler, has given his permission to relate one insightful saying: as we were filing in for dinner past the Butler, a guest asked whether we observed protocol strictly. The question was passed to me and I temporized, 'Oh yes, a certain amount,' I admitted, and not to sound too daunting added, 'But we laugh at ourselves a bit also, don't we, Ron?' 'Yes, sir,' he replied, with his unfailing dignity; 'and with good reason, sir!'

### Oliver Rackham (Fellow), 1958
Although the Senior (non-retired) Fellow and author of the first article in this book, I cannot claim to go back to

*Opposite: Sir George Thomson, Master, 1952–1962.*

*Left: Oliver Rackham.*

1352 on personal reminiscence. I first encountered Corpus Christi College as a shivering scholarship candidate in December 1957.

My performance in the examinations convinced me that I would never see Corpus again, and had better make the most of my brief experience of life in Cambridge. I see from my diary that I was fascinated by dry rot in the New Court and its ecology. The College in the 1950s had treated its historic buildings with clumsiness. New Court had been cleaned by soaking the stonework with thousands of gallons of water. Wilkins, the original architect, who evidently had a soft spot for the dry-rot fungus, had favoured counter-battened construction, with hidden timbers buried in the brick core of the walls, which gave it an excellent habitat once the moisture content had been brought up to a certain level.

Whilst astonished to have been accepted, the transition to Cambridge came as a liberation. My schooldays had been oppressive but at Cambridge I entered the free world. Nobody noticed, still less cared, whether I went through the motions of playing rugby on a Thursday afternoon or not. Independence was no longer a vice to be hidden. An interest in fungi or medieval Latin no longer had to be cultivated secretly and alone.

My first action in Cambridge was to halt before my door and read my name painted on the lintel – *painted* by a craftsman who did such things, not as now printed by a computer on to a bit of sticky tape. My second was to enter my rooms, now part of the Development Office, and marvel at how a mere student was expected to expand and fill such a stately lodging. My poor books, delivered in a trunk by the railway lorry, took up less than one shelf of the built-in bookcases. My third action, prompted by a smell issuing from the bedroom, was to draw my knife and plunge it to the hilt in the suspiciously cracked skirting-board. I thereupon sent for the Bursar and informed him of an outbreak of dry rot. His workmen thereupon pulled the room to pieces (we would now call it 'refurbishing'), soaked it in Wykamol®, and departed, warning me not to smoke in bed until the fumes had dissipated, which I took as an insult. As a result, I was let off paying room-rent for that year. (The College accounts included a special Dry Rot Fund until c. 1970.)

Others will pay better tribute than myself to the distinguished people who crowded the College in 1958. Sir George Thomson, the Master, combined generous hospi-

*The 1968 May Ball – The present Master and his wife are seated fifth and sixth from the left.*

tality and terrifying learning; he gave lunch to every undergraduate in the course of a year; his conversation was what one would expect of the discoverer of electron diffraction and a Nobel Prize-winner, and was all the more impressive to one like me who was trying to be a physicist. It was Tom Faber who gave me the very sound advice to become a botanist. My tutor at first was John Lucas, who interrupted a distinguished career at Merton College, Oxford for that purpose. George Carter – whose infant head had been patted by Alfred Russel Wallace, discoverer of evolution – was my Director of Studies. John Harley-Mason was my formidable supervisor in organic chemistry, a man of wit and raconteur of strange experiences. Theodore Boorman, Quaker and Roman Catholic, rode to hounds and was a harper and a remarkable performer upon his beautiful harpsichord. The Dean of Chapel was Peter Walker, who (as he put it) was a freshman like me,

and is a lifelong friend. Geoffrey Styler, if he will allow me to say so, has changed little over the years, except for the gradual perfecting of his gifts as divine, preacher, precentor, and pianist. Among College staff I remember with particular affection my bedmaker, Hilda Schweitzer, an exile from Austria, who was delighted to encounter a student who spoke Austrian-German.

The climax of the Cambridge year was in November, with Poppy Day coming hard on the heels of Guy Fawkes Night. Guy Fawkes Night was the last vestige of the unhappy centuries when the students would go out and beat up the townspeople. Riots centred on the market place: stalls and huts would ignite, and the home-made fireworks, year after year, came more to resemble home-made bombs. Fire-engines and ambulances were busy. Ever-increasing threats and persuasions from the College authorities, proctors, and police

had no visible effect, and it seemed inevitable that someone must be killed, until, in 1961, this desperate event mysteriously collapsed – to be replaced, many years later, by the peaceful and magnificent civic fireworks on Midsummer Common.

Poppy Day was an occasion of pomp and pageantry for the ostensible purpose of collecting alms for Earl Haig's Fund for Distressed ex-Servicemen. The present Rag Day is but a pallid shadow of its glory. My own part was that of a humble seller of roast chestnuts, but the College was adorned with Henry VIII and sundry of his wives, occupying the empty niches on the façade of New Court. Bizarre events involved a contest in piano-smashing: reducing a scrap pianoforte (against time) to fragments which would pass through a nine-inch pipe.

As a Scholar, I attended College feasts, which introduced me to unknown realms of pleasures of the flesh.

189

The food was not noticeably superior to what it is now, although different. Turtle soup, awash with curious little gobbets of green meat, appeared on the menu until the mid-1960s; a great turtleshell, labelled for the Commemoration of Benefactors 1910, then still hung in the kitchens and now languishes among the College archives. The wine was fabulous. The menu for the Commemoration of 1959, which lies before me as I write, shows that Château Margaux 1947 passed down my unappreciative throat.

Wine in general was better than it is now. Château d'Yuqem itself could be had over the Buttery hatch, but, alas, a poor student could not run to 15 shillings a bottle. There was less variety then, and wines from other hemispheres were unknown. As far as I remember, the acidulated fluid now mysteriously called College Port had not been invented. However, people could be prevailed upon to attend sherry parties, standing around for hour after hour sipping cheap sherry and doing nothing in particular.

Another change is the decay of New Court. My undergraduate photographs show that (apart from the replacement of the pinnacles and certain parapets) the Ketton stone, after cleaning in 1952, was almost perfect as Wilkins had left it. Since then the carved features have been attacked by surface solution, exfoliation, and cavernous decay, and the College has been involved in expensive and drastic replacement. Why should the stone have lasted 140 years and then fallen to pieces in the next 40? Acid rain is not the answer: it was almost certainly more prevalent before 1960 than since. In Old Court the clunch stone, badly decayed by 1920, changed little from then on until a slight resumption of decay in the 1990s. Clare College, the oldest Ketton building in Cambridge, more than twice the age of New Court, is still almost perfect.

*Geoffrey Bushrell, Sir Duncan Wilson and Oliver Rackham show Prince Philip part of the College Plate.*

*The area between the west range of the Old Court and Corpus Buildings, formerly a series of back-yards, has become an irregular quadrangle of more distinguished appearance than some people had anticipated, with the new Combination Room at the South end, and the Old Court – cleaned down and repointed but not rough-cast – on the East. It has been decided to rebuild the bridge connecting P staircase with 58 Trumpington Street, which was never intended for display, to make a satisfactory North side; and the College has to find a name for the new little Court.*

*On a site somewhat to the south of this stood Saint Bernard's Hostle, which was purchased by the College for an hundred marks during the mastership of William Sowode (1523–44), about which time the hostles were disappearing or being merged in colleges. That it was subsequently used for the accommodation of students appears from a College Order dated July 27th, 1624, whereby any Fellow, scholar or student of what degree soever who went in or came out by the door of the hostle after the doors of the College were locked was ordered to pay a fine of a book or books worth twenty shillings to the library. But by Masters' time, St Bernard's Hostle had disappeared, for he says in his History that is 'stood in the back-yard (still called the Hostle-yard) fronting the Great Street (of which probably the present Stables were some part).'*

*The Executive Body has decided to revive this old association, without reintroducing the seventeenth-century gate-fine, and the new Court is to be known as Hostle Yard.*

My career as a student was largely determined by members of other Colleges: I am forever in debt to Clifford Evans, Peter Grubb, and the late David Coombe, William Palmer, Harold Whitehouse – and Sir Harry Godwin, in whose company I find myself pictured in the corresponding volume for Clare College. But Corpus, then as now, was a small College with people of many talents and interests, willing to share their knowledge with those outside their fields of specialization, hospitable to dissidents and people with unconventional combinations of interests. It was to be the perfect home for a general practitioner of science, such as myself.

## Robert McCrum, 1972

I was born in 1953 at 8, King's Parade. My father, Michael, was the recently-married Senior Tutor. For a happy family, Cambridge in the fifties and sixties was a kind of paradise. Possibly the highlight of what, in hindsight, seems like one long summer was the long hot day in 1961 when my father led an undergraduate work party to clear the wilderness at the bottom of the garden in the newly acquired Leckhampton. I remember the excitement when, almost a scene from a children's fairytale, the crumbling stonework of that lost Victorian swimming pool emerged from beneath the brambles.

When I came up as an undergraduate in 1972, the Leckhampton garden had been tamed and the pool restored to its former condition. Quite a few of the Fellows I remembered from childhood, especially Geoffrey Styler, Garth Moore and John Harley Mason, were still very much in residence; their presence made the place (already a kind of home to me) seem doubly familiar. Some of the College servants, notably Mr Bert Lawrence and loyal Mr Ormond Jones, were another comforting reminder of the 50s. Albert Jaggard had become Head Porter, but I was dismayed to discover that our previous acquaintance made him no more indulgent to my undergraduate misdemeanours.

As a freshman in 1972 I became involved in staging a production of Marlowe's *Tamburlaine The Great* in the College Hall. It was then that my year left its mark. We discovered, during the dress rehearsal, that the chandelier suspended above High Table was casting an irritating shadow on the features of Tamburlaine (Michael Bywater) and his captive king Bajazeth (Francis Maude). There was only one thing to be done. Someone went to a hardware store and bought a meat hook. With a tremendous effort, we used the hook to loop the chain suspending the chandelier back on itself, lifting it clear of the spotlight's beam. None of the Fellows on the High Table beneath ever noticed, and the hook was still in place when I came down in 1975.

To my secret delight, the hook remained *in situ* throughout my third decade of Corpus memories. This was during my father's decade as Master. Previously, my perspective on the College had been as a child, and as a student. Now I was seeing it from the secure and comfortable vantage point of the Lodge. With its beautiful garden and splendid public rooms, this must be among the best addresses in Cambridge, a house brilliantly designed (by

*Newnham House.*

Wilkins) to catch the light throughout the day and, behind that rather unpromising front door in the dankest corner of the New Court, to provide the Master and his family with a home at the heart of the College.

### Michael Patrick Spens, 1960

I arrived at the College in 1960, to read Architecture. By then I had deferred entry by a year in order to spend two years as an infantry officer abroad. I had won distinction rowing at Eton, but in those two years contrived to forget the sport and never joined the College Boat Club or even found the Boat House. Architecture became a life, supported by Corpus connections, tutored by Sandy Wilson (later Professor Sir Colin St John

Wilson RA), and imbued with the excellence of that vintage. I soon found my way to Newnham House, where the Lawrence family discreetly reigned, and despite their wise counsel, and that of the Fellows, I got married early in my third year, ushered by Peter Cavanagh, Billy Whitbread, Hughie Gathorne-Hardy, Nick Hare and, with much head-shaking, by Jack Stanley (who added brilliantly to my jazz collection). At Newnham House we stuck together through thick and thin, a wonderful community within the larger family of the College. The tolerant civility of the College Tutor, Michael McCrum, of John Harley-Mason, Pat Bury and the Reverend Peter Walker enabled us mostly to fulfil their hopes.

**Emma Wilson, 1995**

I was a student at Newnham College, living in Old Hall and, one summer, in 2 Wordsworth Grove. I used to love walking down Maltings Lane to the Mill Pond and over to Newnham village. When I arrived as a Fellow at Corpus in 1995, it was with pleasure and nostalgia that I moved into a flat in Newnham House. Janet Allen, Reader in Pathology, lived there before me and I remember visiting her in the flat one Sunday afternoon.

*View from Hostel Yard into Stable yard.*

I've lived in Newnham House for seven years now, surviving student parties and the strange Escher-like layout of the corridors and stairwells. My rooms are densely clustered with books, cards and flowers. Supervisees seem most absorbed by my film collection which grows exponentially in piles of videos and DVDs. I supervise students here in French literature and contemporary film. Newnham House has felt like home to me, offering a room of my own, airy, light and hard-wired.

**Dr Robert Lefever, 1958**

In my first year at Corpus Christi I was privileged to have two rooms on the ground floor of C staircase, looking across New Court to the Parker Library. In my professional life as a doctor I have come to specialize in the treatment of alcoholism and other addictive behaviours. Recently, on returning to Corpus, I find that my former rooms are now incorporated in the College bar – *Sic transit gloria mundi.*

# The Master

## Haroon Ahmed

*The Master's garden.*
Although I have been 36 years at Corpus, my most persistent memories are the early ones. When I came to live in the College as a Fellow in February 1967 I dined regularly on High Table, and was soon introduced to the duties of a Junior Fellow. In those days the curious custom of 'remainders' entitled a Fellow to an extra glass of port if the decanter emptied as he filled his glass. It was my duty to fetch the extra glass from the store cupboard and to fill it to the meniscus lest I be accused, as I once was, of short changing, as the bulk of the volume of a conical glass is in the upper section. This custom has lapsed along with the decline in consumption of port.

Another vivid memory is of my consternation at the reaction when I announced to a group of Fellows that Anne, who had been seen frequently in my company, had agreed to marry me. Expecting warm congratulations I was taken aback by the response: 'Oh, well done my dear chap, we shall look forward to receiving your wedding fine'. I then had no idea that a fine was inflicted, and still is, if a Fellow decides to marry – a custom dating from about 1880 when Fellows, after many centuries, were reluctantly given the right to retain their Fellowship after they had succumbed to matrimony.

Participation in sport soon made me many friends among the undergraduate and postgraduate members of the College. There were leisurely Sunday afternoons of tennis at the sports ground, occasionally with the then Master, Sir Duncan Wilson, followed by Leckhampton tea. On most Sundays all eight grass courts could be in use and a court had to be reserved for the use of Fellows only. Sometimes Sir Duncan and I challenged under-

graduates to play doubles against us but the students were usually not only more skilful but always fitter than us. Our occasional triumphs were aided by my whispered comments to our opponents that they should keep their first serves to a modest pace against the Master. Sir Duncan had a fierce forehand drive against a moderate serve which frequently enabled a winning interception at the net. Where have all the tennis players gone in recent years? My favourite cricket memory is being given decidedly 'not out' by the Master, Sir Frank Lee, who was officiating as umpire, when I clearly felt that I had snicked the ball to the keeper. I was playing for the Fellows against the undergraduates in the Long Vacation and Sir Frank explained, when I reached his end, that we might not get enough runs to make a game out of it if I got out too early. He considered it my duty to bat for a while until he felt that a decent match was secure. Sir Frank had an excellent reputation as a sensible and pragmatic administrator, not only in the Civil Service but also as Master.

Living in College brought me into contact with the College gyps, and in particular Mr Ormond Jones. He unpacked my clothes when I first arrived and there followed an incident straight out of a Jeeves encounter. I had summoned up the courage to ask, after a week in residence, where my favourite working trousers had gone. They were excellent, in my opinion, for working in the laboratory, but over the years had become a little worn in certain areas from constant friction with the cycle saddle as I cycled to and from the Engineering Department. Mr Jones replied, 'Those trousers, sir. I have disposed of them, but before I took this step I showed them to the gentlemen's outfitters across the road and they confirmed they were no longer suitable for a gentleman to wear.' From then on I was resigned to subjugation to the gyps on matters of sartorial elegance. Tom Saunders, the second gyp, told me once of his life working in a Cambridge College a few years after the end of the Great War. At the age of ten he had been the Master's 'garden boy'. His job was to be in the garden in the afternoons, but to remain out of sight, hidden behind bushes while the Master took his constitutional walk around his garden. An occasional shout of 'Boy!' would bring him running out to pick out a weed that the Master indicated in the lawn with his walking stick. Alas there are no garden boys or afternoon walks for twenty-first century Masters!

As Senior Treasurer of the May Ball Committee, I encountered the most streetwise of the undergraduates of the late sixties and early seventies, who were adept at pulling the wool over my innocent eyes on more than a few occasions. I particularly recall that once they persuaded me into supporting a cabaret show. The details of the show were presented to me as a bland routine of song and dance. On the night, however, the act took a somewhat risqué turn in the early morning performance due to the participation of a very scantily clad female entertainer. Those who were present at this Ball will no doubt recall the occasion: the rest I leave to the imagination. There was much tut-tutting among the senior Fellows and unrestrained glee among the students in the audience. I just about retained my Fellowship but became very popular with the undergraduates. After the event I decided to resign from the Committee and retreat to the safer post of Assistant Tutor.

In my early years the College took its first steps towards acknowledging the position of women in our University. Fellows were given the right to invite women as their guests on High Table and I took advantage of this opportunity to invite Anne. She was one of the first women to dine on High Table in our history of more than six centuries. It is hard today to imagine the strength of feelings that existed in the College during the sixties on this issue.

*Robert Beldam with HRH Prince Phillip.*

My association with Leckhampton began well before my election to Corpus. This was in the time when I had finished my student days at King's, and although appointed to a University lectureship, I was not accepted by the conservative College ethos of the sixties into a Fellowship at any of the Cambridge colleges. I was friendly then, as I am still, with a group of Canadian Corpus postgraduates working for PhD degrees at the Engineering Department, who invited me as Captain of the Engineering Department Cricket Team to raise a team to play them at softball on the Corpus grounds. The matches were both exciting and entertaining. The cricketers learned to bowl underarm and to hit with a cross bat, while some of the softball players took up cricket and proved to be remarkably good fielders and excellent pinch hitters in limited-over matches. These matches led to a happy association with Leckhampton and to my first encounter with the formidable first Warden, Christopher Longuet-Higgins, when I was invited as a dinner guest of one of the Canadian students. Leckhampton continued to play an important part in my life after I became a Fellow of Corpus, with Sunday teas, croquet and as an adventure playground for my children while they were growing up. It was a great honour for me when the College elected me Warden in 1993. In my five years as Warden my wife and I made many friends not only among the graduate students but also among the Visiting Fellows, with some of whom we continue to retain the most cordial of relations many years after their departure from Cambridge. I returned to cricket for the Leckhampton team for a year or two as Warden and had the satisfaction of achieving a batting average of 33 in one of the seasons. A Visiting Fellow from Canada, of English origin and obviously a fine cricketer in his younger days joined me in several partnerships, much to the consternation of our opponents from other colleges who did not expect two elderly 'postgraduates' to be competent cricketers. Excellent teas were provided by postgrads ably led by Vanessa Conte and Leckhampton life was much envied by visiting teams of postgrads from other colleges.

The Leckhampton community was in transition in the mid-1990s. The original 'Leckhampton Fellows' had all either retired or died and the many excellent traditions and customs they had instituted to make Leckhampton such an attractive graduate campus had been eroded. Changes in society and the availability of convenience foods continued to threaten the formal arrangements and numbers coming in to dine in Leckhampton declined each year. The Stephen Hales Society which had been started in the time of the first Warden was also declining in popularity with postgraduate students. Two new societies came into existence in my time as Warden. Achim Kempf, a Research Fellow started the Cross-Talk Society to cater for the needs of the growing post-doctoral community in the University, some of whom had been elected to Research Associateships at Corpus. Using the advantages of email for disseminating University-wide announcements he established a lively society which meets at Leckhampton to discuss issues over a wide range of research disciplines. At the same time the need was felt for a society for postgraduates doing research in the humanities and social sciences who tended to work in isolation compared to science students who had more communal activities in their laboratories. The Leckhampton Society was established to provide a forum for postgraduates to talk to each other about their research. Initially the membership was confined to the 'Arts' students but I received a letter accusing me of creating an Arts/Science divide at Leckhampton and realised quickly that the Society would be popular with all the students and scientists were immediately invited to attend and contribute.

Living in College in the Master's Lodge over Christmas when there is no one else in College reminds me of my time in the Old Court over the two Christmas periods in the sixties when I thought that I was the only resident in the College. This was an eerie experience at a time in the year which is regarded as the haunting season for the Corpus ghosts of Henry Butts and the unfortunate Elizabeth Spencer. These experiences laid the foundation for my ghost stories that have become part of the Leckhampton Christmas dinner entertainment over the years.

Finally, as Master, the event that my wife and I recall most often, and somewhat ruefully on occasions, is the fateful telephone call from the Senior Fellow. It came one evening when, anticipating my retirement from my University post, we were in our garden planning the siting of a greenhouse as part of our intention to take up gardening as a serious shared activity. The telephone rang to inform me that the College wished me to be the internal candidate for the Mastership. We abandoned the greenhouse discussion to consider 'what if ?' for the next few hours, but we plan to return to the greenhouse discussion in the future when the time permits. Nonetheless, my 35 years at Corpus have brought much pleasure and many memories and I can conclude by saying that for me there has been no happier chance in life than that which brought me to the College in 1967, and no greater honour than my election as Master in 2000.

## Postscript

Change, sometimes radical, but never at the expense of our 'laudable customs', might best describe the history of Corpus over the eighty years or so covered by the memories in this book. Scattered through the pages you will find descriptions and images of some of the many developments which have taken place within our traditional community in more recent times. These include the admission of women in 1983, after more than six centuries, the creation of Leckhampton following the

demands for more attention to the needs of the increasing numbers of postgraduate students coming to the University, the construction of the Beldam building and Botolph Court and the reconstruction of Newnham House to allow for a modest expansion in undergraduate numbers.

At this moment in our history we look forward to the realization, in the near future, of two of our greatest ventures: the completion of our project for the Parker Library to give greater access while enhancing the security of our precious collection of manuscripts and early printed books, and the re-location, modernisation and substantial expansion of our inadequate student library. We also plan to refurbish our sports pavilion and to install a gym at the sports ground in Cranmer Road. The student bar and JCR are also in need of renovation and expansion and will be the focus of our attention once the library projects have been com-

*The Beldam Building student accommodation.*

*The Natwest Bank on the corner of King's Parade and Bene't Street is the site of the new student library.*

pleted, as too will our plans to provide additional pur-pose-built accommodation for postgraduate students at Leckhampton.

The transformation which has taken place in the manner in which we select those to be admitted to the College as undergraduates and postgraduates must also be stressed. We, together with all other Cambridge col-leges, are following the University's declared policy by widening access to the College from all sectors of sec-ondary education, although, as the reminiscences of Sir Fred Lawton from the 1930s show, Corpus has always been open to the academically gifted, regardless of the financial and social circumstances of the families from which they come. One thing is certain, if the Old Members who have so vividly recorded their time in College so many decades ago were miraculously to find themselves freshers in the Corpus of 2003, they would find their time here no less enjoyable and rewarding.

# INDEX OF NAMES

# SUBSCRIBERS

The following members and friends of the College subscribed in advance to ensure the success of this project:

| | | | | | | | |
|---|---|---|---|---|---|---|---|
| Nigel Adams | 1970 | Robin Benn | 1982 | David R. Brigstock PhD | 1984 | Ray Chan | 1959 |
| Demetrios Agoropoulos | 1979 | Chris J. Bennett | 1954 | John MacD. Broadhead | 1937 | Stan Chan | 1985 |
| Elizabeth Alam (née Shaw) | 1987 | Dr Robert Bennett | 1986 | Michael Broke | 1954 | Jennifer A. Chapman | 1999 |
| John Alderson | 1981 | Timothy Bennett | | Dr D.J. Brown | 1981 | Graham Charlton | 1932 |
| Katy Alexander | 1999 | Andrew and Gemma Benson | 1973 | Dr M.F. Brown | 1977 | Alistair Chesser | 1984 |
| Stephen Allan | 1949 | Frank Benson | 1946 | Quintin Brown | 1953 | J.D. Chick | 1963 |
| Philip Allen | 1946 | Kate Benton | 1987 | Ronnie Brown | 1935 | David Chiesman | 1950 |
| Dr D.J. Allison | 1969 | Mark L. Berlin | 1979 | V.W. Brown | 1942 | Jin Chin | 2001 |
| Martin Amherst Lock | 1977 | Peter Bernstein | 1993 | Robert F. Browning | 1948 | Dr Robert Chivers | 1997 |
| Dr Davina Anderson | 1983 | Dr John Bertalot | 1955 | Richard J.H. Brownlie | 1987 | Chor Yee Lok | 1980 |
| J.H.F. Angas | 1949 | Roy Bery | 1935 | Steven Brumby | 1961 | Anup-Singh Choudry | 1980 |
| Guy Arnoux | 1952 | Dr Darryl R. Biggar | 1984 | Mr Michael Buckle | 1943 | Youssef M. Choueiri | 1982 |
| Rob Ashmore | 1991 | Mark William Bingham | 1997 | Graham Budd | 1987 | J.R.A. Christie | 1979 |
| John Assheton | 1938 | C.E. Bingley | 1958 | Prof David Buisseret | 1955 | Canon Thomas Christie | 1950 |
| H.J.A. Astley | 1938 | J.W. Binns | 1949 | John Bull | 1955 | Zhikang Chua | 2000 |
| D.I. Atcheson | 1996 | Alex Birch | 1982 | Jonathan Burchfield | 1972 | John M. Clark | 1957 |
| Dr Harry H. Atkinson | 1955 | Sir John Birch | 1956 | Michael Burke | 1999 | Andrew Clarke | 1967 |
| Dr Jules Attard | 1980 | D.B. Bird | 1951 | Dr John Burkinshaw | 1931 | Edward Clarke | 2000 |
| Hannah F. Austin | 2001 | Benedict Birnberg | 1951 | Gemma Claire Burnett | 2001 | Roger Clarke | 1957 |
| Dr Dominic Ayers | 1988 | James Bishop | 1950 | Robin Burns | 1976 | Sandy Clarke | 1957 |
| P.J. Bacon | 1952 | Professor David Black | 1980 | Martin J. Burton | 1977 | J.E. Clayson | 1958 |
| John Baden | 1948 | Jeremy Blacker | 1961 | Andrew Bush MD. FRCP. FRCPCH | 1972 | Conrad F.J. Clifford | 1977 |
| David A. Baer | 1994 | Professor Colin Blakemore | 1962 | The Revd G.V.A. Buss | 1985 | Colin A. Clifton-Ince | 1989 |
| David G. Bailey | 1974 | John F.F. Blandford | 1933 | Lucy Butler | 1999 | Professor Christopher Colclough | 1967 |
| W.A.C. Baker MBE | 1935 | Nicholas Bliss | 1978 | J.Anthony Cable | 1954 | A.L. Coleby | 1955 |
| Mr M.P. Baker | 1974 | Lance S. Blockley | 1974 | David D. Caldwell | 1958 | Dr and Mrs R.J. Collier | 2000 |
| Nicholas Baldock | 1997 | John Blundell | 1941 | Neil Manson Cameron | 1985 | Ian Collin | 1946 |
| Robert Baldock | 1999 | Elisabeth and Ben Blundson | 1987 | Neil Campbell | 1984 | Sir John Conant | 1946 |
| Antony W. Baldwin | 1953 | Bob Boas | 1957 | Graham Campbell-Smith | 1949 | Dr Stephen Coniam | 1968 |
| Dr D.V.T. Baldwin | 1938 | John Bolton-Maggs OBE | 1939 | Jamie Camplin | 1965 | J.A.Y. Conway | 1951 |
| Mr R.J. Bamford | | The Revd Edward Booth OP | 1949 | Ms Gill Cannell | | Martin Godfrey Cook | 1999 |
| Mike Bancroft | 1964 | John Boreham | 1954 | Dr Peter M. Cannon | 1981 | Sir Alan Cook | 1940 |
| Richard Barber | 1960 | Christopher Bouckley | 1975 | The Revd John Caperon | 1978 | George A. Cooke Jr | 1973 |
| Rodney Barber | 1965 | Robin Boudard | 1943 | Mr Gregg M. Capon | 2000 | Louise Cooper | 1999 |
| Alex Barrett | 1998 | The Revd Mark Boughey | 1983 | Julian Carlisle | 1950 | William A. Cooper | 1941 |
| The Revd Robin Barrett | 1952 | Gemma L. Bourne | 2001 | Antony Carr | 1955 | Canon Charles McAester Copland | 1929 |
| J.C. Barry | 1945 | Professor David Bowen | 1941 | J.R. Carr | 1964 | Dr H.M.C. Corfield FRCA | 1942 |
| Canon A.M. Barton | 1954 | Robert Bowles | 1968 | Brian Carter | 1964 | Anthony Cory-Wright | 1969 |
| Ian M. Barton | 1948 | James Bowsher | 2001 | Danielle Caulfield | 2001 | Dr Daniel C. Coster | 1977 |
| Peter D. Barton MNZM | 1949 | Stephen E. Bradforth | 1984 | Ray Cave | 1985 | Robin J.M.G. Coupar | 1952 |
| Eric Q. Bashforth | 1958 | John M. Bradshaw | 1959 | Dr H.A. Chadwick | 1964 | Peter Coupland | 1982 |
| Michael Bedwell | 1955 | Isabella Brewerton | 1998 | Ella Chaitow | 2001 | G.H.R. Couzens | 1966 |
| Gordon Bell | 1956 | Dr Natalie Brewerton | 1992 | Anita Chakraborty | 1989 | Graham Coy | 1971 |
| Keith Bell | 1960 | The Hon. Mark Bridges | 1973 | M.V.D. Champness | 1941 | Mr A.N. Craven MA | 1941 |

| Name | Year |
|---|---|
| M.Kennedy | 1969 |
| Andrew Kerr | 1973 |
| Ian Kerr | 1959 |
| James Y.K. Kerr | 1955 |
| A. Stanley Kiaer | 1951 |
| Christopher King | 1959 |
| Wing Cdm John King | 1931 |
| Peter J. King | 1972 |
| Tania King | 1974 |
| David Kinnersley | 1944 |
| Philip Kinnersly | 1965 |
| R.A. Kinnersly | 1926 |
| Gachao Kiuna | 1999 |
| Sir Alister Kneller | 1948 |
| Nik Knight | 1964 |
| Richard Knowlton | 1969 |
| Klaus Koenigshausen | 2000 |
| Philothei Kolitsi | 1991 |
| Martin Kubelik | 1967 |
| Andy Kulessa | 1984 |
| Alison W.L. Kwan | 1994 |
| Stuart Laing | 1967 |
| Edward Lake | 2000 |
| H.G. Lambert | 1929 |
| Sir Stephen Lamport | 1970 |
| C.J. Lane | 1947 |
| Mr Allan Lang | 1994 |
| Kate and Ed Langford | 1983 |
| Neil Langlois | 1983 |
| Richard Larcombe | 1959 |
| Harold Last | 1935 |
| Roderick J. Latham | 2000 |
| Nicholas Lavender | 1983 |
| Andrew Lawrence | 1991 |
| Emma Lawrence | 2000 |
| William Lawrence | 2001 |
| W.David Lawrie | 1963 |
| The Hon. H.de B. Lawson-Johnson | 1931 |
| Alexandra Lawton | 1996 |
| Tony Lawton | 1930 |
| Tristram Lawton | 1999 |
| Marcus G.J. Laycock | 1985 |
| Jan Leaver | |
| Dr B.K. Lee | 1953 |
| Dr Jason T.C. Lee | 1994 |
| K.W. Leech | 1939 |
| Dr Robert Lefever | 1958 |
| F.J. Leishman | 1937 |
| Professor Robert J. Lenardon | 1971 |
| John Lennard-Jones | 1944 |
| Wen Pin Leow | 2001 |
| Dr Peter Lewis | 1960 |
| Keum Keow Lim | 1995 |
| Timothy R. Linton | 1964 |
| Katherine Anne Liversidge | 2000 |
| James H.M. Lo | 2000 |
| James Lockhart Smith | 1999 |
| Matthew Bird Lohse | |
| John P. Long | 1956 |
| Nigel Long | 1974 |
| Alec Loten | 1944 |
| David Loy CBE | 1948 |
| Jonathan Lubran | 1969 |
| J.R. Lucas | 1956 |
| N.G. Lucas | 1966 |
| Peter Luff MP | 1974 |
| Victoria Lung | |
| K.R.R. Lunn | 1966 |
| Denzil Lush | 1982 |
| James Lynch | 1999 |
| Christopher Mabley | 1977 |
| The Revd Brian J. Macdonald-Milne | 1955 |
| Dr Julian M. Mace | 1978 |
| Professor Samuel L. Macey | 1972 |
| Colin Mackinnon | 1956 |
| Major J.F. MacKinnon MC.DL.JP | 1946 |
| Thomas Maclean | 2001 |
| Geoffrey Maddrell | 1957 |
| Rodney Mahon | 1961 |
| Matthew Mailey | 2001 |
| Maurice Maling | 1931 |
| Desmond Malley | 1959 |
| Roger Mangnall | 1946 |
| Dr R.J. Mann | 1968 |
| The Revd Richard Mapplebeckpalmer | 1953 |
| Andre K.v Mayer-Marling | 1926 |
| David C. Marsh | 1983 |
| A.R. Marshall | 1975 |
| Charlotte Marshall | 2000 |
| Sir Peter Marshall | 1943 |
| Dr Nicholas Marston | 1977 |
| Christopher J. Martin | 1979 |
| Douglas Mason | 1990 |
| W.R. Matthews | 1949 |
| Henri P.M. Mayoux | 1950 |
| Hannah Z.R. McConkey | 2001 |
| W.Bruce McAdam | 1955 |
| Kevin McCloud | 1978 |
| Clare McCoubrey | 1992 |
| Michael and Christine McCrum | 1946 |
| Beverley McKeon | 1992 |
| K.Robin McLean | 1955 |
| Dr Brian McNeil | 1970 |
| Roger Mears | 1962 |
| Anthony Meehan | 1997 |
| Dato' Malek Merican | 1953 |
| Tony Merriam | 1946 |
| John Michell | 1961 |
| Roger Middleton | 1956 |
| Ivan Milatovic | 1992 |
| Dr Patrick Mileham | 1985 |
| Grahame B. Miles | 1956 |
| Katie Miller | 2000 |
| Oliver Prewett Miller | 2001 |
| Tim Millington | 1951 |
| Dr D.E. Mills | 1974 |
| Andrew Mitchell | 1987 |
| Harry Mitchell QC | 1950 |
| Rebecca Mitchell | 2000 |
| Samantha Mitchell | 1999 |
| Ben Monaghan | 1990 |
| C.B. Moncrieff | 1973 |
| Tony Moorwood | 1964 |
| Hugh More | 1999 |
| Isabel Moreton | 1995 |
| M.P. Morris | 1991 |
| Richard Morton | 1974 |
| Charlie & Natalie Mount | 1989 |
| Jessica Moxham | 1999 |
| S.J. Munasinghe | 1953 |
| Andy Murphy | 1982 |
| Genevieve Murphy | 1999 |
| Sir Richard Mynors | 1966 |
| Dr Jeremy Mynott | 1961 |
| Dennis Napier | 1955 |
| J.A.F. Napier | 1969 |
| Paul and Judith Nathanail | 1982 |
| John T.P. Neild | 1941 |
| John Neilson | 1977 |
| David A.Neish | 1952 |
| Paul Nelson | 1975 |
| D. Nelson-Smith | 1957 |
| Don Neville | 1973 |
| Dr Chris Newbery | |
| Jim Newsome | 1943 |
| Bill Newton | 1959 |
| David I. Newton | 1980 |
| Paul Ng | 1999 |
| Dr James Nicholson | 1983 |
| Peter G. Nicholson | 1953 |
| Justice Robert Nicholson AO | 1997 |
| Alasdair Noble | 2000 |
| Ana-Maria Norbury (née Mills) | 1990 |
| Luke Norbury | 1989 |
| P. Norman | 1968 |
| Dr Catriona O'Connell | 1986 |
| Professor David T. Okpako | 1973 |
| M. Ollier | 1989 |
| Jacinta S.T. Khoo | 1987 |
| Jonathan Opie | 2001 |
| R.A.N. Orange-Bromehead | 1945 |
| Dr Tony Ottridge | 1973 |
| Michael Overbury | 1972 |
| Tony Overton | 1955 |
| Edward Owen | 1924 |
| Philip Pacey | 1964 |
| Mr Pratapaditya Pal | 1962 |
| Christopher Andrew James Palmer | 2000 |
| Mr J.V. Parker | 1973 |
| Captain Cedric Parrish OBE, Royal Navy | 1961 |
| Mr Brian L. Parry | 1982 |
| Mr Harivadan A. Patel | 2000 |
| T.J.M. Paterson | 1963 |
| Dr R.C. Paul CBE | 1955 |
| Graham Pawley | 1986 |
| Prof Stuart Pawley | 1956 |
| Dr Scott Peake | 1998 |
| Leonard Pearcey | 1959 |
| Dr Richard Peckover | 1965 |
| P.E.E. Pemberton | 1982 |
| Mark Pender | 1982 |
| Allan Pengelly | 2001 |
| C.K.M. Percival MA.MICE | 1938 |
| P.W.S. Percival | 1956 |
| Robert H.H. Peto | 1968 |
| Peter Petrie | 1953 |
| Joanna Phillips | 1999 |
| B.Phillipson | 1971 |
| Alan Phipps | 1969 |
| Hitomi Maruyama | 1996 |
| T.G. Pierce | 1960 |
| Mr Andrew Pillidge | 1977 |
| S.N. Pitchford | 1983 |
| Andrew Plowman | 1971 |
| Mike Polke | 1964 |
| Keith R. Poole | 1954 |
| Harry C. Porter | 1945 |
| I.J.W. Pratt | 1961 |
| Graham Preskett | 1967 |
| John Press | 1938 |
| C.M. Preston | 1971 |
| Rebecca Preuveneers | 1998 |
| John Price | 1966 |
| Lionel Price | 1964 |
| The Rt Revd Anthony Priddis | 1966 |
| P.N.A.M. Prince | 1988 |
| Michael Proudfoot | 1963 |
| J. Pryce-Jones | 1965 |
| Dr A.M. Purves | 1974 |
| Adrian Quarry | 1973 |
| Andrew Quartermain | 1993 |
| Stephen Quigley | 1958 |
| Adam Quinton | 1980 |
| Howard Raingold | 1975 |
| Christopher Ramsey | 1982 |
| Canon Edmund Randall | 1938 |
| Priya Rao | 2000 |
| Christopher Raper | 1978 |
| John E. Ratcliffe | 1956 |
| Earl C. Ravenal | 1952 |
| Dana K. Raydan | 1993 |
| John Reddaway | 1944 |
| Roger Redding | 1961 |
| Mr B.W.S. Reed | 1996 |
| Christopher Rennie | 1982 |
| William Paul Renwick | 1948 |
| E.J. Rice | 1948 |
| Maurice J. Richardson | 1942 |
| Michael Richardson | 1971 |
| Pierre V.E. Riches | 1946 |
| John A. Rickards | 1959 |
| Alex Riddell | 2001 |
| Gerard Ridgway | 2001 |
| Patrick Ridgwell | 1953 |
| Dr Paul Rimmer | 1984 |
| Dr Peter S. Ringrose | 1964 |
| R.B. Ritchie | 1955 |
| Canon Bill Ritson | 1956 |
| Professor J.P.C. Roach | 1938 |
| Bill Roberts | 1956 |